Paul Ricoeur and the Poetic Imperative

SUNY series in Theology and Continental Thought

Douglas L. Donkel, editor

Paul Ricoeur and the Poetic Imperative

The Creative Tension between Love and Justice

W. David Hall

State University of New York Press

Cover art: Kelli Williams, *Deeply*, 1991,
acrylic on paper, (17.5 x 15).

Published by
State University of New York Press, Albany

Printed in the United States of America

For information, address State University of New York Press,
194 Washington Avenue, Suite 305, Albany, NY 12210-2384

Production by Kelli Williams
Marketing by Anne M. Valentine

Library of Congress Cataloging-in-Publication Data

Hall, W. David (William David), 1965
Paul Ricoeur and the poetic imperative : the creative tension between love and justice / W. David Hall.
p. cm — (SUNY series in theology and continental thought)
Includes bibliographical references and index.
ISBN-13: 978-0-7914-7143-2 (hardcover : alk. paper)
ISBN-13: 978-0-7914-7144-9 (pbk. : alk. paper) 1. Ricœur, Paul.
2. Ethics. I. Title.

B2430.R554H35 2007
194—dc22

2006101100

10 9 8 7 6 5 4 3 2 1

In memory of Harold Lee Watts

1949–1994

Contents

Acknowledgments

Many hands and minds have contributed to this project, more than I can name explicitly. Several deserve special mention, however. First I should thank Carole Blair who made me first read Ricoeur as an undergraduate majoring in rhetoric at California State University, Sacramento. I owe a tremendous debt to William Schweiker whose oversight and often painful, but always constructive criticism was instrumental in bringing to fruition the dissertation that grounded this book, and to David Klemm and David Tracy who served as readers on my dissertation committee. I also want to thank Bill Schweiker for continued friendship and encouragement in bringing the book itself to fruition.

While at the University of Chicago, I benefited greatly from the insights of peers and teachers, among them Eric Bain-Selbo, Chris Gamwell, Paul Griffiths, Michael Johnson, Kevin Jung, Robin Lovin, Chuck Mathewes, Joe Petit, Rick Rosengarten, Kristin VanHeyningen, John Wall, Darlene Weaver, and Brent Wilmot. Special thanks go to Kristine Culp who made my return to Chicago after a brief hiatus easy, and who has served at various times as employer, teacher, critic, mentor, and valued friend. Special thanks are also due to Elmer Almachar, Paul Dehart, and Mark Wolf whose companionship kept me sane and alive through graduate school and whose insight and criticism made me a better thinker. There are surely too many others associated with my time at Chicago who helped along the way for me to be able to adequately thank all.

I have benefited from insightful and supportive colleagues in my time at DePaul University and Centre College who deserve mention. Special thanks to Jeff Carlson who first hired me as an adjunct instructor at DePaul and to Frida Furman who offered me my first full-time position. Jim Halstead's mentorship and dedicated friendship were instrumental in making me a teacher and scholar (and, I hope, a better human being). Centre College has been a place where I have been able to flourish as a teacher and a scholar. I am especially indebted to Rick Axtell, Rob Colter, Brian Cooney, Ruben Dupertuis, Beth Glazier-McDonald, Tom McCollough, and Milton Scarborough for critical insights and personal friendships, and to John Ward whose support, both moral and financial, as academic dean of Centre College has been steadfast. Two people have had an important hand in the editing and preparation of this manuscript, Kristin Henze and Zeke Goggin.

Finally, I must acknowledge my family whose influence on the completion of this project is immeasurable. My parents, Gary Hall, Peggy and Don Allan, and Harold Watts provided a safe and loving environment to grow up in. This was often not adequately appreciated, but it is now and I hope they are proud of their work. Most importantly, my love and thanks to Sarah and Lilli who make everyday worth getting out of bed.

Chapter One

Introduction

> But I think our question—and we understand it better after Marx, Nietzsche, and Freud—is: what is man? Do we know man better than we know God? In the end, I do not know what man is. My confession to myself is that man is instituted by the word, that is, by a language which is less spoken *by* man than spoken *to* man. . . . Finally, what constitutes our answer to the apology of Necessity and resignation is the faith that man is founded, at the heart of his mythopoetic power, by a creative word. Is not The Good News the instigation of the *possibility* of man by a creative word?
>
> —Paul Ricoeur, "The Language of Faith"

Paul Ricoeur's publications spanned nearly six decades from the latter half of the twentieth century to the first decade of the twenty-first. His *oeuvre* crossed an unbelievable range of scholarly topics and philosophical perspectives that included existentialism, phenomenology, psychoanalysis, hermeneutic theory, theories of metaphor and symbol, narrative theory, and political philosophy. His influence on the contemporary philosophical scene is immense, even if the recognition for this influence is not as explicit as one might like. Given the breadth and texture of his career, any attempt to provide a coherent account of Ricoeur's corpus seems folly. Nevertheless, functioning under the adage "nothing ventured, nothing gained," this book attempts to provide such a coherent and reasonably comprehensive account.

The overarching argument of this endeavor is that Ricoeur's religious writings offer an important context for interpreting his philosophical project. His project (provided that there was only one project, as opposed to a multitude of them as many have argued and as Ricoeur himself frequently seemed to imply) became more theological in character as he directed attention more explicitly toward ethics at the end of his career. This theological turn was most profoundly manifest in what Ricoeur called "communal ethics in religious perspective," at the heart of which resides a creative tension between the ideals of love and justice. This focus on the creative tension between love and justice was a late manifestation, and Ricoeur's articulation of it was spread out among a series of seemingly disconnected and occasional articles that were usually addressed to other topics. While this dimension of his work received very little systematic attention, it is my claim that it ought to be viewed as a central feature of his overall project. This creative tension between the ideals of love and justice reaches its highest pitch and greatest level of productivity in the confrontation between the ideas of autonomy and theonomy, the centerpiece of which is the love command, particularly as this is understood by Jewish philosopher Franz Rosenzweig. The love command lends an imperative structure to the ideal of love that opens it to moral judgment in general and ideals of justice in particular. However, the imperative structure of the love command is not reducible to a moral imperative in the Kantian sense. Rather, the love command employs a poetic use of the imperative that draws its meaning from a surrounding matrix of biblical symbols, metaphors, and narratives.

There are many reasons to suggest that this creative/tensive structure of the poetic use of the imperative provides an important perspective on Ricoeur's later writings and on his thought in general. At the level of epistemology, the structure of creative tension runs throughout Ricoeur's philosophy. He always relied on the creative tension released by bringing together apparently incompatible positions to make his points. Creative juxtapositions of existentialism and phenomenology, reflexive philosophy and Nietzschean genealogy, and Aristotelian and Kantian ethics were among his most fruitful explorations. He argued that theology and religious discourse function in a similar way relative to philosophy: biblical symbols, metaphors, and narratives offer a sort of poetic resolution to philosophical impasses that defy speculative resolution. This notion of poetic resolution is significant for understanding how Ricoeur believed theological discourse in general *means*. Theology is figurative discourse; or, more accurately stated, biblical texts are poetic texts, that is, figurative linguistic structures that are productive as much as expressive of meaning.

This epistemological analysis opens onto an ontological one. A significant organizing theme that arose early in Ricoeur's work was a sort of creative tension between activity and passivity that resides at the heart of human agency. This creative tension takes many forms, from the reciprocity of the voluntary and involuntary structures of will and action, to the voluntary servitude of the will in moral fault, to the structure of summons and response in his analysis of moral conscience. This active-passive structure takes on a deepened sense when touched by theological and biblical expressions which poetically configure ideas as diverse as the origin and end of existence (creation and eschaton) and the presentation of a voice that summons the individual to responsible selfhood in the theological interpretation of moral conscience. Biblical symbols, metaphors, and narratives open dimensions of the meaning that are not accessible at the level of pure philosophical speculation.

At the level of ethics, the creative tension at the heart of Ricoeur's ontology of selfhood appears at a higher register under the aegis of responsibility. Like the theme of activity and passivity, the moral dimensions of selfhood emerged quite early in Ricoeur's thought. The problems of affective fragility and moral fault undergirded his earliest work. More importantly, however, he located a fundamentally moral dimension of capable agency in the ability to keep one's promises. What begins as an aspect of self-constancy—my capability to project initiative into the future by remaining true my word—takes on ethical and moral overtones once the idea of promising is introduced into the interpersonal world of interaction. Promising is not simply a matter of remaining true to myself but also one of keeping fidelity to another; someone expects me to follow through on my promise. Thus, selfhood is opened to a range of moral determinations that are characterized in a broad sense as responsibility. Once again, the poetic matrices of theological discourse and biblical textuality fund a deepened sense of these moral dimensions of selfhood. I previously cited the place that a theological interpretation of moral conscience played in Ricoeur's thought. To this, one can add such expressions as the covenant that establishes the relationship with a liberating God, and particularly, the love command that is constitutive of selfhood both ontologically and morally.

My central claim that theology and religion are important to Ricoeur's philosophical project as a whole entails four basic presuppositions that may be open for debate. For reference, I list them in ascending order of importance. First, I argue that Ricoeur's *oeuvre* can in fact be reasonably and responsibly interpreted as a single coherent project. While his ideas evolved and moved in a number of different and new directions over the course of fifty years, there were several general concerns that guided and continued to direct his thought. Second, Ricoeur never completely left the phenomenological method that was centrally important to his early thought. While his project took a decidedly linguistic and hermeneutical turn, the structure of phenomenological method continued to work beneath this turn. Third, Ricoeur's project is fundamentally a philosophical anthropology; his concerns ultimately lay in the question of the identity of self-reflective agency, whether through the lens of reflexive philosophy, existentialism, phenomenology, psychoanalytic theory, or narrative. Finally, and perhaps the most disputed assumption, is that a closer relationship existed between Ricoeur's philosophical explorations and his religious thought than he typically admitted. While he outlined a number of points of approach between philosophical and theological discourse, his overall tendency was to hold the two at arms length from one another. My claim focuses on the possibility that several fundamentally religious themes are located throughout Ricoeur's thought, and that the influence of these themes becomes most pronounced at the level of ethical concern. I will expand on these presuppositions in situating my interpretation.

Situated Reading

Among other things, this book is intended as a *critical constructive interpretation* of Ricoeur's *oeuvre* with particular emphasis on uncovering the importance of his theological explorations for interpreting his philosophical project as a whole. I am not interested only in what Ricoeur wrote, but in what his writings tell us about what it means to be human. His philosophy can be viewed as a singular project which is centrally concerned with this question of human meaning. Having said this, it should be noted that I am not attempting to offer the *one true account* of Ricoeur's corpus. By placing this limit on the project, it may seem that I am hedging my bets, if not resorting to blatant cowardice. However, I believe this is not the case for several reasons.

First, the scope of Ricoeur's thought is so vast and so varied that the one true account, if there is such a thing, may remain forever elusive. This limiting factor is compounded by Ricoeur's continued evasion in offering self-appraisal of his work; this is particularly the case with regard to the effect of religious sentiment on his philosophical project. For example, in an interview Ricoeur claimed the following:

> I am very committed to the autonomy of philosophy and I think that in none of my works do I use any arguments borrowed from the domain of Jewish and Christian biblical writings. . . . But if someone says, "Yes, but if you weren't Christian, if you did not recognize yourself as belonging to the movement of biblical literature, you would not have been interested in the problem of evil or, perhaps, in the poetic aspect in the broadest sense, or the creative aspect of human thought." Well, to this objection, I make all the concessions one wants by saying that no one knows where the ideas which organize oneself philosophically come from. . . . Certainly, a reader could be much more sensitive than I am to the secret religious motivation in my work.

> What I claim, what I argue forcefully, is that this motivation is always put in parentheses in order to allow the formation of philosophical arguments which are aimed at all rational beings capable of discussion, no matter what their position on the question of religion.[1]

Ricoeur claimed again and again that the author is not the best interpreter of his/her work, nor the best judge of its motivation or significance. This may seem as if he gives the reader carte blanche to interpret the text however s/he sees fit and in the interests of any ideological stance s/he wishes to advance. Once again, I believe this is not the case; Ricoeur would most certainly argue that there are more or less adequate interpretations, more or less *responsible* readings of any text, his own no less than others.

The question of adequate, responsible interpretation raises a second justification for the limits I place on my project. Ricoeur's hermeneutical philosophy was profoundly influenced by the criticism of romanticist hermeneutics advanced by Hans Georg Gadamer. Ricoeur himself became one of the most outspoken advocates of the need to move hermeneutical enquiry away from the search for authorial intention. Thus, the creative potential for meaning resides not in the search for the authorial genius "behind" the text, or in the attempt to know the author better than s/he knows him/herself, as Friedrich Schleiermacher and Wilhelm Dilthey would have argued. The creative potential for meaning is opened by the engagement of the reader with the text, the *sense* of the text, and the *world* that the text presents "in front of" itself. That is to say, the text is an autonomous source of meaning, which is constantly open to new engagements, new interpretations, and *new appropriations of meaning*.

Once again, however, the notion of textual autonomy does not give the reader carte blanche to bend interpretation in any direction s/he wishes. Rather, the text is a *structure* that guides interpretation and imposes its own limits on the scope of legitimate interpretation. If the movement away from romanticist hermeneutics has consigned scholars to the realm of the conflict of interpretations, the conflicts are not unadjudicable, even if adjudication is always tentative and never final; the structure of the text itself allows one to argue the merits of more or less adequate interpretations, more or less responsible appropriations, more or less *convincing* readings. My desire in this book is to offer an adequate, responsible, and reasonably comprehensive interpretation of Ricoeur's thought. My intent is to be guided by his writings, though not uncritically, in articulating the relationship between his hermeneutical philosophy of the self, that is, philosophical anthropology, and his theological interests, particularly regarding the problem of evil, biblical configurations of creation and redemption, and the commandment to love one's neighbor.

As I previously claimed, my interpretation is situated around four basic presuppositions about Ricoeur's philosophy. The first three of these presuppositions principally concern the philosophical reception and interpretation of Ricoeur's work. The fourth focuses specifically on the theological dimensions of his work. Thus, I will situate my reading under separate headings.

Philosophical Orientations

My first assertion is that Ricoeur's writings can be interpreted as a single, coherent collection that spans from his early phenomenological orientation to the work he completed at the end of his life. In this vein, Charles E. Reagan, citing a private conversation with Ricoeur, stated:

> I recently asked Paul Ricoeur if we would ever see the promised *Poetics of the Will*. . . . He told me that either there would be no *poetics* of the will, or that his work on metaphor and narrative constituted it. Then he asked me, "Do you hold me to completing a plan I made when I was a very young man, some thirty-five years ago?" The whole of Ricoeur's work is more the result of the twistings and turning's of a journey than the completion of an architectonic drafted many years ago. At the end of each of his major works, he lists the unanswered questions, the unsolved problems, the new directions which will occupy him in the next work. This does not mean that there are not certain themes which are fairly constant in his work.[2]

These themes, around which Ricoeur's thought cohered, are in many respects the basis of the three remaining presuppositions that orient my interpretation. Before moving on to discuss these other presuppositions, however, I want to pause and note a possible point of disagreement with Reagan's assessment concerning Ricoeur's original architectonic and proposal for a *poetics of the will*: I suggest that Ricoeur did not abandon the notion of a poetics of the will, but rather, that this project is an exceedingly complex one that has of itself introduced the twistings and turnings of a journey into his work.

My second presupposition is that Ricoeur never completely left the phenomenological method that governed his initial systematic works. Ricoeur long held a connection between phenomenology and hermeneutics. Phenomenology serves to direct hermeneutics to the question of meaning in general and away from the mind of the author; by the same token, hermeneutics serves to "liberate" phenomenology from an idealistic epistemology. But my interpretation seeks to do more than situate Ricoeur within the trajectory that leads from Husserl to Gadamer; in orienting this interpretation, I am placing myself in league with a group of commentators on Ricoeur, most notably Don

Ihde, who argued that Ricoeur pushed phenomenology itself into the realm of hermeneutics. Ihde argues:

> Ricoeur's application of phenomenology to language or his transformation of phenomenology into hermeneutics finds its justification in a need to elaborate concepts *indirectly* and *dialectically* rather than directly and univocally. Out of the whole range of linguistic "sciences," Ricoeur chooses to address himself to a certain set of symbolic structures (and myths) by which man may better understand himself. This indirect route via symbol and through interpretation constitutes the opening to a hermeneutic phenomenology.[3]

Therefore, Ricoeur's overall project should be viewed as a *hermeneutic phenomenology*; by this I mean, a philosophical exploration of the *interpretive encounter with phenomena*. This encounter is interpretive because objects of perception, thought, etc., rise to meaning in linguistic and cultural expressions that *mean* more than they *say* and, therefore, demand interpretation.

Once again, however, I wish to pause and note a slight divergence between my understanding of Ricoeur's project and Ihde's. He tends to divide Ricoeur's project into two broad orientations: structural phenomenology, indebted to Husserl, and hermeneutic phenomenology, beginning, generally speaking, with the analysis of symbols in *The Symbolism of Evil*. I, on the other hand, want to hang on to Ricoeur's own threefold division of *eidetics*, *empirics*, and *poetics* of the will. This is a divergence more than a dispute; I think the difference in divisions is a matter of different emphasis on the degree to which the "structural" orientation of Husserl's method remains a key aspect of Ricoeur's hermeneutical expansion of phenomenology. A hermeneutics of figurative discourse is inextricably tied to Ricoeur's account of the structure of the will.

My third presupposition is that Ricoeur's project is most adequately thought of as a *philosophical anthropology*. This is certainly the least disputed of my presuppositions, and I will not treat it at length here. Suffice it to say, Ricoeur's project has always been concerned about the nature of the self, and more particularly, with the capable self. Ricoeur's accounts modified and deepened with the introduction of different perspectives and methods, but the emphasis on human capability remained the constant in his thought. However, the emphasis on human *capability* raised another set of issues that became progressively more important in Ricoeur's corpus: those of ethics and morality. For this reason, Ricoeur's philosophical anthropology must also be recognized as a *moral anthropology*. The ethical and moral questions surrounding the issue of selfhood will become the central concern of the second half of this book. In addressing the last of my presuppositions I turn directly to theological issues.

Theological Issues

My final assertion was at one time disputed, but has become progressively less so. I argue that it is possible to locate a much deeper connection between Ricoeur's philosophical writings and his religious and theological writings than he himself typically assigned. I am by no means alone in my interest in Ricoeur's religious thought. In fact, few other philosophers have garnered as much attention from theologians and scholars of religion as Ricoeur has. And the various engagements with the religious and theological dimensions of Ricoeur's thought have yielded various conclusions. I want to begin by surveying a portion of the field of religious and theological approaches to Ricoeur's thought before I situate my own reading.

Few scholars of religion or theologians have taken interest in Ricoeur's early phenomenological works, unlike philosophers, who have been especially interested in the place of this work in Ricoeur's corpus. While mention is made of these works in nearly all treatments from the perspective of religion and theology, few make it a central issue.[4] For obvious reasons, Ricoeur's later work on symbol, metaphor, and narrative tend to be the principal interest of religious and theological treatments. This is somewhat unfortunate, however, because Ricoeur's later turn to the hermeneutics of symbols and metaphors, and to narrative theory are of a piece with his early presentation of a poetics of the will, as I hope to show over the course of the proceeding studies. Additionally, it is not always clear whether theological appropriations of Ricoeur seek to advance a theological understanding of Ricoeur's ideas or use Ricoeur to advance a separate position that is more or less consonant with his ideas. Dan Stiver, for instance, seems less interested in articulating Ricoeur's positions than in reforming a vision of Ricoeur that can be appropriated in the service of defending contemporary evangelical Christianity.[5] John Wall adopts the structure of Ricoeur's *Oneself as Another* to explore the idea of a human creative moral capacity, but does little to tie this structure to the rest of Ricoeur's *ouvre*.[6] Others attempt to remain closer to Ricoeur's own ideas; my own project follows in the steps of these latter approaches.

Religious and theological treatments can be divided, without too much oversimplification, into two primary camps. On the one side are positions that are interested in Ricoeur for purposes of Christian apology. That is to say, these perspectives see Ricoeur's work as possessing valuable resources for exploring a specifically Christian identity and for defending an "orthodox" view of Christianity in what they label the postmodern situation.[7] On the other side are positions that explore Ricoeur's work for the poetic and redescriptive opportunties that he presents for the study of religion and theology in a context that is not exclusively Christian.[8] One is tempted to label these two camps conservative/evangelical and liberal/progressive, but this *would* be an oversimplification.

Rather, I will call these two approaches to Ricoeur's religious and theological thought the *apologetic* and the *poetic*, respectively.

An abiding interest among apologetic appropriations of Ricoeur's thought is his relation to what has often been called the New Yale Theology, indebted to the theology of Karl Barth and represented by contemporary figures Hans Frei and George Lindbeck.[9] While Frei has criticized Ricoeur for making the Biblical narrative subservient to philosophical speculation, many apologists argue that Ricoeur's thought need not be interpreted so.[10] However, while these thinkers appear to believe that Ricoeur's ideas can be redeemed, they criticize Ricoeur himself for taking a too poetic approach and/or for relying too much upon philosophy at the expense of a more robust account of distinctly Christian sensibilities. For instance, Kevin VanHoozer complains that Ricoeur's metaphorical treatment of the resurrection, as well as other aspects of Christian doctrine, does not sufficiently account for the Christian understanding of the new being initiated by the Christ event: "It would appear that for Ricoeur, the resurrection power is more a matter of metaphorical than historical reference. It is the metaphor—an event of discourse rather than history—that saves by redirecting our imagination and refiguring our existence."[11] As such, Ricoeur presents the resurrection as a poetic event that reveals an existing, though hidden, possibility for new life, rather than the historical event that makes new life a novel ontological possibility. James Fodor questions the relative priority that Ricoeur gives philosophy over theology:

> Are hermeneutical or methodological questions capable of being displayed independently of the particular texts in question or are they internal to the practices of biblical exegesis, commentary, exposition, and proclamation? That is, in what sense does describing the Bible as a poetic, metaphorical text significantly illuminate its function as the Word of God? Indeed, if the Bible is just one more instance of a poetic text, perhaps even the most central text in the Western world, how might a Ricoeurian hermeneutic account for its specificity, especially its distinctive truth claims?[12]

In all cases, the concern is whether or not Ricoeur's reliance upon philosophical hermeneutics and characterization of the Bible as a species of poetic text effaces Christian distinctiveness and biblical authority. This line of questioning has real teeth; Ricoeur clearly wanted to preserve the distinctiveness of the Bible, even as he described it as a species of poetic text and compared its redescriptive capacities to those of literary fiction. But the real question is whether such claims to distinctiveness are warranted given the general shape of Ricoeur's thought.

The very aspects of Ricoeur's thought that the apologists find so troubling are what those in the poetic camp find of such value in his thought. David Klemm and William Schweiker point to the multiplicity of perspectives, and to Ricoeur's critical hermeneutics of the biblical texts in particular, as the most salient aspect of his thought:

> In some of the writings in which he interprets the biblical word, Ricoeur critically appropriates the Word of God theologies that dominated dogmatic and ecclesial theological reflection earlier this century; in other such writings, he appears to approach more current forms of narrative theology. . . . That we have always already been "spoken to" means for Ricoeur that we do not have cognitive clarity concerning who or what the human being is, since to be human is in part to be constituted by what is spoken to us. Moreover, the hermeneutics of text and the various explanatory methods an interpreter uses in examining religious symbols and myths do not exhaust the possible import of these discursive forms for understanding the human condition. In fact, they provoke further detours of interpretation on the way to understanding the truth of the ambiguity we are. That truth, it seems, is bound up in the Word spoken to us.[13]

Richard Kearney speaks approvingly of Ricoeur's insistence that belief pass through the critical gaze of philosophical criticism. In Kearney's estimation, this critical gaze is necessarily entailed in Ricoeur's presentation of biblical myths as a species of poetry: "In maintaining a poetical fidelity to the great (and small) myths of tradition, we retain a questioning attitude. Without fidelity we become disinterested spectators of a cultural void; without questioning we become slaves to prejudice. If myth is to remain true to its promise, it must pass through the detour of critical enlightenment."[14]

My approach will fall squarely within the camp that finds the most promise in exploring the poetic possibilities of Ricoeur's religious and theological writings. Not only do I find apologetic appropriations of Ricoeur's work suspect, I argue that they attempt to place restraints upon those dimensions of his thought that offer the most potential for human liberation in light of the biblical texts. Indeed, I agree with David Klemm's assessment that it is important "to remove the constriction Ricoeur places on religious discourse." The point is not to defend the uniqueness of the Bible, but to explore what it reveals about the human condition. "Religious discourse," Klemm continues, "in the nature of the case is not merely biblical discourse, but any instance of language, which drives thinking and experiencing to the limits by means of limit expressions."[15] Thus, the criticisms of apologists such as VanHoozer and Fodor, that

Ricoeur was unable to coherently articulate the uniqueness of the Bible, are correct. But then again, his attempts to privilege the Bible, to defend its distinctiveness and unique authority, went against the more hopeful possibilities for describing new life that his thought offered.

So, to lay out my final presupposition again, I assert that there is a close connection between Ricoeur's philosophical writings and his religious and theological ones. Not only this, but his religious views offer an important interpretive key to understanding his *ouvre* as a whole. There are, dispersed throughout Ricoeur's writings, points of approach between philosophy and theology; the problem of moral evil was among the foremost of these. Within these points of approach, philosophy comes upon speculative impasses that it cannot resolve, though philosophy can advance "approximations" of religious meanings and experiences. In this sense, philosophy opens theological claims to the possibility of rational speculation, though philosophy cannot cross the divide that separates it from religious witness.

I do not wish to question this divide; I have no desire to collapse philosophy into theology, or vice versa. However, I do want to argue that Ricoeur's religious and theological writings offer an important interpretive key to the overall coherence of his thought. One need not go so far as to claim that there is "a secret religious motivation" in his writings. Ricoeur was certainly not a theologian, but he was, by admission, a careful listener to the Christian witness. I argue that these commitments answer to the philosophical impasses that he went to such lengths to highlight; theological discourse and biblical texts, considered as species of poetic configuration, offer figurative resolutions to the impasses encountered within philosophy, even if one recognizes, as I believe one must, the difference between theology and philosophy.

This "poetic crossing" becomes most apparent at the level of moral deliberation. I pointed to the idea of a poetic use of the imperative that Ricoeur derived from the biblical configuration of the love command. This imperative nature of the love command arose from his treatment of the ideas of Jewish philosopher Franz Rosenzweig. On Rosenzweig's account, the love command, conceived as a direct address from the divine to the individual soul, is the grounding for all other commandments, all laws, and all ethical orientations. In this sense, the love command serves a function within Rosenzweig's thought similar to Kant's proposal of the categorical imperative. Yet Ricoeur argued that the imperative structure of the love command cannot be reduced to a simple moral imperative. Rather, the love command derives its very meaning from the poetic dimensions of the biblical texts that surround it. I intend to expand on this notion with the proposal of a *poetic imperative*, which draws together the key themes that concern the relationship between love and justice. Briefly put, I will explore Ricoeur's ideas in this arena along a trajectory that leads from the competing logics of equivalence and superabundance, through the confrontation between the golden rule and the love command, to the tension between autonomy and theonomy. This trajectory is explored in more detail below.

Interpretational Structure

Once again, the thesis I am arguing is that Paul Ricoeur's religious and theological writings provide important perspective on his philosophical project as a whole, and I have gone to some lengths to outline what is entailed in this claim. The book is composed of four analytic chapters, which are organized by a threefold organization that runs throughout. In chapter 6, I conclude with the constructive proposal for a poetic imperative and the novel features that this idea introduces into our understandings of Ricoeur's work. This threefold organization is composed of the interconnected categories of *basic structure*, *configuration*, and *experience*, and is intended as a sort of revised phenomenological analysis. I characterize this structure as a revised phenomenological analysis in order to encompass both the analytical rigor and the influence of Husserl's phenomenology in Ricoeur's early thought, and the linguistic and hermeneutical orientation that Ricoeur lent to phenomenology. These interrelated levels of analysis organize the progression of each of the four main chapters.

Chapter 2 addresses the topic of *human agency*. Unlike other philosophical perspectives that have exerted a profound influence on contemporary thought on the nature of the self, for example, Descartes and Hegel, Ricoeur's central anthropological category was not reason or mind, but will. In this sense, he was an heir to Nietzsche's critique of a self-founding, transparent rational faculty. However, while Ricoeur was in fundamental sympathy with the suspicion of transparent rationality, he was unwilling to follow Nietzsche in dissolving selfhood into pure will-to-power. If selfhood is displayed in the exercise of will, that is, in action, selves are *capable* agents because they can reflect upon and choose different courses of action.

I address the basic structure of agency in terms of *capability*. I unfold this idea through Ricoeur's understanding of the reciprocal relationship between the voluntary and involuntary structures of will and action. On this account, human action is not pure spontaneity; rather, the voluntary is receptive to involuntary structures, which make volition itself possible. That is to say, capability is both limited and empowered by involuntary structures in the face of which capability is passive and receptive. The analysis of agency enters another stage in the attempt to configure the *identity* of the agent. Like capability, the notion of identity is not simple and univocal, but composed of a relationship. Identity is characterized by a dual designation of *idem*, or sameness, which encompasses the dispositions and characteristics that allow one to identify individuals as remaining the same over time, and *ipse*, or selfhood, through which agency displays itself beyond the confines of sameness. Identity is irreducible to one or the other of these designations, but exists, rather, at the intersection of both. At a final level of analysis, I address the experience of agency in terms of *attestation*. I believe that this designation of *experience* is faithful to Ricoeur's definition of attestation as the assurance of being oneself acting and suffering. I address the character of attestation through Ricoeur's understanding of initiative as it is traversed by various forms of passivity.

Chapter 3 takes up the issue of what I call *meaning* or, more accurately, meaningful existence. A sort of conceptual bridge spans this analysis and the preceding one: the recognition that human agents are beings who reflect on their existence. The structure of agency is revealed in a capability that is configured as identity and attested to in the experience of acting and suffering. In the analyses that composed the topic of agency, it was possible to bracket the question of the self-reflective meaning of agency in the interest of offering a conceptually clear and rigorous account. In moving to the question of meaningful existence, therefore, I remove this first set of brackets in order to explore the manner in which selves *make sense* of themselves as agents.

Meaning becomes a problem by virtue of the fact that human existence is a "thrown" temporal project, that is, the self *finds* itself in an existence for which it is responsible. In more Ricoeurian terms, selfhood is a task that is lived in the mode of possibility. This account of selfhood as a task aimed at possibility introduces two closely related notions into the problematic of meaningful existence: temporality and potentiality. First, human existence is a temporal phenomenon. This idea is hardly earth-shattering; all existence is temporal. Yet, human existence is temporal in a distinct way; humans "wrestle" with time in the attempt to make sense of themselves. How does one experience time? How is it that one can account for an identity, whether one's own or another's, that remains the same despite change over time? These and other questions are avoided so long as one remains within the realm of pure structures. Once the question of meaning moves to the fore, so does the problem of temporality. Second, the problematic of meaning introduces the question of potentiality; Ricoeur characterized selfhood as a task, as a reality that humans are on the way toward. Of course, humans are already selves, that is, capable agents with identities to which they attest. But the *meaning* of selfhood is never finally fixed; self-reflection, in its profoundest dimension, is directed toward future possibilities that represent potential meanings for my existence. In the attempt to account for this deeply temporal character of human existence, Ricoeur turned to the configuring capacities of narrative, and this dimension of his work is a central component of this chapter.

Once again, I address the configuration of meaningful existence through three related levels of analysis that I label *understanding*, *possibility*, and *affirmation*.

I designate the structural aspect of meaningful existence as understanding in order to encompass both the phenomenological character of meaning and the hermeneutical dimension that Ricoeur introduced. On this account, understanding is wrought out of the active-receptive synthesis in imagination of the appearance of objects, actions, and inherited ideas.

Reflection on existence within a world does not yet signal *self*-reflection, however. The meaning of one's own existence remains only a possibility in the recognition of a meaningful world. An adequate account of self-reflection requires another level of analysis: the configuration of meaningful existence in *possibility*. Here, Ricoeur's reflections of the function of narrative in self-understanding move center stage. Narration becomes a centrally important factor in this movement by virtue of the "fusion of horizons" that takes place between the world of experience that a reader brings to a text and the world of possible meanings that the text presents to the reader.

However, this reflection on one's own possibility marks a place where reflection on the meaning of one's existence departs from narrative emplotment. If it can be claimed that meaningful existence is lived in the mode of possibility, and I believe that one must claim this in light of the projected task of selfhood, then the question of meaningful existence shifts from the imaginative variations opened by narrative to the ontological character of selfhood as *actuality* and *potentiality*. In light of this problem, Ricoeur suggested that the meaning of selfhood takes shape against a "ground of being at once actual and potential." The introduction of the notion of an ontological ground of being against which human possibility comes to light is extremely beneficial for my attempt to show the connections between Ricoeur's philosophical anthropology and his theological writings because, I will argue, it represents a philosophical approximation of the idea of God. At the final level of analysis of this chapter, which I label *affirmation* of the experience of meaningful existence, I introduce Ricoeur's philosophical writings to a set of theological ideas as they are construed biblically by a hermeneutics of testimony.

Chapter 4 takes up the issue of ethics proper in Ricoeur's writings via the idea of *practical experience*. The conceptual bridge that leads from the configuration of meaningful existence to practical experience is what I have labeled public life. By the term *public life* I mean to encompass, once again in fidelity to Ricoeur's thought, the fact that human existence is lived with others within the context of institutions, that is, shared languages, social-cultural mores, political and economic structures, etc.. With the introduction of public life, the reality of other persons, or more accurately expressed, the recognition of a general experience of otherness, enters the experience of selfhood. Indeed, Ricoeur claimed that otherness is the phenomenological correspondent to the experience of passivity that is a guiding theme of the project. However, in all cases, the experience of otherness is not ancillary to the experience of selfhood; rather, the experience of otherness is instrumental in the understanding and constitution of selfhood.

As with the preceding two, this chapter is governed by the threefold organization of structure, configuration, and experience. I label the three analyses that compose this exploration of practical experience *responsibility*, *ethics*, and *witness*. My examination of the basic structure of responsibility diverges somewhat from Ricoeur's own explicit statements on the idea, though I do not believe that this divergence signals a fundamental disagreement. Ricoeur himself discussed the notion of responsibility in a rather narrow sense of *holding oneself responsible* for one's actions. This narrow focus by no means exhausts the meaning of moral responsibility; Ricoeur introduced two other terms in order to fill out the topic of moral obligation: *imputation* and *solicitude*. In offering an expanded account of the idea of responsibility, I make a distinction between responsibility *for* actions and responsibility *to* persons. This distinction places the ideas of imputation and solicitude both under the umbrella of responsibility and, in so doing, gives both a less abstract and more ethically robust sense.

What does this account of responsibility as the structure of practical experience entail for practical action? Here, I move to a second level of analysis: the configuration of practical experience in terms of *ethics*. Ricoeur's most explicit formulation of ethics entailed a threefold movement that (1) places a priority on an ethical aim for the good life, which (2) necessitates the imposition of norms of obligation due to the possibility of violence, and which, in turn, (3) demands recourse to the aim due to the impasses that arise within the formation of norms of obligation themselves. The first two movements are the focus of this section of the chapter; the third is the focus of the final section. Though given priority status, a teleological orientation toward the good life, in an Aristotelian mode, is not of itself adequate, in Ricoeur's estimation, for a complete determination of ethicomoral judgment. The aim must be buttressed by a deontological moment, in a Kantian vein, within which all particular aims are subjected to a test moral obligation.

This Kantian moment within the overall drift of the good life gives rise to a set of fundamental philosophical impasses within moral judgment, which necessitate a return to the teleological dimension of the good life. Ricoeur argued, therefore, for the need to return to the concern for the good life, which I address in the final section of this chapter under the heading of *witness*. Nevertheless, this return to the ethical aim is neither a simple return nor a disavowal of the deontological moment; rather, the moment of moral judgment gives the quest for the good life a critical edge and a perspective on the possibilities of violence. Ricoeur called this critical return to judgment conviction, which directs moral judgment to specific situations characterized by fidelity to others.

The philosophical articulation of conviction and fidelity goes some way toward articulating practical experience. However, philosophical speculation does not do complete justice to experience; philosophy points to a value within specific situations that draws attention, but the shape of this value remains somewhat undetermined. Likewise, philosophy comes up short in addressing experience of moral conflict and tragedy, which hound convictions. The attempt to provide an adequate account of practical experience opens onto the concerns of theological ethics. Thus, the conceptual bridge that leads from practical experience to the next level of theological ethics, the topic of chapter 5, is precisely the recognition of moral value despite moral conflict and the experience of tragedy. Ricoeur's own convictions were shaped by the Christian witness; in pointing to this fact, I am not imposing Christian claims into his thought. Rather, I am attempting to introduce his own claims about this witness as an interpretive key to his philosophical project as a whole.

I address Ricoeur's theological and ethical concerns under the category of *conscience.* But why conscience? I adopt this term for two reasons. First, he defined conscience as the capacity to relate oneself to an instance qualified by the distinction of good and evil, that is, qualified by moral values. Second, Ricoeur offered several important and potent investigations of the theological meaning of conscience. In this sense, conscience represents a natural point of entrance into theological claims.

My exploration of Ricoeur's theological perspective follows the same threefold organization that functions throughout the rest of the project. At the level of basic structures, I address the creative tension between a *logic of equivalence* and a *logic of superabundance*. The first outlines the basic sentiment at the heart of the concern for justice; equivalence is the logic upon which notions of equality and reciprocity are built. The logic of superabundance, the paradigmatic example of which is the Sermon on the Mount in the gospel of Matthew, in many ways calls into question the reciprocity grounded in equivalence. It does not contradict equivalence, but forces one to redefine it in terms that do not succumb to a sort of reactive reciprocity (do unto others as they do unto you) or an equally perverse instrumental reciprocity (I do this so you will do that).

This corrective relationship between equivalence and superabundance becomes more manifest at the second level of the configuring orientations of the golden rule and the love command. The golden rule functions along the lines of a formalization of the ideal of reciprocity which governs justice. In many ways, the love command opposes this ideal with a demand to forgo reciprocity in the interest of the other; that is to say, the love command introduces into our relations with others a fundamental generosity that seeks the good of the other, in many cases over the good of the self. Once again, however, the tension between the golden rule and the love command does not signal contradiction, but rather a mutual implication that offers a deeper understanding of both.

The final level of analysis addresses the ideas of autonomy and theonomy. In many respects, this level of analysis represents the greatest point of tension between the ideals of love and justice by virtue of the fact that ethical theory since Kant has placed the possibility of moral discernment in the existence of a self-sufficient autonomous will. The idea of theonomy seems to introduce a dimension of heteronomy into morality that contradicts his moral foundation of autonomy. However, Ricoeur sought to disarm this conflict by conceiving theonomy in such a way that it did not rule out, but rather empowered, freedom. The notion of the poetic imperative enters at this level of analysis.

In chapter 6, I offer concluding reflections on the overall character of the idea of the poetic imperative and what this idea introduces into Ricoeur's philosophical anthropology. I will begin by addressing an idea that arose in Ricoeur's discussion of the logic of superabundance: the notion of an "economy of the gift." This idea is exceedingly ambiguous due to an intuitive urge to pose "economy" and "gift" as contradictory concepts. Indeed, Jacques Derrida played on this intuition, positing economy and gift not just as contradictories, but as "impossible others," ideas that cancel each other out, yet cannot be thought without each other. Derrida, among others, will be a principal dialogue partner in the attempt to uncover what Ricoeur might have meant by economy of the gift. The exploration of this idea will give some purchase on the relationship that Ricoeur sought to establish between love and justice.

It is important to emphasize that the relationship between the ideals of love and justice is, on Ricoeur's accounting, a creative tension and not a static opposition. They do not cancel each other out; rather, the establishment of a relationship offers the possibility of a mutual reinterpretation that yields a deeper understanding of both love and justice. While the generosity demanded by the love command turns justice, conceived in terms of the golden rule, away from its perversion into retribution and utility, the abiding demand that justice be done assures that the generosity of love does not devolve into self-denigration and self-negation. My concluding reflections on the idea of the poetic imperative are more exploratory in nature. At issue is the manner in which love can be imperative, that is, how it can serve as a foundation for action, and capable of redescribing reality in the sense that Ricoeur speaks of poetry. My hope will be to open future lines of enquiry.

Chapter Two

Agency
The Structures of Selfhood

The focus of this chapter is principally descriptive: my purpose is to uncover the basic structures of Ricoeur's account of the agent with the intention of laying the groundwork for following chapters. My turn to the questions of meaning, practice, and conscience in the following chapters will not signal an abandonment of the question of the agent but a deepening of this exploration of the nature of the self who is revealed in action as an agent. I will explore the question of agency in Ricoeur's writings in three stages that I label *capability*, *identity*, and *attestation*. By organizing this initial set of analyses in this manner, I am attempting to trace out, at a formal level, what Kathleen Blamey has called Ricoeur's philosophical itinerary "from the ego to the self." Referring to Ricoeur's later work, Blamey states, "Emphasis has shifted from the earlier discussions of 'ego' and 'subject' to a preference for the 'I' and the 'self.'"[1] The movement from capability, through identity, to attestation marks an itinerary from a rather formal account of the capable subject to one of a self who attests to itself in its capability.

The idea of capability delineates the kind of freedom that is available to humans. Ricoeur posited a reciprocal relationship between freedom and "nature," between the voluntary and the involuntary, which characterizes human willing. The reciprocity between the voluntary and the involuntary is the basic structure of capable agency. Within this reciprocity, Ricoeur defined human existence in terms of "incarnate freedom." As an incarnate, "only human" freedom, human capability is not absolute: human willing is not pure act but active *and* passive. Humans are made capable on the basis of structures that they do not choose, but in the face of which they are passive and to which they are receptive, for example, needs and desires, physical abilities, and laws of nature.

The basic structure of human capability is configured into a meaningful account of the identity of the agent through the creative tension that exists between the ideas of *idem* and *ipse*, or sameness and selfhood. These two dimensions of the identity mark out what can be called, at risk of some oversimplification, the objective and subjective conditions of the identity of the agent. Ricoeur configured the relation between these two dimensions of selfhood through the relative concepts of character (*caractère*) and self-constancy. In the analysis of character, sameness overlaps selfhood to the point where they are indistinguishable. At the level of self-constancy, selfhood establishes itself beyond its support in sameness.

At the final level of analysis, I will address the question of agency from the experiential perspective of *attestation*. For Ricoeur, attestation delineated the kind of assurance one has of himself as an agent. If one can no longer follow Rene Descartes in positing, beyond any doubt, the sovereign ego, neither can one follow Friedrich Nietzsche in casting all doubt on the existence of an integral self. Behind all suspicion about the self, and the philosophical analysis that attempts to banish the question of the nature of selfhood, another question asserts itself and demands an answer: How does one account for the experience of being a self? For Ricoeur, this experience is defined by the idea of attestation as *the assurance of being oneself acting and suffering*. Human will is not a sovereign, "noumenal" freedom but an incarnate, that is, embodied, freedom. Ricoeur defined the kind of freedom open to incarnate agents as *initiative*, that is, as the ability to initiate a series of events within a causal structure. Initiative is the nature of human activity. This account of human activity as initiative forces one to recognize the limits of human agency: humans not only act but are subject to various forms of passivity, for instance, necessity, temporality, violence. Humans are acting *and* suffering beings. The recognition of this creative tension between activity and passivity reveals the profound significance of the act of attesting as an assurance of being oneself in both *acting* and *suffering*.

These three dimensions mark out the itinerary of the chapter, which is a progression from basic structure, through configuration, to experience. Before proceeding, however, the broad outlines of Ricoeur's account of agency must be explored.

The Structure of Agency

Ricoeur's account of selfhood was always bound to the question of agency. To answer the question of the nature of the self is therefore to offer an account of agency:

> Every act, in the strong sense of the term, possesses at the same time an objective intending and a relation of "imputation" which appears clearly in a decision; in making up my mind, I impute to myself the action, that is, I place it in a relation to myself such that, from then on, this action represents me in the world; if it is asked: "Who did this?" I hold myself ready to respond: "It is I who did this, *ego sum qui feci*." . . . Thus I posit myself as the agent in the intending of the action to be done. . . . My power-to-be manifests itself in my power-to-do and this power-to-do is revealed to itself in the projects which it forms concerning things in the world.[2]

It is important not to underestimate the significance of this fact because it oriented Ricoeur's entire philosophical project in a very important direction. Ricoeur claimed that selfhood is attested to in the capacity to act and in the abilities of the will to leave its traces on the course of events in the world. In this sense, Ricoeur was one of the heirs to the attacks leveled at the naiveté of an overly self-assured reason. If Descartes can be credited for positing this self-assured rational faculty, Nietzsche must be considered the progenitor of current attacks on the self-founding certainty of reason. Ricoeur was in fundamental sympathy with the suspicion that has been cast upon the self-founding *I* by various late-twentieth-century philosophical perspectives.

This sympathy is not complete, however. While he recognized the problematic character of the account of a self grounded solely in the idea of transparent reason, Ricoeur was unwilling to follow the inheritors of Nietzsche's campaign against the rational faculty in reducing the self to a mere confluence of external or internal forces. Unlike various forms of philosophical voluntarism such as existentialism, he refused to replace the self-reflective *I* with the sovereign act of an unencumbered will. Likewise, in opposition to philosophical trends that attempted to deny the possibility of a cohesive, reflective self (and with it, the possibility of agency), for example, poststructuralism and deconstruction, Ricoeur's project doggedly sought to establish the place of a self that reflects on its existence, is motivated by needs and desires, and acts freely. Ricoeur resisted the temptation to erase the question of the self-reflective *I*. Rather, he argued that the capacity for self-reflection is revealed in action. That is to say, *selfhood is attested to in action*: the *I* is, first and foremost, an agent.[3]

Establishing the structure of agency is important for many reasons, but most especially for ethical reflection. Ethics depends upon an account of the agent for two reasons. First, the topic of agency allows an approach to the subject to whom one can ascribe moral predicates. There must be a subject who is an agent in order to be able to engage in ethical reflection at all. For this reason, Ricoeur's philosophical project was most profoundly a philosophical *anthropology*. His was a project that sought to address the nature and character of acting selves. In a second way, agency designates the subject of ethics to the extent that ethics is a discipline concerned with the question of morally responsible agency. Ricoeur's project was concerned, implicitly if not always explicitly, with moral questions. If it is possible to locate an agent capable of responsible action, then the question of responsible limitations on action follows closely behind. Thus, Ricoeur's explicitly ethical writings were the necessary outcome of a long philosophical career. For this reason his philosophical anthropology must be understood at the same time as a *moral* anthropology.

In point of fact, the two sides of the question of agency are inseparable; to locate an agent is to locate one who is responsible and, therefore, subject to moral injunctions. This connection between capable subject and moral injunction signals Ricoeur's profound debt to Immanuel Kant, a debt he shared with thinkers as diverse as Emmanuel Levinas, Jürgen Habermas, and John Rawls. Yet, where Levinas claimed that selfhood was constituted through "the other" in answer to the moral injunction embodied in the "face" of the other, Ricoeur argued that there must first be a self who is capable of recognizing the other and his/her moral claim. While Habermas located moral autonomy in an ideal speech communication situation devoid of particularizing conventions, Ricoeur founded human capability in the critical convictions individuals hold and through which they bring their particular concerns to the situation of argumentation. Rawls articulated citizenship in terms of the ability to recognize procedurally agreed upon principles of justice that arise out of a postulated "original position" governed by a "veil of ignorance." Ricoeur, on the other hand, claimed that citizenship rests on mutual indebtedness and power exercised in common. Ricoeur's philosophical anthropology was, in every sense of the word, a philosophy of capability enmeshed in the vicissitudes of existing. This chapter focuses precisely on articulating the structures of this embodied, reflective, capable agent.

Capability: The Voluntary and the Involuntary

Ricoeur set the question of the agent within the reciprocal relationship between the voluntary and the involuntary, which, I claim, presents the basic structure of agency as capability. He consciously adopted this strategy in order to escape the kind of dualism that effected Kant's account of self. While Kant discussed the self in terms of a phenomenal/noumenal duality (natural causality/free causality) which places the voluntary and involuntary structures of action in epistemologically unrelated realms of existence, Ricoeur argued that the voluntary structures of action only make sense when considered in their relation to the involuntary.

In the opening pages of *Freedom and Nature*, Ricoeur described the polemical relation between the voluntary and the involuntary in the following terms:

> [T]he initial situation revealed by [phenomenological] description is *the reciprocity of the involuntary and the voluntary*. Need, emotion, habit, etc., acquire a complete significance only in relation to a will which they solicit, dispose and generally affect and which in turn determines their significance, that is, determines them by its choice, moves them by its effort, and adopts them by its consent. . . . Only the relation of the voluntary and the involuntary is intelligible.[4]

To paraphrase, the voluntary exists only by virtue of the motives, affections, and constitutional and physical limitations that condition it and embody it. Those same involuntary conditions only become understandable as such in relation to a will that chooses, moves, and adopts on the basis of those conditioning factors. This reciprocity is the structure within which Ricoeur's understanding of human agency comes to light.

Ricoeur attempted to trace the structure of human freedom across three arenas of the involuntary, which he labels *decision*, *motion*, and *consent*. At the first level of decision, his principal interest was to unearth the description of action as a motivated project. What sets an action apart from a random event is the fact that an action seeks an end: *when we act, we seek a desired result*. For example, I decide to go to the refrigerator, take an orange, and peel it because I want to relieve my hunger. But the recognition that an action is a motivated project points to a deeper structure within decision itself; the impetus for our motives to act are *received*; we are motivated to act out of the needs and desires of the body. My hunger is not voluntary, but my decision to eat an orange is a voluntary response to an involuntary need for nutrients.

In the second arena of motion, the received character of volition is even more pronounced. *To act is to move one's body*. This fact is so endemic to voluntary action that it tends to escape conscious reflection. My decision to eat an orange only becomes an action when I physically move my body to the refrigerator, physically move my arm to the shelf, move my hand to peel the orange, etc. My capability to act is conditioned by the abilities of the body; the body is, in the profoundest sense, the *received* organ of my freedom. I do not choose my body, and I only have a limited control of its native abilities. My volition confronts my body in the form of effort, that is, moving my body entails exerting effort upon it; the body is both a constellation of physical abilities and brute physical inertia. This fact is lost from sight in mundane examples such as taking something from the refrigerator. But the recognition of the effort it takes to move one's body enters consciousness again when we consider more strenuous activities, for instance, learning a sport. I can learn to move my body in such a way that I can throw a basketball through a hoop; indeed, the more effort I put into this activity the more natural it becomes (hence, receding from consciousness again). But the learning is an effort to which the body puts up resistance.

The final arena of consent represents the point at which volition confronts pure limitation. In decision I confront the givenness of need and desire which I direct toward a project; in movement I confront the inertia of the body upon which I direct effort; *in consent I confront the experienced necessity which conditions my possible action*. While I can teach myself, train my body, to shoot a basketball, I cannot train my body to dunk a basketball. (At a height of 5'8" and a vertical leap of well under 48", it is simply impossible that I will ever dunk a basketball so long as the rules of basketball dictate that the hoop is ten feet high.) This is not to say that the experience of external necessity on me cancels out my freedom. It is to say, however, that experienced necessity is the context for capability. To consent to experienced necessity is quite simply to recognize the scope of capability.

The first point to make clear, therefore, is that human freedom cannot be reduced to the voluntary. Freedom is not characterized by volition, which stands in opposition of the involuntary. Once again, only the *relation* of the voluntary and the involuntary is intelligible. As I suggested, this is one of the principal places where the anthropology of capability that Ricoeur espoused parts company with a Kantian anthropology. While Kant posed the question of the self in terms of a phenomenal/noumenal dichotomy, that is, noumenal, voluntary freedom versus a phenomenal body that is subject to causality (free causality versus natural causality), Ricoeur located human capability in the relation between voluntary and involuntary structures of action and will. For Ricoeur, freedom is not a transcendental presupposition. Rather, freedom is human capability that traverses the structures of a project motivated by needs and desires, of movement that exerts effort on bodily resistance, and of voluntary consent to the limitations upon action. Therefore, human freedom is an embodied, *incarnate* freedom.

A second point follows: the entity that Ricoeur called *cogito* or the *I* in his early work is not a transcendental presupposition set in opposition to the phenomenal body, but the experience of a will conjoined to a body that is both its organ and its condition. "The nexus of the voluntary and the involuntary does not lie at the boundary of two universes of discourse, one of which would be reflection concerning thought and the other concerning the physical aspects of the body: Cogito's intuition is the intuition of *a body conjoined to a willing which submits to it and governs it*. It is the meaning of the body as a source of motives, as a cluster of capacities, and even as necessary nature."[5] *Cogito* becomes the locus around which the idea of an "only human freedom," that is, a freedom that is conditioned by the involuntary structures that make it possible, congeals. Of this freedom, Ricoeur stated that it "is not a pure act, it is, in each of its movements, activity and receptivity. It constitutes itself in receiving what it does not produce: values, capacities, and sheer nature."[6]

This characterization of incarnate freedom only becomes understandable, he argued, against a set of regulative ideas, which serve as the first point of entrance onto a second level of analysis, that of configuration. Ricoeur adopted Kant's postulates of pure practical reason, particularly the presupposition of the existence of God, to serve as limit concepts in delimiting an "*only* human freedom." The presupposition of a transcendent, divine freedom presents the limit concept of a fully enlightened, completely spontaneous freedom against which the conditioned character of human freedom is set in relief. "These limit concepts have no other function here than to help us understand, by contrast, the condition of a will which is reciprocal with an involuntary. . . . At least such limit concepts complete the determination of a freedom which is human and *not* divine, of a freedom which does not posit itself absolutely because it *is not* Transcendence."[7] Here is one place that Ricoeur's philosophical project comes up against a theological horizon, even if a purely formal one. The introduction of the regulative idea of God is a formal requirement at this point in the argument. In order to make sense of a freedom that is embodied and receptive, a freedom that is transcendent and absolute must be imagined. In this sense, God is the context against which humans recognize their freedom.

By setting of human freedom within the context of a transcendent, perfect freedom, Ricoeur was already attempting to make sense of the basic structure of human capability. The turn to a regulative ideal is an attempt to configure the structures of the voluntary and the involuntary, that is, the active and the receptive sides of human capability, into a meaningful account of agency. In what follows, I will explore one of Ricoeur's more mature attempts: the configuration of the identity of the agent in terms of *idem* and *ipse*.

Identity: *Idem* and *Ipse*

I have argued that the structure of Ricoeur's account of agency can be characterized by capability that exists at the point of convergence between the voluntary and the involuntary structures of will and action. Therefore, these voluntary and involuntary structures are not opposed but rather fundamentally related. At the end of this exploration, the structure of agency is revealed by a capability that is both active and receptive; my abilities are affected by structures that I do not control. My decisions are motivated by the needs and the desires of my body. Motion is the effort I exert on the abilities and the resistances of my body. My freedom is won through consent to the conditions of experienced necessity.

In this second part, I follow Ricoeur in configuring these basic structures into an understandable account of the identity of the agent. The reciprocity between the voluntary and the involuntary is meaningfully configured as identity by Ricoeur's delineation of a creative tension within identity itself. This tension is signaled by two accounts of permanence in time: *idem* and *ipse*, or sameness and selfhood. Ricoeur concluded by relating these two dimensions of identity with the relative terms of character (*caractère*) and self-constancy.[8]

The attempt to configure the complex relationship between sameness and selfhood raises the critical question of the *temporality* of the self. The preceding analyses of Ricoeur's work have bracketed the question of time. However, selves exist in time; the identity of the agent is a personal history that makes agency itself possible. The principal question to ask here is the manner in which the identity of the agent perseveres in time and how agency is configured within time. Posing the identity of the self in terms of sameness and selfhood, therefore, is Ricoeur's attempt to account for the *permanence in time* of the self both as a body and as an agent.

At the lowest level, one can account for identity in time as sameness. Sameness delineates the characteristics of a self that allow one to recognize it as the same self, as selfsame, over time. Sameness exists in manifold forms: from *numerical* identity—this is *one and the same thing* now as it was then—to *qualitative* identity—these two, or more, temporal things are *similar in important characteristics*—to *uninterrupted continuity*—there is a temporal relation of continuity in this thing which appears differently than it did then. This characteristic of sameness can account for the identity of objects such as bodies and persons, which change over time. However, it cannot account for the characteristic of selfhood whereby a self actively affects and inhabits its own history, where the self maintains itself in initiative. Indeed, identity as selfhood, as *ipse*-identity, is lost behind the identification of a body that remains the same despite change. The relation between these two dimensions of identity is precisely what Ricoeur wished to plumb. In doing so, he adopted two relational concepts: *character* and *self-constancy*. Speaking of character (*caractère*), Ricoeur claimed, "I would say, barely skirting paradox, that the identity of character expresses a certain adherence of the 'what?' to the 'who?' Character is truly the 'what' of the 'who.'"[9]

The first place that the character of the self rises to the surface is in dispositions, or the patterns of behaving and acting, that cling to the self. Outside the objective *physical* characteristics and limitations of the body, persons are recognized through their particular mannerisms, their habituated, identifiable actions. In this way, personal dispositions become *character traits*, enduring signs by which persons are recognized as the same over time. One can define character broadly as a certain "style" of existence. Secondly, Ricoeur discussed character in terms of the acquired identifications that serve as communal models or ideals for emulation: "To a large extent, in fact, the identity of a person or a community is made up of these identifications with values, norms, ideals, models, and heroes *in* which the person or the community recognizes itself. Recognizing oneself *in* contributes to recognizing oneself *by*."[10] These identifications represent a sort of cultural deposit, which lends itself to the ethos of persons and communities, of persons within communities. Character traits and acquired identifications form an existential correlate to the physical traits by which persons are recognized as the same over time. However, if character inclines perspective toward the sameness of the person, the selfhood of the person is not lost from view. The fact remains that it is selves who form dispositions and habits, who recognize themselves in the identifications that contribute to the ethos of their social-culture surroundings. Character represents not the *absence* of *ipse*-identity, but the "over-lapping" of *idem* and *ipse* to the point where the latter becomes indiscernible from the former. In a metaphorical sense, selfhood remains hidden behind sameness as the principle around which dispositions and identifications cluster. But, selfhood is also the potential for initiative, which can spring forth from character.

In initiative, selfhood announces itself as self-constancy and frees itself from sameness. One of the principal places where Ricoeur located capability as initiative is in the ability to keep one's promises. This is likewise one of the principal places where he located selfhood as self-constancy:

> There is, in fact, another model of permanence in time besides that of character. It is that of keeping one's word in faithfulness to the word that has been given. I see in this keeping the emblematic figure of an identity which is the polar opposite of that depicted by the emblematic figure of character. Keeping one's word expresses a *self-constancy* which cannot be inscribed, as character was, within the dimension of something in general but solely with the dimension of "who?" . . . The perseverance of character is one thing, the perseverance of faithfulness to a word that has been given is something else again.[11]

In giving a promise, I display the ability to intend myself into the future with the intention to make good on the word I have given in the present. Thus, there is a profound link between selfhood and agency. *The self is an agent who maintains him/herself in remaining true to his/her word.*[12]

Nevertheless, human freedom is not pure volition; human action is not pure act. Human capability is embodied, incarnate, and as such one's action is limited by the obstacles both within and outside of the body. Actions arise within interconnected systems of cause and effect. Thus, initiative is not an *absolute beginning*, but the initiation of a series of events within a larger series. Even at the level of keeping one's promises, where the capability of the self announces itself at its most profound, individual initiative is a limited one. Therefore, one cannot reasonably promise to do something that is beyond his/her capability. Selfhood finds its structural support within sameness, even if selfhood lays claim to itself beyond structures of sameness.

At this point, however, I have already begun to delve into the question of the experience of being a self, which Ricoeur called attestation. I claimed that Ricoeur meaningfully configured the identity of the agent in terms of the creative tension between the ideas of sameness and selfhood and their relationship in character and self-constancy. In the realm of experience, this creative tension will take on a deepened meaning in the experience of another creative tension that exists between initiative and passivity. I took, as the basic structure of human agency, the idea of capability. However, capability itself, to the degree that it is structured by the reciprocity of the voluntary and the involuntary structures of will and action, reveals agency as both active, hence free, and receptive, hence limited.

Moving to the question of the experience of capable agency, I will follow Ricoeur in formulating attestation as *the assurance of being oneself acting and suffering*. Suffering will be defined in the broadest possible sense—from the mere fact that I cannot control all the effects that issue from my action to the incapacity inflicted on me through violence.

Attestation: Acting and Suffering Selves

Ricoeur defined attestation as "*the assurance of being oneself acting and suffering*."[13] It is important to realize the degree to which this assurance of oneself, this experience of being a self, is related in the same way that I have spoken of agency in general, namely, in terms of activity and passivity. I recognize myself and lay claim to myself in action. The experience of passivity—for example, suffering the actions of others, or confronting the fact of brute necessity—does not destroy the experience of selfhood. Passivity, "suffering" in the broad sense, is as much a dimension of agency, even at this experiential level, as is activity.

Recall that in posing the question of the self and freedom in terms of capability, Ricoeur attempted to locate the question in a particular place within the history of philosophical speculation on the self. Or, perhaps more adequately expressed, he attempted to dislodge the question from its particular "place" in the debate between Enlightenment and postmodern perspectives on the subject. This place, which both the Enlightenment and post-Enlightenment positions "share," is that of the transcendental ego. Ricoeur credited Descartes as the first to carve out this space and occupy it. Through the exercise of radical doubt about the existence of anything, Descartes posited the one inescapable truth to be the existence of the *I*: "*Cogito, sum*." Yet while Descartes took the certainty of the *cogito* to be that last and only bastion against radical doubt, Nietzsche was the philosopher to extend this radical doubt even to the *cogito*. Ricoeur explained:

> To understand this point, one must keep in mind the attack on positivism; where positivism says, There are only facts, Nietzsche says, There are no facts, only interpretations. In extending the critique to so-called internal experience, Nietzsche destroys in its principle the exceptional character of the cogito with respect to the doubt that Descartes directed to the distinction between the world of dreams and the world of waking. . . . In the exercise of hyperbolic doubt, which Nietzsche carries to its limit, the "I" does not appear as inherent to the cogito but as an interpretation of a causal type. . . . He bears witness in this way to the fact that nothing resists the most fantastic hypothesis, at least as along as one remains within the problematic defined by the search for a certainty that would be an absolute guarantee against doubt.[14]

Ricoeur sought to displace the question of selfhood from this quest for epistemic certainty, for positivity, that governs the debate between philosophies of *cogito* and philosophies of "anti-*cogito*."

If he was willing to follow Nietzsche in extending the interpretive task even to the question of selfhood, he was unwilling to follow him in interpreting the self in terms of pure vitality, that is, will-to-power. If the way has been closed to approaching the question of selfhood on the basis of positive certainty—existence/illusion, being-true/being-false—there is another kind of certainty upon which one can hang the experience of selfhood. Ricoeur called this change of perspective the *alethic* dimension of attestation; one attests to selfhood in and on the basis of the interchange between trust and suspicion.[15] If it is no longer possible to posit the self as an objective, transcendental reality outside change and causality, I nonetheless attest to an experience of selfhood within the flux, an experience I trust in spite of my suspicions.

This change of perspective bears witness to the profoundly existential dimension of Ricoeur's philosophical anthropology. It is possible to locate descriptively or analytically the places in which the question of selfhood rises to the surface, thus opening the space for attestation. But the being of that self is comprehended only within the effort to exist, only in the formation of projects and in concrete acts. That is to say, I attest to my power to *be* through my power to *do*. Or, as Ricoeur stated elsewhere, "attestation is the assurance—the credence and the trust—of *existing* in the mode of selfhood."[16]

This analysis of the experience of being an agent places one at the crossroads of another creative tension between initiative and passivity. While the polarity between these two ideas is more pronounced at this level of exploration, it remains a nondualistic account. Passivity is not the other of agency. Rather, passivity is a dimension of agency itself, a passing within agency that both complicates and deepens the idea of agency. Here I address the configuration of agency in two movements. First, I will address Ricoeur's understanding of free action as *initiative*, then I will address some of the privileged forms of passivity that cling to his account of agency.

Initiative

If human capability is not unbridled, if human willing is not pure act, how does one make sense of the kind of freedom that is open to human agents? Ricoeur related human agency in terms of initiative. In the most descriptive sense, human freedom is *the ability to initiate a series of events within a causal structure*. His analysis of initiative traversed four interrelated phases, which he characterized as such: "first, I *can* (potentiality, power, ability); second, I *act* (my being is my doing); third, I *intervene* (I inscribe my act within the course of the world: the present and the instant coincide); fourth, I keep my promises (I continue to act, I persevere, I *endure*)."[17] The first of these phases is the most closely related to the idea of incarnate freedom. In the footsteps of Maurice Merleau-Ponty, Ricoeur discussed human agency in terms of a phenomenology of the "I *can*," or a phenomenology of the *flesh*. Under this heading, human initiative, in the most profound sense, is recognized *in the flesh*. Ricoeur stated, "My own body, in this sense, is the coherent ensemble of my powers and my nonpowers; starting from the system of possibilities of the flesh, the world unfolds as the set of hostile or docile instrumentalities, of permissions and obstacles. The notion of circumstance is articulated here on that of powers and nonpowers, as that which surrounds my power of acting, offering the counterpart of obstacles or of workable paths for the exercise of my powers."[18] Circumstance, necessity, and all those aspects to which one consents are not absolute obstacles, but avenues within which one channels his/her powers. That is to say, the body, the flesh, is the point of commerce with the world; it is the place where I affect and am affected by the world. Human freedom is incarnate because the experience of being capable is an experience of the body in the world.

Secondly, Ricoeur addressed initiative in terms of action, proper. To employ the language of action at all is to utilize a semantic apparatus, a set of words that convey the sense of action such as project, motive, and intention. The recognition that humans act and that human action is a motivated project introduces a fracture into the deterministic account of necessity as an observable closed system. This fracture is introduced by virtue of the distinction between happening and "making happen," that is, between impersonal event and motivated project. Humans "make" things happen through their actions; they introduce change into the system. Ricoeur explained this paradox of action as such:

> Making something happen is not . . . an object of observation; as the agent of our actions, we produce something that, strictly speaking, we do not see. . . . We cannot be at the same time observer and agent. It follows that we can think only of closed systems, of partial determinisms, without being able to extend them to the universe as a whole, under penalty of excluding ourselves as agents capable of producing events, of making things happen. In other words, if the world is the totality of what is the case, action does not allow itself to be included within this totality. In yet other words, action *makes* reality incapable of being totalized.[19]

In the recognition that action makes things happen, affects the system, one also recognizes that no system is ultimately or completely closed.

To put this fact in even more pointed terms, humans *intervene* in the course of things. In the third phase, Ricoeur addressed G. H. von Wright's account of "systems theory" as the point of intersection between agency and causality. Citing von Wright, Ricoeur argued, "No action would happen and in particular, no scientific experiments would occur, without this confidence and this assurance that through our intervention we can produce changes in the world. . . . Von Wright is correct when he states 'in the idea of putting systems in motion the ideas of action and causation meet.'"[20] Scientific investigation, that is, putting the system in motion, intervenes in the functioning of the system itself. Therefore, action cannot be entirely encapsulated within a complete network of causation.

Finally, Ricoeur described initiative in terms of *promising*. I followed Ricoeur in locating the ability to keep one's promises as the premier place where selfhood disengages itself from sameness. Promising signals the point at which future action touches upon the idea of capability in the form of commitment. The commitment to a future action opens analysis to the fact that agents are capable *toward* the future. In this sense, promising is not only a point of initiation, that is, an intervention in the course of things, but also an orientation toward the future that secures my understanding of my capability. If I were incapable of initiating the course of action I promised, the promise itself would be meaningless.[21] The ability to keep one's word links up here with Nietzsche's *Genealogy of Morals*. Recall that the promise marks the point of entrance, for Nietzsche, of responsibility and the birth of the bad conscience. The ability to keep one's word, that is, the "right to make promises," marks the beginning of the slippery slope that runs through responsibility, to guilt, to debt, to the spectacle of cruelty surrounding the exaction of the debt, to bad conscience, and the social straightjacket of peaceful society. Keeping one's word signals the first step into non-freedom. However, while Nietzsche railed against the "morbid softening and moralization through which the animal 'man' finally learns to be ashamed of all his instincts,"[22] Ricoeur developed the capacity to keep one's word in a positive direction. This was largely due to different understandings of the nature of freedom. For Nietzsche, the human animal is only truly free when allowed to discharge its "powerful instincts." That is to say, freedom is synonymous with the will-to-power. For Ricoeur, on the other hand, the individual is only free to the degree that s/he can be responsible for his/her actions in light of the moral expectations of another. This will become the central aspect of chapter 4.

Therefore, initiative is the defining mark of human capability. Human agency is bound within conditions that both limit and empower it, conditions against which agency is passive and to which it is receptive but not *incapable*. Before addressing these forms of passivity within initiative, it will be useful to pause and discuss the importance of this dimension of passivity in Ricoeur's philosophical anthropology. The recognition that human agency is not characterized by pure activity, but also by passivity and receptivity, is significant. In the first place, Ricoeur's analysis of the dimensions of passivity at the purely descriptive, structural level seems indisputable. If one is to make sense of freedom, I believe one must follow Ricoeur in locating freedom within the involuntary structures of action and will, and within the structures of temporality, history, etc., "outside" of subjective freedom. These radically non-chosen structures are part of the theoretical/epistemological background *within* which one is forced to address freedom. However, as more existential and experiential dimensions of passivity are approached, these dimensions themselves serve to deepen Ricoeur's account of selfhood. As the experiences of being an agent in terms of meaningful existence (chapter 3), practical experience (chapter 4), and the religious dimensions of conscience (chapter 5) are approached, these deepened senses of passivity lend themselves to a deepened understanding of selfhood. In the conclusion of this initial chapter, I will offer something of a thumbnail sketch of these forms of passivity that will follow us through the rest of the project.

Forms of Passivity

The passivity that clings to agency is manifold, and it is necessary to analyze the various forms of passivity that affect, even assail, agency. At risk of oversimplifying this issue, I suggest that the idea of passivity be assigned two broad categories: external passivity (where external factors place limitations on acting), and internal passivity (where passivity seems to arise from within agency itself). These forms of passivity traverse the points of entrance of passivity into activity and deepen the experience of passivity within agency.

The most immediate form of external passivity is the experience of *suffering* that arises as an effect of violence. Indeed, the genesis of violence and suffering produces the most debilitating effects on agency. Ricoeur claimed:

> The occasion of violence, not to mention the turn toward violence, resides in the *power* exerted *over* one will by another. . . . The power-over, grafted onto the initial dissymmetry between what one does and what is done to another—in other words, what the other suffers—can be held to be the occasion par excellence of the evil of violence. The descending slope is easy to mark off, from influence, the gentle form of holding power-over, all the way to torture, the extreme form of abuse. . . . In all these diverse forms, violence is equivalent to the diminishment or the destruction of the power-to-do of others. But there is something even worse: in torture, what the tormentor seeks to reach and sometimes—alas—succeeds in destroying is the victim's self-esteem . . . . What is called humiliation—a horrible caricature of humility—is nothing else than the destruction of self-respect, beyond the destruction of the power-to-act.[23]

Violence, and to this one must add social and political oppression and the manifold expressions of nonphysical violence, borders on the complete destruction of agency. In this sense suffering represents the most direct experience of passivity in the face of external factors.

Yet, there are other forms of external passivity that fall short of the suffering caused by violence. For instance, the social, systemic character of action itself; once I act, my actions produce a string of effects that advances beyond the boundaries of what I intended. Likewise, natural necessity puts up resistance to and places limitations upon my power to act. For example, I am not at liberty to ignore the law of gravity, nor can I walk through solid objects. Humans are largely passive in the face of natural laws and physical objects; their existence is something to which I must consent if my actions are to be meaningful. In this sense, passivity seems to go hand in hand with *limitation*.

However, there is a more intimate sense in which individuals are confronted by necessity: in the form of *finitude*. At this point one begins to cross into what I have termed the internal forms of passivity. Finitude is perhaps the most profound sense of Ricoeur's understanding of agency as incarnate freedom. The body itself introduces into the experience of an agency a fundamental passivity. I have an experienced sense of bodily necessity, such as the need for rest or nourishment. Furthermore, it is through the body, with all its physical, habitual, and emotional inertia, that actions occur. That is to say, the body is the organ of action. More intimately still, the body is both the site of interaction with the world and the source of the motivation to act. This point is profoundly important in virtue of the fact that human action is a motivated project in the world. Freedom's association with the body inserts an inescapable note of passivity and receptivity into agency. Agency is characterized as an "only human" freedom because it is finite.

But there is a passivity within agency that is even more intimate than the experienced receptivity of the body and, at least philosophically, as debilitating as the suffering that assails agency from the outside. This passivity, which borders on incapacity, is associated with the experience of *moral evil.* Moral evil, sin, is internal to the will itself and represents one of the principal places where theological concerns crossed Ricoeur's philosophical anthropology. Ricoeur was indebted to Kant for his analysis of moral evil. Of this experience, Ricoeur claimed,

> I discover the *nonpower* of my freedom. (Curious nonpower, for I declare that I am responsible for this nonpower. This nonpower is completely different from the claim of an outside constraint.) I claim that my freedom has already made itself not-free. This admission is the greatest paradox of ethics. It seems to contradict our point of departure. We began by saying: evil is what I *could have* not done; this remains true. But at the same time I claim: evil is this prior captivity, which makes it so that I *must do* evil. This contradiction is interior to my freedom; it marks the nonpower of power, the nonfreedom of freedom.[24]

Moral fault is a passivity experienced at the heart of freedom itself. Hence, it is a fundamental aspect of agency. But this passivity is paradoxical in that it is a choice on the part of freedom that makes freedom unavailable; it is a *choice* that makes agency *incapable.*

While the other figures of passivity can be approached from the angle of a philosophical anthropology that defines agency in terms of capability, the radical passivity of moral evil at the heart of agency is incomprehensible so long as one remains solely within the bounds of philosophical speculation. It is simply inconceivable that a will should choose a principle of action that undermines its own freedom. Citing Kant, Ricoeur stated, "If we may think in conceptual terms of radical evil as the supreme maxim that grounds all the bad maxims of our free will, the *raison d'être* for this radical evil is inscrutable (*unerforschbar*): 'There is then for us,' Kant says, 'no conceivable ground from which the moral evil in us could originally have come.'"[25] Equally baffling is the question of how freedom might be restored once the will has chosen its own servitude. If philosophical speculation stumbles on the problem of moral evil, mythical narratives make sense of this problem through the symbol of the bound or servile will; theological speculation on the nature of hope witnesses to a possible restoration of moral goodness, which is eschatologically oriented. However, it is important to recognize that the incapacitation of freedom, the bondage of the will, is a function of agency itself. Moral evil is a self-binding, a voluntary servitude. This is what links it to the other figures of passivity that cross the idea of agency.

In this chapter, I began with the claim that capability, as it is structured by the reciprocity between the voluntary and the involuntary, is the basic structure of Ricoeur's account of selfhood as agency. I followed Ricoeur in configuring the identity of the agent in terms of the distinction between sameness and selfhood. I concluded by analyzing what I characterized as Ricoeur's understanding of the experience of being an agent in the idea of attestation as the assurance of being oneself acting and suffering. While I have been able to distinguish these two fundamental modes of the being of the agent, conceived broadly as activity and passivity—voluntary and involuntary, sameness and selfhood, initiative and forms of passivity—I have done little to discern, other than in purely formal terms, what the relationship between them is. To do this, however, Ricoeur entered another mode of analysis, that of narrative. He argued:

> This new manner of opposing the sameness of character to the constancy of the self in promising opens an interval of sense which remains to be filled in. This interval is opened by the polarity, in temporal terms, between two models of permanence in time—the perseverance of character and the constancy of the self in promising. . . . Now it is this "milieu" that, in my opinion, the notion of narrative identity comes to occupy. Having thus situated it in this interval, we will not be surprised to see narrative identity oscillate between two limits: a lower limit, where permanence in time expresses the confusion of *idem* and *ipse*; and an upper limit, where the *ipse* poses the question of its identity without the aid and support of the *idem*.[26]

This statement marks the end of my descriptive approach to the question of agency. From this point, I enter the realm of meaning where the self makes sense of itself and its possibility by, among other processes, narrating its existence.

Chapter Three

Meaning

The Narrative Configuration of Existence

In chapter 2, I argued that agency represents the structure of Ricoeur's account of the self. His philosophical anthropology focused attention on the capacities of the will rather than on the capacities of mind or reason. In this sense, his philosophical project diverged in important ways from Enlightenment accounts of the self, which, following Descartes, locate selfhood in a self-transparent rational faculty. Ricoeur took very seriously the post-Enlightenment critique of transparent reason initiated by Nietzsche. However, while sympathetic to this critique, he did not dissolve the question of the self into either the force that will exercises or to the force that is exercised on the will.

Human persons are acting agents, but they are also beings who strive to make sense of their existence. In this chapter, I will follow Ricoeur's argument that *existence is meaningfully configured via the mediation of narratives*. In unfolding the idea of narrative mediation, I will follow a similar itinerary to the one I adopted in the last chapter: structure, configuration, and experience. I will address the structure of meaningful existence under the heading of *understanding*, the configuration of meaningful existence under the heading of *possibility*, and the experience of meaningful existence under the heading of *affirmation*.

The move from the basic structure of agency to the configuration of meaningful existence is bridged by the idea of reflective agency, that is, the fact that human agents are beings who reflect on the meaning of their existence. I bracketed this sense of reflective agency in the last chapter in order to uncover the basic structures that make reflection on existence possible. The removal of these brackets allows the formal, structural account of agency to be deepened by questions of meaning and self-understanding. Ricoeur's account of the narrative configuration of meaningful existence mediates between the content-rich encounter with a world of meaning and an equally rich sense of self-understanding conceived in terms of possibility.

As it was in the last chapter, passivity is a central aspect of the structure of meaningful existence. Here, I will focus on the idea of receptivity, which is immediately recognizable at the level of understanding. In advancing the claim that human understanding is grounded in receptivity, I simply claim that humans do not make up meaning *ex nihilo*. Human understanding is receptive to structures of perception, to ideals of a complete life, to traditions of thought and artistic production, etc.. Humans come to understand their existence within a realm of meaning to which they are receptive; however, like the passivity encountered at the level of the basic structures of agency, human receptivity to the realm of meaning is not absolute passivity. This receptivity is an *active receptivity*. In other words, humans *actively understand* on the basis of the meanings they receive: they *create* new meaning out of received meaning. Active receptivity reveals itself first at the level of the body when humans actively make sense of received perception. This same active receptivity arises at the second level of meaningful action where human initiative strives, on the basis of what it receives from the body, for self-understanding and self-realization. Finally, active receptivity grounds meaningful existence in the dialectic of sedimentation and innovation that governs the ongoing formation of traditions of thought and practice.

Moving to the problematic of configuration, I will explore meaningful existence under the heading of possibility. In the last chapter, the ideal of self-constancy indicated the manner in which agents are capable of keeping their promises and the manner in which the actuality of the self is oriented by future possibility, or potentiality. In this chapter, emphasis will be placed on how existence becomes meaningful in light of potential for future self-actualization. Narrative configuration is a central feature of this orientation toward future possibility. Self-narration casts both a retrospective glance on existence, gathering together my past experiences into a meaningful whole, and a prospective glance orienting my future aspirations. In this second capacity, narrative serves to broaden the "practical field of action" through the imaginative variations that are offered to the reader. Narratives configure the practices that direct individual and communal lives. Likewise, narratives configure future possibilities in the form of life plans that direct future strivings. These narrative futures are composed in light of a practical horizon that Ricoeur called "the narrative unity of a life." The purpose of this exploration is to account for the manner in which narrative constructs a bridge between the past, present, and future of experience and, in so doing, constructs a bridge between the actuality and potentiality of the self. Selfhood, Ricoeur argued, is recognized as much in its potentiality, in its future possibility, as in its actuality. Yet, if this is so, a problem arises in that selfhood as potentiality can only be conceived as future possibility, that is, as *not yet* in existence. This fact *decenters* one's ruminations on the self toward what Ricoeur called "a ground of being at once potentiality and actuality." It would not be an overstatement to suggest that this ground of being represents a philosophical correlate for the divine. Thus, the location of a purposeful existence in an ontological ground of being is a premier place where my claim that Ricoeur's philosophical project has important theological sensibilities comes to the forefront.

In chapter 2, I argued that Ricoeur's account of attestation is attestation to the experience of being an agent. This experience resides in the recognition of an initiative traversed by various experiences of passivity However, attestation to the assurance of being a self points beyond the pure fact of this assurance to another experience. This is the point at which the experience of attestation opens onto what I label the experience of meaningful existence, or affirmation. To attest to an experience of being an agent is *to testify to one's desire to be a self*, or what Ricoeur called "primary affirmation" (*l'affirmation originaire*).

Because selfhood is an experience of fundamental possibilities, attestation to the experience of acting and suffering opens a dimension of potentiality toward which one is compelled by desire. I affirm the existence of an ideal self I want to be precisely because I am *not yet* that self. Therefore, primary affirmation is also an experience of lack of identity because one's present state is not identical to the ideal; the actuality is inadequate to the projected potentiality. This lack of identity becomes a source of anxiety once it is introduced to the affective level of consciousness. The experience of inadequation between the actual self to which I attest and the projected ideal self, which I affirm, becomes an experience of disproportion and a source of misery. This experienced disproportion within the self, the disproportion of the self with itself, becomes the path of least resistance for the entrance of moral evil in human existence. "Affective fragility," the name that Ricoeur gave to the experience of disproportion, becomes the point of entrance for moral evil. In the last chapter, I followed Ricoeur in defining moral evil, in Kantian fashion, as the choice of an evil maxim to guide actions. Hence, in choosing moral evil, I paradoxically choose a principle that makes me unfree. Seeking a resolution to this enigma, Ricoeur turned to biblical sources and to theological speculation. Again in a Kantian fashion, he addressed the problem of evil to a theology of redemption and the idea of gracious assistance as the possibility of a restoration of freedom. In a complementary fashion, Ricoeur formulated a theology of creation that served to secure a sense of value in the self and creation in general. I will conclude by addressing what this foray through theological speculation offers to the experience of meaningful existence. In underscoring Ricoeur's reliance on the configuring capacities of narrative for self-understanding, the path to an exploration of biblical texts as a source of such understanding is laid open. I engage this argument through an examination of his idea of the hermeneutics of testimony.

The itinerary of this chapter mirrors that of the last, progressing from an account of *understanding* as the basic structure of meaningful existence, through the narrative configuration of meaningful existence in terms of *possibility*, to an *affirmation* of the possibility of meaningful existence in a hermeneutics of testimony. Before proceeding, it will be useful to set the context of this exploration. Narrative provides an initial answer to a fundamental problem: the discordant experience of temporality. Therefore, I must pause and explore the relationship that Ricoeur established between temporality and narrative activity.

The Configuration of Meaning

The discussion of sameness and selfhood in the last chapter introduced the dimension of temporality into the account of agency. The examination of the distinction between sameness and selfhood was meant to lend perspective on the question of *permanence in time*. Character develops *over time* as habituated modes of behavior and as identification with cultural ideals and values. Self-constancy manifests itself in the project of *possible futures* toward which one aims. More pointedly, existence is lived *within time*. The turn toward temporality brings new problems, however. Indeed, temporality exercises a disorienting and disintegrating effect on thought and agency as much as it does an orienting and integrating one. Analysis is shielded from this aspect of temporality as long as one remains at the level of the structures in isolation from the question of meaning.

This chapter marks a shift in concern from basic structures to the configuration of meaningful existence. This exploration involves two important claims: First, individuals make sense of existence through the stories they tell about themselves. Life narratives cast a retrospective glance over existence from the past to the present; the story I erect around the events that have happened to me organizes my existence into a meaningful whole. By the same token, personal narratives cast a prospective glance from the present into the future. Desires and aspirations are narrated in the form of anticipations of future possibilities. However, narrative configures meaningful existence in a second way. Self-narration does not happen in a vacuum; existence is carried out with others in social-political institutions. Social existence takes place within a cultural context that is itself profoundly narrative in nature. Factors such as history, artistic genre, philosophical and religious tradition affect my self-understanding and self-narrating activity. Thus, the configuring capacities of narrative must be addressed as both an individual and a cultural phenomenon.

Ricoeur introduced the first volume of *Time and Narrative* with the rather bold statement that "what is ultimately at stake in the case of the structural identity of the narrative function as well as in that of the truth claim of every narrative work, is the temporal character of human existence. The world unfolded by every narrative work is a temporal world. Or, as will often be repeated in the course of this study: time becomes human time to the extent that it is organized after the manner of a narrative; narrative, in turn, is meaningful to the extent that it portrays the features of temporal experience."[1] Time becomes human time, that is, experientially meaningful time, through the configuring capacities of narrative structure. I have already noted the importance of temporality for Ricoeur's understanding of agency, but time resists attempts to make sense of it. The experience of time is, Ricoeur argued, fundamentally discordant.

In order to plumb this discordant experience, Ricoeur turned to Augustine's *Confessions*. Augustine exclaimed: "What, then, is time? I know well enough what it is, provided that nobody asks me; but if I am asked what it is and try to explain, I am baffled."[2] What puzzled Augustine was time's "impending state of *not being*," that is, the fact that past *is no longer*, the future *is not yet*, and the present constantly *is passing out of existence*. He did not question *whether* time is experienced, but *how* it is experienced.

This encounter with the seeming nonbeing of time launched Augustine on a series of skeptical arguments on the existence of time. His answer to skepticism was the notion of the *distentio animi*: rather than experiencing time as past, present, and future, he suggested that temporal experience is that of a *threefold present*. The soul experiences time because it is extended over time, or rather, distended across time: "It might be correct to say that there are three times, a present of past things, a present of present things, and a present of future things. Some such different times do exist in the mind, but nowhere else that I see. The present of past things is the memory; the present of present things is direct perception; and the present of future things is expectation."[3] In each case, the answer to skepticism was an appeal to experience, and this was what interested Ricoeur in Augustine's discourse. Augustine adopted the act of reciting a poem as an analogue for the idea of the threefold present, and this move was advantageous for Ricoeur for several reasons. First, it relocated the discussion from the external passage of time to its internal effect, that is, the sense impression that this passage leaves on the mind. This focus on the internal impression also highlights the active, intentional aspect of temporal consciousness. Ricoeur argued:

> To compose beforehand, to entrust to memory, to begin, to run through—these are all active operations dependent upon the passivity of the sign-images and the impression-images. But it would be to

> mistake the role of these images if we failed to stress that reciting is an act that moves from an expectation turned first toward the entire poem, then toward what remains of the poem, until the operation is completed. In this new description of the act of reciting, the present changes its meaning. It is no longer a point, not even a point of passage, it is a "present intention" (*praesens intentio*). . . . [T]here would be no future that diminishes, no past that increases, without "the mind, which regulates this process". . . .[4]

Yet, for all the advantages taken from Augustine's example, one is not completely relieved of the enigmas surrounding the consciousness of time; most pointedly, one ought to consider what relationship exists between the experience of time *in* the mind and the passing of time *outside* the mind.

Paradoxically, this impasse is the second advantage that Ricoeur drew from his engagement with Augustine. It signaled his turn to Aristotle: "It is to this enigma of the speculation on time that the poetic act of emplotment replies. But Aristotle's *Poetics* does not resolve the enigma on the speculative level. It does not really resolve it all. It puts it to work—poetically—by producing an inverted figure of discordance and concordance."[5] What Aristotle's theory of *muthos* (emplotment) provides is a structure in which the discordance of temporal experience is subsumed under an ultimate concordance of events in an unfolding narrative. While Augustine's discourse was marked by a fundamental discord in the experience of time, Aristotle's *Poetics* offers resources for making sense of that discord by placing it within a structure that accents concordance over discordance.

Augustine's example of recitation was, in many ways, a precursor to Ricoeur's analysis of emplotment. The act of emplotment (*muthos*), that is, the representation of possibilities for existence (*mimesis*), configures a concordant structure around seemingly discordant events. The pair *muthos/mimesis* must be understood in this active sense: *muthos* is the active organization of events into a plot; *mimesis* is the active representation of characters and their actions. This active dimension of poetic composition was central to Ricoeur's adoption of narrative: "When Aristotle . . . says that the muthos is 'the organization of the events [*e ton pragmaton sustasis*]', we must understand by *sustasis* . . . the active sense of organizing the events into a system, so as to mark the operative character of all the concepts in the *Poetics*. . . . Imitation or representation [*mimesis*], therefore, must be understood in the dynamic sense of making a representation, of a transposition into representative works."[6] None of this is to say that the active emplotment of events and the active representation of characters banishes discord. Indeed, discord is an important element in the unfolding of the plot itself. Dramatic narrative does, however, adopt discord in the service of concord.

Discordant events are brought into concordance, retroactively, at the close of the narrative.

But what does the active pair *muthos/mimesis* lend to understanding of the discordant experience of temporality, not to mention the understanding of existence as an agent? In articulating the nature of the interaction between *muthos* and *mimesis*, the locus of activity shifts from composing the work to engaging the work. The principal character is no longer the writer, but the audience. Ricoeur's principal interest was what the reader takes away from the narrative work, an effect that Hans Robert Jauss called an *aesthetics of reception*.[7] Understanding of the narrative work and self-understanding overlap; to receive and understand the work is also to receive an understanding of self and the complexity of temporal existence. The relationship between narrative and the understanding of temporal experience is characterized by the intersection between the world of the narrative composition and the understanding that the reader brings to the engagement with the text.

As I stated, this chapter is devoted to an exploration of the manner in which narrative configures meaningful existence. This initial exploration of Ricoeur's idea of the narrative configuration of temporal experience sets the course. Before directly addressing narrative configuration, however, it is necessary to explore the structure of understanding, that is, the active/receptive confrontation between a self and a world.

Understanding: Active Receptivity

The phenomenological/hermeneutical idea of understanding serves to structure meaningful existence. Reflective agency takes on a particular determination at this level of analysis; within the structures of understanding, reflection takes the form of a recognition of existence within a world that presents itself to perception. In the previous chapter, I defined the structure of agency in terms of capability as this was revealed in Ricoeur's understanding of the reciprocal relationship between the voluntary and involuntary structures of action and will. In a similar way, the exploration of the idea of understanding progresses via the convergence of polarities. At the level of *bodily perception*, the polarity between finite perspective and the seemingly infinite possibilities of signification structures the analysis. At the level of *meaningful action*, the polarity between what Ricoeur called the constituted partiality of character and the infinite demand for happiness governs analysis. At the level of social and cultural *traditions*, the creative tension between historical sedimentation and creative innovation directs the examination.

I will explore the structure of understanding in two steps. First, at the level of basic understanding, the manner in which understanding is directed toward objects and actions will be the principal interest. In relation to objects, or rather, the objectival character of things, understanding will take the form of an imaginative synthesis that functions as an intermediary between bodily perception and the power of signification. In relation to action, understanding arises in the idea of humanity as the figure of meaningful existence that mediates between the constituted partiality of individual existence and the total demand for happiness. Second, the communal context of understanding will come to light through the process of the formation of traditions of thought and practice. Ricoeur's complex presentation of tradition grounds social and historical understanding within the process of sedimentation and innovation in which humans critically appropriate shared meanings through the interpretative strategy of distanciation and appropriation. These two approaches delineate the "basic" and the "social-historical" structures of understanding, respectively.

Basic Understanding: Meaningful Objects, Meaningful Actions

It is important to point out that for Ricoeur, like Kant, understanding was a synthetic operation of the imagination. At the level of basic understanding, objects and actions become understandable through the synthetic operation of the imagination, which mediates the receptivity of experience and intentional striving for meaning.[8] In much the same way that he located human capability in embodied freedom, Ricoeur located human understanding in the perception of the body: the body is the receptive pole in the understanding of the object. The body is, first and foremost, my opening onto the world, my point of commerce with the world. Ricoeur argued that this openness of the body "makes my body an originating mediator '*between*' myself and the world; it does not enclose me, like this bag of skin which, viewed from the outside, makes it seem like a thing in the midst of things. It opens me onto the world, either allowing perceived things to appear or making me dependent on things I lack and of which I experience the need and desire because they are elsewhere or even nowhere in the world."[9] This presentation of the body as an opening on the world gives it two important characteristics with regard to understanding, which Ricoeur called *receptivity* and *point of view*.

The body is my receptive organ onto the world. This fact is so commonplace that it too frequently escapes consciousness. My existence in and understanding of the world is made possible because I interact with the world through my bodily senses. In more phenomenological terms, there is a world for me because a world discloses itself to my senses. All my judgments about the world are dependent on the fact that a world first appears to me. Ricoeur argued that the receptivity of the body "is what makes things appear. The desirable, the fearful, the practical, the useful, and all aesthetic and moral predicates of the thing are secondary strata of primary appearing."[10] In other words, I am affected by the world at the level of the *flesh.*

But this receptive opening onto the world that is the body is a limited, finite opening. My receptivity is, at the same time, my point of view on the world. Ricoeur intended the phrase "point of view" in the broadest sense, as the spacial and temporal location of my body in relation to the world that appears to my senses: "This aspect of the appearance, which refers me back to my point of view, is the perceived object's insurmountable and invincible property of presenting itself from a certain angle, unilaterally. I never perceive more than one side at any given time, and the object is never more than the presumed unity of the flux of these silhouettes. . . . [M]y perceiving body is not only my openness onto the world, it is also the 'here from where' the thing is seen."[11] This recognition of the inescapably perspectival nature of receptivity to the world has several important implications for the analysis of understanding. First, understanding is always limited, always perspectival. This is not to say that the adequacy of my understandings cannot be judged; indeed, I can move my body, change my position, in order to gain a better *sense* of the object that confronts me. But I can only *view* the object from one particular angle at any given time. In drawing connections between the various silhouettes that appear to my perception, I draw conclusions about the object itself. This fact points to a second important implication of understanding: understanding of the object of perception is an *interpreted understanding*. Indeed, the inferred connection between the silhouettes of the perceived object is itself an interpretation. This recognition is profoundly important for the idea of understanding as active receptivity.

However, the process of analytically disengaging the experience of perceiving from the perspectival character of perception signals a movement that transgresses the limited, finite nature of perception as such. To give a phenomenological account of the perceiving body is to take a perspective on perspective, and this opens the way to an account of understanding as signification. The power of signifying represents a transgression of limited perspective in virtue of the fact that to signify is to *say* more than I *see.* Ricoeur argued:

> [I]t is *upon* the thing itself . . . that I apprehend the perspectival character of perception, namely, *upon* the object's obvious property of always showing itself from only one side, then another. It is also upon the thing itself that I transgress my perspective. In point of fact, I can *express* this onesidedness only by *expressing* all other sides that I do not currently see. . . . I anticipate the thing itself by relating the side which I see to those which I do not see but which I *know*. Thus I judge of the

> entire thing by going beyond its given side into the thing itself. This transgression is the intention to signify.[12]

I do not advance an interpretation of my perception, of the silhouettes that confront me one at a time in perception, but of the thing itself. In speaking, I offer an interpretation of the being of the thing I confront in perception. Thus, to speak of the thing is to offer an ontological interpretation of its being, and this act delivers my interpretation up to the realm of verifiability.

My statements are open to judgments of truth and falsity because they are not released into a vacuum. Signification is an intention to truth, an intention to *say* something true about the thing. In offering up an interpretation of the thing I am are opening my perception to a public world. Thus, my interpretations engage the interpretations of others: "In effecting this process of verification, [the other's] body will provide a *different* perspective, a *different* structuration of the mutual signification of colors through sounds and smells. But it is the same expressed signification that will be verified in a *different* perspective."[13] In short, when I speak of the object that I perceive, I intend a meaning that can be verified in the perspective of another.

Thus, with regard to the realm of objects, Ricoeur claimed that understanding is the imaginative synthesis of the object's appearance in perception *and* an ascribed meaning:

> Consciousness makes itself an intermediary primarily by projecting itself into the thing's mode of being. It becomes a mean between the infinite and the finite by delineating the ontological dimension of things, namely, that they are a synthesis of meaning and presence: here consciousness is nothing else than that which stipulates that a thing is a thing only if it is in accordance with this synthetic constitution, if it can appear *and* be expressed, if it can affect me in my finitude *and* lend itself to the discourse of any rational being.[14]

Understanding is always understanding of something I try to make sense of. Therefore, the basic structure of understanding is a hermeneutical mediation of sense and presence. Understanding is active receptivity, that is, the active ascription of meaning (sense, expressibility) to the received object of perception (presence, appearance).

Ricoeur's account of selfhood as agency or will followed this same basic structure of mediation between opening and limit, or finitude and infinitude. He sought to give a meaningful account of the will that is, at the same time, an account of meaningful action. This account of meaningful action takes up, logically speaking, where the discussion of capability in the last chapter left off. The finite, limited pole of practical existence, which Ricoeur called character [*caractère*], is quite simply an approach to the idea of capability at a different level of analysis. Ricoeur translated this finite pole of existence into the perspectival language that ordered the synthesis of the object: character is made up of two perspectival orientations of *affective perspective* and *practical perspective*.

Under the title of affective perspective, Ricoeur addressed the nature of action as a motivated project, that is, as an aim that is directed by the needs and the desires of the body. Recall that judgments about the world are dependent on the fact that the world first appears to sensibility. My judging and valuing activity proceeds from this affective perspective:

> Motivation brings into view a new kind of "receptivity" wherein my finitude is inscribed. It is no longer the sensory receptivity of seeing and hearing, but the specific receptivity which signifies that I do not create my projects radically from nothing, no more than I produce my objects through creative intuition. I posit my actions only by letting myself be influenced by motives. . . . It is this attraction grasped on the thing itself, over there, elsewhere, or nowhere, which makes desire an openness onto . . . and not a presence to the self closed on itself."[15]

Just as perception is my opening onto the world, affective perspective is, above all, my motivated openness to things. Just as perception is a limited opening directed by point of view, so affective perspective is a limited opening by virtue of the specificity of needs and desires; it is an opening that is narrowed by my specific emotive and affective "viewpoints." "Practical perspective," like sensible perception and affective perspective, is a limited opening onto the world. My practical abilities are an opening in the sense that in acting, that is, in moving my body, the body itself becomes the intelligible point of interaction between I who act and a world that I act upon. But this opening is once again limited by virtue of the materiality of the body and the narrowing of capability in habituated action.

These two perspectival orientations of the practical life constitute the finite pole of character. I addressed the idea of character at several important points already, most notably in the discussion of sameness and selfhood. There, character functioned as a descriptive term to relate the twofold nature of the agent. Here, character is presented more broadly as a "field of motivation" that opens capability to the possibility of practical existence. By systematically linking the limited opening of character with the limited opening of sensible perception, Ricoeur opened the structure of capability to an experiential world. He claimed: "My character is the primal orientation of my total field of motivation, and this *field is my openness to humanity*. Thus, step by step the most 'destinal' aspects of finitude are recaptured in the dialectic of narrowness and accessibility to which the perspective of perception has given us the key."[16] This more comprehensive understanding of character introduces capability to the realm of meaningful action that Ricoeur called *happiness*. In a discussion that was thoroughly indebted to Aristotle, Ricoeur claimed that happiness is the destiny of our meaningful action; it is the ultimate aim of meaningful action. This aspect of agency will be a central concern of the next chapter.

In order to make sense of the idea of happiness as a destiny, it is necessary to dissociate the idea of happiness as a "total demand" from the naive idea of happiness as pleasure or satisfaction. To this end, Ricoeur explained, "The investigation of human action and its all-embracing and most ultimate aim would disclose that happiness is a termination of destiny and not an end of individual desires. It is in this sense that it is a *whole* and not a *sum*; the partial aims and disconnected desires of our life stand out on its horizon."[17] Happiness represents a total field of orientation for our discrete aims and satisfactions. However, this understanding of happiness as the total demand of a completed destiny forces one to recognize that happiness is never finally accomplished, but aimed at. Just as Aristotle argued that happiness can only be achieved over the course of an entire lifetime and never in a single action, Ricoeur argued that "happiness is not given in experience; it is only adumbrated in a consciousness of direction. No act gives happiness, but the encounters of our life that are most worthy of being called 'events' indicate the direction of happiness."[18] Thus, if happiness is the total aim of meaningful action, then meaningful existence becomes a task rather than an achievement. I am always on the way to meaningful existence.

This sense of always being "on the way" presents a problem for the attempt to understand meaningful existence. I am always "in transit" toward it and, hence, always trying to understand something that *isn't yet*. It is precisely at this point of difficulty that the synthetic activity of understanding as active receptivity steps in. On Ricoeur's accounting, meaningful existence is ultimately represented in the idea of the *person* as a synthesis of the constituted partiality of character and the total demand for happiness:

> What we must first establish is that the person is primarily a project which I represent to myself, which I set before me and entertain, and that project of the person is, like the thing but in an entirely irreducible way, a "synthesis" which is effected. . . . This project is what I call *humanity*, not in the collective sense of all men but the human quality of man, not an exhaustive enumeration of human beings but the comprehensive significance of the human element that is capable of guiding and regulating an enumeration of human beings. . . . Humanity is the person's personality, just objectivity was the thing's thingness; it is the mode of being on which every empirical appearance of what we call a human being should be patterned.[19]

Humanity represented the figure of meaningful existence in Ricoeur's thought. As the possibility of meaningful existence, humanity arose out of the active receptivity of understanding. In understanding, one actively recognizes the meaningful possibilities that reside in his/her received constitution.

In significant ways, however, an account of the basic understandings of things and of actions remains an abstract analysis. In reality, basic understandings arise within a social context itself structured by shared meanings that lend themselves to understanding. It is to this social context of shared understanding that I now turn.

Traditions: The Social-Historical Context of Understanding

Basic understanding, I claimed, is structured as active receptivity, which is revealed in the synthetic operation of imagination that mediates between finite opening onto the world and infinite intentionality toward meaning. In perception, this active receptivity takes the form of the imaginative synthesis of the object in the mediation between oriented perception and the capacity to give expression to that perception, that is, signification. At the level of practical life, active receptivity is at work in the imaginative synthesis of the idea of humanity, which mediates between the limited opening of character and the infinite demand for happiness. In both cases, understanding served an intermediary function between an inescapably perspectival orientation and an equally inescapable move that transcends limited perspective. The introduction of the social-historical context of understanding lends its own perspectival slant to understanding. The sense of perspective reveals itself in the fact that all understanding is historical; humans are born into a historical context that orients understanding. In this sense, the analysis that I am turning to attaches itself to the preceding analysis of basic structures of understanding.

However, if the social-historical context of understanding is taken seriously, one is forced to recognize the abstract character of the previous analysis. The encounter with objects in perception is already informed in significant ways by one's social-historical location. If I do not advance interpretations into a vacuum, neither do I form them out of a void. At the very least, I participate in a natural language that makes signification possible. By the same token my understanding of the total demand of happiness does not come from nowhere; I encounter figures of the happy life that are profoundly shaped by social and cultural ideals. Thus, the recognition of the social-historical context of understanding pulls the active-receptive structure of understanding out of phenomenological abstraction and places it in a realm of shared meanings that precedes any particular attempt at understanding.

The introduction of historical experience into understanding makes more pronounced the the hermeneutical character of understanding as such: "The 'lived experience' which [hermeneutics] is concerned to bring to language and raise to meaning is the historical connection, mediated by the transmission of written documents, works, institutions and monuments which render present the historical past."[20] This presence of the historical past is what grounds the sense of shared meanings that precedes understanding. The *historicity* of meaning is the "perspective" of an inherited context of meaningful existence that has the potential of rising to understanding. Thus, the same active-receptive structure is at play at the level of social-historical context as at the phenomenological level of basic meaning.

Ricoeur conceived this inherited context of meaning in its broadest sense through the idea of tradition. In this sense, Ricoeur's understanding of the inherited context of meaning was inescapably communal; traditions represent the shared space in which one confronts the possibility of meaning and understanding. He conceptualized traditions not as static entities that govern meanings, but as dynamic, evolving structures. He articulated the process by which traditions are formed through three distinct but related dimensions that he called *traditionality*, *traditions*, and *tradition*.

Under the heading of traditionality he addressed what might be called a general structure of historical experience. With the idea of traditionality, it becomes possible to analyze the manner in which the present is influenced by the past. Speaking of the quality of traditionality in terms of Hans Georg Gadamer's "fusion of horizons," Ricoeur stated:

> The past is revealed to us through the projection of a historical horizon that is both detached from the horizon of the present and taken up into and fused with it. . . . It is in projecting a historical horizon that we experience, through its tension with the horizon of the present, the efficacity of the past, for which our being-affected by it is the correlate. Effective-history, we might say, is what takes place without us. The fusion of horizons is what we attempt to bring about. . . . In this first respect, tradition, formally conceived of as traditionality, already constitutes a broadly significant phenomenon. It signifies that the temporal distance separating us from the past is not a dead interval but a transmission that is generative of meaning.[21]

In a very real sense, the fusion of horizons that occurs between the present and the historical past is something one affects in the attempt to make sense of the past. Historical study itself is an active process of projecting current understandings onto past events *and* allowing current understandings to be affected by our interpretations of the past.

If the first dimension of the idea of tradition lays out the formal characteristic of traditionality, the second dimension is addressed to the content of traditions itself. The plural designation is important here because it is as a plurality of past representations that inherited meanings confront one. At this level of plural traditions that proceed from out of the past into the present, it is possible to locate the "chains of interpretation and reinterpretation," by which the past informs present understanding. But this engagement with traditions, this reception of inherited meanings is an active process. "The past questions us to the extent that we question it. It answers us to the extent we answer it."[22] Receptivity of the past is, in all cases, an active receptivity.

The final dimension in the process of formation of traditions presents Ricoeur's account of the abstract ideal of tradition as such. If one abstracts from the contents of plural traditions, s/he recognizes the sedimentation of interpretation and reinterpretation that directs the formation of traditions. This sedimentation is not just a compilation of meanings, but an overall intention to truth. Traditions are, most basically, historical-cultural attempts at the meaning of things in general. I access these historical-cultural truth intentions any time I engage a tradition of thought. In important ways I cannot avoid such engagements to the extent that my existence is lived out within broad social-historical communities; my very commerce with society already involves me in participation in one or more traditions of thought and practice at any given time. As Ricoeur claimed, "Every proposal of meaning is at the same time a claim to truth. What we receive from the past are, in effect, beliefs, persuasions, convictions; that is, ways of 'holding for true,' to use the insight of the German *Für-wahrhalten*, which signifies belief."[23] In a very real sense, participation in a culture is *appropriation* of a given context of meaning.

However, the fact that one already belongs to a context laden with cultural expressions of conviction and belief demands a kind of active receptivity that is more intentional in nature. There is a demand for intentional hermeneutical engagement with inherited cultural meanings because of the constant threat of violent and oppressive forms of ideology. As Karl Marx and others revealed, an inherited context of meaning can serve to mystify as well as inform understanding. Critical engagement with one's social-cultural inheritance strips understanding of its naivete in acceptance of that inheritance. Such critical engagement begins "when, not contented to belong to transmitted tradition, we interrupt the relation of belonging in order to signify it."[24] Deeper understanding is won through the back and forth movement between appropriation, suspicion, and reappropriation. Traditions, therefore, are never static entities; they change and evolve through a process of sedimentation and innovation. If sedimented tradition is the inherited context of meaning which lends itself to understanding, that is, the receptive dimension of understanding, critical engagement with those sedimented meanings produces an innovation within tradition itself. I actively affect tradition in the process of critically appropriating it. As always, understanding is structured by active receptivity. Humans do not make up understandings out of nothing. They first exist in a world, both a physical and cultural world, which offers itself to the capacity for meaning. The world that confronts them is always a potentially meaningful one.

This exploration of understanding as the structure of meaningful existence is only a first step. To this point, the notion of understanding has been directed toward things in the world, that is, objects that confront perception, ideals that direct actions, inherited meanings that ground the social context of meaning. What cannot be approached at the level of basic structures is the question of the one who perceives, who directs action toward an ideal, who critically appropriates inherited meanings. The examination of the basic structure of meaning allows one to address understanding in terms of active receptivity; it does not, however, allow one to address understanding as *self-understanding*. The synthesis of the object in understanding is consciousness, Ricoeur argued, "but that it is not *self-consciousness*. . . . Consciousness spends itself in founding the unity of meaning and presence 'in' the object. 'Consciousness' is not yet the unity of a person in itself and for itself; it is not one person; it is no one."[25] If the term *meaningful existence* is to become truly meaningful, it must be brought into the realm of the self-consciousness.

Ricoeur's claim that narrative meaningfully configures existence comes to center stage at this point. His principal interest was what narrative theory and narrative configuration lend to self-understanding. I have already hightlighted the role of narrative in mediating temporal experience. In what follows, I will explore the role that Ricoeur assigned to narrative in self-understanding in general.

Possibility: Actuality and Potentiality

Narrative, Ricoeur argued, is a fundamental structure of self-understanding. It casts both a retrospective glance and a prospective glance over one's existence, and in so doing, erects a configuration around what are otherwise random events. He claimed that this narrative self-understanding "is the only kind that escapes the apparent choice between sheer change and absolute identity. . . . In place of an *ego* enamored of itself arises a *self* instructed by cultural symbols, the first among which are the narratives handed down in our literary tradition."[26] If the identity of the agent is configured by the dual designation of sameness and selfhood, the configuration of meaningful existence via narrative offers reflective purchase on that identity in its orientation toward future possibilities. The reader of the narrative is invited to adopt the world it presents as his/her own realm of possibilities.

I will explore the connection between narrative and self-understanding in three steps. First, I will address the manner in which Ricoeur's account of narrative configuration mirrors the active-receptive structure of understanding.

Particular attention will be paid to the manner in which the formation of (and engagement with) a narrative plot is a similar kind of synthetic activity to the active receptivity of understanding. Narrative emplotment goes beyond basic understanding by virtue of the manner in which a reader engages a text. While the text offers a figurative world to the reader, the reader brings a "prefigured" set of understandings to the text. When I engage the narrative text hermeneutically, I allow the world I bring to the text, namely, my prejudices, presuppositions, tastes, desires, etc., to be interpreted by the figurative world of the text. Thus, when I engage the narrative text I open myself to new possibilities for self-understandings.

I will proceed to Ricoeur's proposal for a narrative understanding of identity. This discussion links the configuration of identity in terms of narrative to the discussion of agency in terms of sameness and selfhood in the previous chapter. These two dimensions of the identity of the agent are placed in dynamic interaction through the mediation of narrative; narrative *configures* the relationship between sameness and selfhood in meaningful ways. In this sense, one can address emplotment as the synthesis of character, where sameness and selfhood overlap, and the imaginative space opened by the engagement with narratives in terms of future anticipations toward which selfhood orients itself. Narrative lends itself to an understanding of identity through the configuration of the practices within which one lives out existence and in terms of the life plans one constructs.

Finally, the issue of meaningful existence as an opening onto possibility. In a very profound sense, meaningful existence resides in the mode of possibility. The recognition that existence is narratively configured in terms of life plans will necessitate serious consideration of this prospective orientation of self-understanding. Ricoeur claimed that the meaning of human existence in its ontological dimensions is precisely a dialectic between the present understanding of existence and the anticipation of future possibility, between actuality and potentiality. This dialectic configures the relationship between self-understanding and meaningful existence; it "refigures" self-understanding as meaningful existence.

Narrative and Understanding

Narrative lends itself to a discussion of understanding by virtue of the fact that the act of emplotment is a synthetic activity. Perception involves the synthesis of meaning and presence in the object; practical life involves the synthesis of character and happiness in the idea of humanity. Emplotment is, broadly speaking, an operative synthesis of heterogeneous elements. It involves three distinct but related synthetic operations: *the synthesis of multiple elements into a unity*, *the synthesis of discordant experience into concordant structure*, and *the synthesis of successive events into a total configuration.*

First, emplotment gathers together multiple elements into a unitary structure. Of this synthetic unity, Ricoeur claimed that "the plot serves to make *one* story out of the multiple incidents or, if you prefer, transforms the many incidents *into one* story. . . . [T]he recounted story is always more than the enumeration, in an order that would be merely serial or successive, of the incidents or events that it organizes into an intelligible whole."[27] The plot is not a conglomeration of disconnected elements that are recounted in serial order, but a total unity. A narrative plot does not merely add up the elements of the story; it transforms those elements into a meaningful whole. It is not the sum of its parts but a new creation that arises out of the interconnection of the incidents that it synthesizes.

This first synthetic operation of emplotment focuses on the process of actively composing the events and incidents that make up the story. The second operation, the synthesis of a concordant structure out of discordant experience, turns attention toward the reader and the act of following a plot. But to posit this synthesis beforehand circumvents the dramatic aspect of engaging a narrative plot; it is important to pause and address this dramatic aspect of reading. The plot moves by virtue of the manner in which events and characters come into conflict. This clash of events and characters is what holds my attention; I allow myself to be drawn up in the discord that mounts as I progress. As Ricoeur argued:

> [The plot] organizes together components that are as heterogeneous as unintended circumstances, discoveries, those who perform actions and those who suffer them, chance or planned encounters, interactions between actors ranging from conflict to collaboration, means that are well or poorly adjusted to ends, and finally unintended results; gathering all these factors into a single story makes the plot a totality which can be said to be at once concordant and discordant. . . . We obtain an understanding of this composition by means of the act of *following* a story; following a story is a very complex operation, guided by our expectations concerning the outcome of the story, expectations that we readjust as the story moves along, until it coincides with the conclusion.[28]

In this way, a concordant structure is "won" through discordant events, a concordant structure that never completely escapes discord, but rather synthesizes a meaning out of it. In a similar vein, Ricoeur discussed the discordant concordance of the plot as a "retrograde necessity which proceeds from the temporal totality carried to its term."[29]

This last statement points to a final synthesis accomplished through activity of emplotment, the synthesis of succession into configuration. Recall Ricoeur's interest in Augustine's excursus on the experience of time. Our experience of temporality is, on Ricoeur's reading of Augustine, fundamentally discordant. Emplotment establishes a relationship between this passing succession of events and an enduring meaning that arises out of that passage. He concluded, "If we may speak of the temporal identity of the story, it must be characterized as something that endures and remains across that which passes and flows away."[30]

Understanding is gained in the interpretive confrontation with the world synthesized by the plot and presented to the reader. What kind of understanding is gained from the hermeneutical engagement with the text? In an attempt to answer this question, Ricoeur turned to Aristotle's *Poetics*: a well-written story has the capacity to teach us something and, more importantly, to reveal universal characteristics of the human condition. In this sense, the understanding gained through the engagement with narratives is *phronetic* or practical understanding. This account allowed Ricoeur to argue that the text itself is the configuration of possible meaning that is completed by the reader:

> [T]he sense or the significance of a narrative stems from the *intersection of the world of the text and the world of the reader*. The act of reading becomes the critical moment of the entire analysis. . . . To appropriate a work through reading is to unfold the world horizon implicit in it which includes the actions, the characters and the events of the story told. As a result the reader belongs at once to the work's horizon of experience in imagination and to that of his or her own real action. The horizon of expectation and the horizon of experience continually confront one another and fuse together. [Hans Georg] Gadamer speaks in this regard of the "fusion of horizons" essential to the art of understanding a text.[31]

By engaging the text hermeneutically I am touched by the world it presents to my imagination. In reading I imaginatively inhabit the world of text and, I am instructed by what it presents of the human condition. Thus, narrative understanding crosses over into self-understanding: I gain perspective on myself by gaining perspective on the narrative. In this sense, narrative understanding is practical understanding.

But there is an even deeper sense, in Ricoeur's estimation, in which narrative affects understanding. Narrative also functions to structure existence itself, and not just my understanding of it; the configuration of the narrative mirrors the configuration of the identity of the agent. In many ways, what he called the prenarrative quality of experience anticipates the move from narrative self-understanding to narrative identity to which I now turn.

Narrative and Identity

Ricoeur sought to establish a more direct relation between narrative configuration and the dual designation of sameness and selfhood that configures the identity of the agent. Narrative relates sameness and selfhood through two operations: the emplotted synthesis of the character (*personnage*) and the imaginative space opened by the fusion of horizons. The first of these operations deals with the manner in which narratives function to create and develop characters. Characters' actions are one aspect of events that the narratives configure. Turning to the question of narrative identity, Ricoeur argued, "The decisive step in the direction of a narrative conception of personal identity is taken when one passes from the action to the character [*personnage*]. A character is the one who performs the action in the narrative. . . . The thesis supported here will be that the identity of the character is comprehensible through the transfer to the character of the operation of emplotment, first applied to action recounted; characters, we will say, are themselves plots."[32] The identities of the characters are themselves discrete synthetic entities within the overall synthesis of the plot. They develop as the plot itself develops; thus, over the course of the story we come to identify and recognize the characters as persons with certain personality traits and particular ways of dealing with situations and events.

It is necessary at this point to pause and highlight a shift in Ricoeur's terminology that is lost in translation to English. In the discussions to this point the term *character* was expressed in the original French by the term *caractère*. This term has a long history in Ricoeur's *oeuvre*, appearing as early as the first volume of the *Philosophie de la volonté*.[33] *Caractère* expresses what in English would be called the character or nature of an actual person, that is, the particular personality traits and characteristics that allow me to recognize someone from one meeting to the next. As I claimed in the previous chapter, character is a particular, observable manner or style of existing. Turning to narrative, Ricoeur adopted the term *personnage*, also translated into English as character. *Personnage*, however, has a broader spectrum of meanings than *caractère*; this term covers both the sense of particular mannerisms of actual persons *and* literary personae of narrative characters.[34] This is an important point because literary characters have identities just as real characters do: they are, first and foremost, *acting and suffering beings*. Literary characters display their identities through their actions and their reactions to twists of fate, the actions of others, chance encounters, etc. In other words, literary characters behave like selves. What is the benefit of this recognition? Here, Ricoeur offered the idea of the "threefold mimesis."

Exploring the role narrative plays in the understanding of temporal experience, Ricoeur asserted the existence of three intersecting mimetic levels that he called *mimesis*$_1$, *mimesis*$_2$, and *mimesis*$_3$. *Mimesis*$_1$ addressed those aspects of action which have a prenarrative *quality*. He claimed that "literature would be incomprehensible if it did not give a configuration to what was already a figure in human action."[35] This prenarrative or prefigured quality of action is the means through which action rises to meaning. One recognizes acting selves within literary works because action itself is meaningful, *in potentia* if not explicitly, at this descriptive level. *Mimesis*$_2$ signals the narrative composition as such. Narrative plays a mediating role here because it serves to poetically structure or configure what was prefigured at the level of *mimesis*$_1$: the narrative is the actual configuration of what is already prefigured in action. The construction of a narrative plot imposes a meaningful structure on a series of events. "In short," Ricoeur argued, "emplotment [*la mise en intrigue*] is the operation that draws a configuration out of a simple succession."[36] The plot structures random events into a meaningful whole, but narrated actions are meaningful because the reader already understands the basic structure of action itself at a prereflective level.[37]

The value of Ricoeur's development of the threefold structure of mimetic activity only becomes apparent in the final dimension, *mimesis*$_3$. At this third level Ricoeur sought to establish the nature of the relation between narrative and temporal experience. He claimed, "Generalizing beyond Aristotle, I shall say that mimesis$_3$ marks the intersection of the world of the text and the world of the hearer or reader; the intersection, therefore, of the world configured by the poem and the world wherein real action occurs and unfolds its specific temporality."[38] To read a narrative is, Ricoeur argued, to imaginatively inhabit the world that is presented by the text. More importantly, to read is to be taught by the text, to allow one's practical understanding to be guided by the narrative's horizon of experience. This capacity of the narrative to guide practical experience allowed Ricoeur to establish a relationship between narrative understanding and self-understanding. But what, exactly, does narrative lend to the identity of actual selves? Ricoeur claimed:

> In the course of application of literature to life, what we carry over and transpose into the exegesis of ourselves is [the] dialectic of the self and the same. There we can find the purgative virtue of the thought-experiments deployed by literature, not only at the level of theoretical reflexion, but at that of existence. . . . The refiguration by narrative confirms this aspect of self-knowledge which goes far beyond the narrative domain, namely, that the self does not know itself immediately, but only indirectly by the detour of the cultural signs of all sorts which are articulated on the symbolic mediations which always already articulate action and, among them, the narratives of everyday life. Narrative mediation underlines this remarkable characteristic of self-knowledge—that it is self-interpretation. . . . What narrative

> interpretation brings in its own right is precisely the figural nature of the character by which the self, narratively interpreted, turns out to be a *figured* self—which imagines itself (*se figure*) in this or that way.[39]

The manner in which fictional characters (*personnages*) are related to their actions in the construction of a plot lends some understanding of the manner in which personal identities are *configured* in the relationship between sameness and selfhood or, more appropriately, in the relationship between character (*caractère*) and self-constancy.

I argued above that actions become meaningful in light of the ideal of humanity configured abstractly as the synthesis of character (*caractère*) and happiness. In Aristotelian terms, discrete actions aim at an ultimate end called happiness. At this point in the analysis, it is possible to address this abstract understanding of meaningful action to the practical understanding of personal identity: *what is aimed at in self-constancy is a happy life*. Character provides an identifiable support for one's aspirations toward happiness, but the effort of self-constancy aims toward the happiness. It is necessary, therefore, to explore the relationship between action and agent at a less abstract level than I have done so far.

Ricoeur characterized action in terms of a sort of nesting of constitutive units or *levels of praxis*, which can be hierarchized on the basis of increasing complexity. He named these levels *practices*, *life plans*, and *the narrative unity of a life*. While the first two of these are inherent in action itself, the third serves as a limiting idea toward which the agent aims in intentional action. Two significant ideas must be kept in mind in taking this practical approach to action: the distinction between *simple actions and complex actions*, and the necessarily *social nature of action* as such. Both play into the understanding of practices that open onto higher levels of praxis.

Practices are composed of individual basic actions, which are configured by overarching intentions. Games, arts, and professions are examples of such practices. The first movement in the configuration of a practice is expressed by the notion of "constitutive rule." A constitutive rule gives a basic action a meaning it would not otherwise have. Ricoeur explained constitutive rules as "those precepts whose sole function is to rule that, for instance, a given gesture of shifting the position of a pawn on the chessboard 'counts as' a move in a game of chess. The move would not exist, with the signification and the effect it has in the game, without the rule that 'constitutes' the move as a step in the chess game."[40] Constitutive rules highlight the social, interactive dimensions of action. Constitutive rules are socially agreed upon. The meanings they lend to action are open to anyone who knows the rules. In addition, constitutive rules lend an evaluative dimension to practices in the form of "standards of excellence." By posing practices in terms of standards of excellence, one distinguishes between someone who is merely proficient in a given practice and someone who has mastered that practice, for example, the difference between someone who can play chess and a grand master.

The idea of a practice lends a great deal to an understanding of the overlapping of sameness and selfhood in character. In developing a skill, becoming *practiced* in a profession or an art, one becomes identified with a certain practice or set of practices. He or she is recognized as a sculptor or a physician, global practices with characteristically associated basic actions. The practice becomes part of the character of the individual, one of the characteristics by which s/he is recognized. If the concept of practices points in the direction of the formation of character, that of life plans points squarely in the direction of self-constancy.

A life plan serves to mediate between a lower limit of action considered in terms of practices and an upper limit of a projected unity of a life which serves as both horizon of possibility and limit idea for discreet actions. The formation of a life plan is the process of choosing and engaging in those practices that will actualize that plan. Thus, a life plan is composed of constitutive practices, which are themselves directed by the overall plan:

> In this sense, what [Alasdair] MacIntyre calls "the narrative unity of a life" not only results from the summing up of practices in a globalizing form but is governed equally by a life project, however uncertain and mobile it may be, and by fragmentary practices which have their own unity, life plans constituting the intermediary zone of exchange between the undetermined character of guiding ideals and the determinate nature of practices. . . . The practical field then appears to be subjected to a twofold principle of determination by which it resembles the hermeneutical comprehension of a text through the exchange between the whole and the part. Nothing is more propitious for narrative configuration than this play of double determination.[41]

The formation of a life plan opens onto the final level of praxis, the narrative unity of a life.

One must be careful in addressing the move from life plans to the possible narrative unity of a life, however. Ricoeur argued that narrative can provide reflective purchase on experience, but he suggested that it would be grossly inaccurate to claim that life is reducible to narrative structure, that fictional narrative and life share a simple unity of form. Rather, the idea of a narrative unity of a life serves both as a horizon of possibility and a limiting idea for action. Hermeneutic comprehension takes place at the intersection of the work of the text and the world of the reader. Understanding of the text becomes at once self-understanding. In this way one can make sense of the idea of the narrative unity of a life and narrative identity. Ricoeur suggested elsewhere, however, that this unity "is not substantial but narrative."[42] This claim merits further discussion.

In *Time and Narrative*, Ricoeur discussed the limitations internal to the concept of narrative identity. He claimed first of all that narrative identity is not "a stable and seamless identity," because multiple plots might configure the same events: "[I]t is always possible to weave different, even opposed, plots about our lives. . . . Narrative identity thus becomes the name of a problem at least as much as it is that of a solution." Ricoeur also pointed out that narrative identity does not exhaust the question of self-constancy, which was associated with the constellation of choices by which a self maintains itself over time. Narratives can function as an impetus to act, but the response to this impetus is not itself a part of the narrative configuration: "This is when reading becomes a provocation to be and to act differently. However this impetus is transformed into action only through the decision whereby a person says: Here I stand! . . . It is at this point that the notion of narrative identity encounters its limit and has to link up with the nonnarrative components in the formation of an acting agent."[43] Thus, narrative reveals itself not only as a horizon of possibilities, but also as a limiting idea.

However, the limits of narrative theory do not discount its positive, configuring capacities. One might argue that the narrative unity of a life outlines a project that draws action. The constraints of being-within-time preclude the possibility that a life can ever be grasped as a totality. My beginning in birth does not belong to my act of narrating but to that of my parents. Likewise, death, the event which offers closure to life, is, paradoxically, that which results in its dissolution. Once again, I exist only in the narrating activity of others. In this sense, narrative unity is a limit idea, a projection that is never finally reached. On the other hand, the projection itself provides a unifying structure, however fragile, by unifying action toward a goal or ideal. The formation of a life plan, which manifests itself at the level of narrative possibilities, projects actions and practices toward goals and ideals. Despite whatever circumstances may hinder their achievement, or whatever obstacles chance may throw in the way, these projects function as unifying principles. In this respect, narrative offers a mediated unity to life.

In the final part of this exploration, I will address this narrative quality of identity to the idea of possibility, or potentiality, which draws action toward a goal. By way of anticipation, I will say that identity is lived as meaningful existence in its orientation toward potentiality.

Narrative and Possibility

Human existence is lived as possibility. I have addressed this fact at several important points already. First, Ricoeur discussed the futural dimension of agency in the notion of keeping one's word where selfhood announces itself beyond the supports of sameness and where agents attest to their power for initiative. Second, at the level of practical life, the figure of humanity represented the projected synthesis of constituted character and the total demand for happiness which directs discrete actions. Finally, in the analysis of the narrative configuration of identity, the narrative unity of a life represented both the horizon of possibility and the limiting idea that directed identity and action toward the projected ideal of a total life well lived. In a very real way, this orientation toward possibility is what makes a human life a meaningful existence.

The detour through narrative theory has covered much ground toward understanding this orientation of possibility that grounds human agency. The synthetic operation of emplotment offers greater understanding of the manner in which events and actions are directed by an intention toward total configuration. The relationship Ricoeur established between the development of a plot and the development of the literary characters who act and suffer within that plot offers some reflective purchase on the manner in which the identity of agents is "composed" in the process of acting and suffering. Finally, the fusion of horizons between the world of the text and the world of the reader offers the possibility of an imaginative appropriation of the world of the text, which, in turn, offers some perspective on the reader's own creative and active possibilities. In a sense, the projected ideal of the narrative unity of a life is the imaginative appropriation of the figure of humanity as meaningful existence. The horizon of possibility toward which the idea of a narrative unity points is the place where the abstract figure of humanity becomes a practical possibility for a self; against this horizon, the figure of meaningful existence becomes meaningful *for me*. This narrative unity, however, remains a project, a task. The narrative unity of a life is a *unity* to the extent that it is a unified *totality*; but, the unified totality of *my* life remains a task so long as I am in the midst of it. To exist is to aim at a complete life that I am always *on the way* toward. In this sense, human existence is "caught" between the present and the future, between presence and possibility, between actuality and potentiality.

But this account raises serious difficulties in the attempt to address the identity of the agent. If I am always on the way to full existence, how is it possible to account for selfhood at all? Am I not always trying to give an account of something that is not *yet*? By casting identity in the relationship between sameness and selfhood Ricoeur raised the stakes of any account of identity. In a very real sense, the category of selfhood is not an empirical quality.[44]

Human existence is lived as possibility. Another way of putting this is to say that the being of the self resides in both actuality *and* potentiality. This then is the significance of Ricoeur's designation of the identity of the agent in terms of both sameness and selfhood. By relating these terms through the concepts of character and self-constancy, he wove actuality and potentiality into the being of the self. However, in the degree that self-constancy is conceived as the point at which selfhood establishes itself beyond the constraints of sameness, the being of the self is decentered from its position in actuality, but in such a way that actuality is not cancelled out but reassigned. In this way, the self who acts, and who finds its capacity for action in actuality, testifies to its power for being a self in potentiality.

Ricoeur turned here to Baruch Spinoza's idea of *conatus*. Spinoza claimed, in Proposition 6, Part III of the *Ethics*, "*Each thing, in so far as it is in itself, endeavors to persist in its own being*," and follows immediately in Proposition 7, "*The conatus with which each thing endeavors to persist in its own being is nothing but the actual essence of the thing itself.*"[45] Spinoza yoked the essence of each particular thing to activity, that is, to the endeavor to persist in being. The being of things is not confined in static substance. Rather, the essence of anything whatsoever resides in its active endeavor to remain itself, and this applies no more to human existence that to any other existence. Ricoeur placed selfhood in the idea of self-constancy, a type of self-constancy that we experience at the level of initiative. With the introduction of Spinoza's *conatus*, the character of human initiative takes on some ontological weight. I quote Ricoeur at length:

> I realize that this dynamism of living things excludes all initiative that would break with the determinism of nature and that persevering in being does not involve going beyond this being in the direction of something else, in accordance with some intention that could be held to be the end of that effort. . . . We should not, however, forget that the passage from inadequate ideas, which we form about ourselves and about things, to adequate ideas signifies for us the possibility of being truly *active*. In this sense, the power to act can be said to be increased by the retreat of passivity tied to inadequate ideas. . . . This conquest of activity under the aegis of adequate ideas makes the work as a whole an *ethics*. Thus there is a close connection between the internal dynamism worthy of the name life and the power of the intelligence, which governs the passage from inadequate to adequate ideas. *In this sense, we are powerful when we understand adequately our, as it were, horizontal and external dependence with respect to all things, and our vertical and immanent dependence with respect to the primordial power that Spinoza continues to call "God."*

The first part of this last sentence is simply a restatement of the fact, addressed in the last chapter, that human capability is not pure activity, not pure volition. In this sense, I am more free the more I have an adequate understanding of the limits of my capability. In a significant way, the passage through narrative understanding has been an exercise in the conquest of adequate ideas about the possibilities for existence, about a particular mode of persevering in being. Ricoeur concluded, "What finally matters to me more than any idea is . . . on the one hand, that it is in man that *conatus*, or the power of being of all things, is most clearly readable and, on the other hand, that everything expresses to different degrees the power or life that Spinoza calls the life of God."[46] The power to persevere in existence is most readable in human existence because humans have the capacity to reflect on this power; narrative mediation is one of the principal means of doing this. The positing of a relationship to a primordial power introduces something new into this account, however.

Ricoeur suggested that this relation to a primordial power points to "a ground of being, at once potentiality and actuality [*puissant et effectif*] against which human action stands out."[47] This ground of being, Spinoza's life of God, points us toward the last section of this chapter. To attest to my power of initiative is, at the same time, to testify to a power that precedes me and makes my power possible. We encountered this testimony to a preexistent power in the previous chapter: Kant's presupposition of a fully enlightened and completely spontaneous freedom, that is, the presupposition of the divine, served as a limiting idea against which limited human freedom would make sense. In the final section, I will address this idea in more detail.

Affirmation: A Hermeneutics of Meaningful Existence

One of the most important lessons to take away from the previous analyses is that Ricoeur saw human understanding and existence as a hermeneutical engagement with the world. If human existence is meaningful, it is because it is open to interpretation. As he asserted in many places, humans attest to and lay claim to their existence through the interpretation of works that express that existence. In this sense, interpretation represents a further specification of the conceptual bridge of reflection that leads from agency to meaning. In the last chapter, I followed Ricoeur in claiming that agency is experienced as attestation to oneself as an acting and suffering being. Attestation rises to the level of self-reflection in the form of interpretation. In this last section, I turn directly to what I will call a hermeneutics of meaningful existence.

Ricoeur argued that action becomes meaningful in light of a total demand for happiness that serves as the horizon of possibility for all discrete acts. In the synthesis of the idea of humanity, this total demand comes into contact with the finite, constituted character that I am; in this way, humanity is the figure of meaningful existence considered abstractly. The journey through narrative configuration allowed me to claim that the limiting idea of the narrative unity of a life, with which that analysis ended, is the point at which the ideal of humanity becomes a possibility *for me*: the figure of meaningful existence becomes my aim in striving for a narrative unity. However, this narrative unity is a projected ideal; it is not reached so long as I am *in* existence. "Because we do not enjoy immediate self-possession and always lack perfect self-identity, because . . . we never produce the total act that we gather up and project in the ideal of an absolute choice, we must endlessly appropriate what we are through the mediation of the multiple expressions of our desire to be."[48] Narrative is one of the principal modes in which this desire to be comes to expression.

It is important to recognize the role of desire in this account, because it is *in* desire that I strive to appropriate what I am. The ideal concerns me because it is what *I want*. But, this desire is two-edged; the desire to be is both that which directs me toward the attainment of my projected ideal and that which interjects a note of misery and "affective fragility" into my existence. This affective fragility, which is not itself *moral fault*, is the point of least resistance for moral evil on Ricoeur's accounting. The leap from affective fragility to moral fault presents a philosophical paradox, however. While philosophy can account for the structures in the will that provide for the *possibility* of moral evil, the advent of the fault itself is something philosophical speculation cannot fathom. Yet, if moral evil defies philosophical resolution, there remains the possibility of the kind of figurative resolution that Ricoeur continually assigned to poetic discourse and narrative. In the attempt to offer some productive resolution to the enigma of moral evil, Ricoeur turned to biblical texts. His engagement with biblical texts manifested itself at the intersection of two trajectories of biblical interpretation: a theology of *redemption* and a theology of *creation*.

In a profound sense, biblical witness held a privileged position in Ricoeur's thought. This concluding analysis of the notion of affirmation is most profoundly manifest in this encounter with the biblical configuration of the relationship between humans and the divine. In many respects, this relationship is a theological corollary to the philosophical idea of a ground of being against which human action stands out. I will explore affirmation in three steps that I label *primary affirmation*, *biblical worlds*, and *the hermeneutics of testimony*.

Primary Affirmation

Humans are oriented in existence by desire. My striving toward selfhood is directed by an intended goal that motivates me. In order to express this orientation of desire, Ricoeur adopted the idea of "primary affirmation" (*l'affirmation originaire*) from French reflexive philosopher Jean Nabert. Primary affirmation signals the fact that I take an affirmative stance toward some ideal, at least implicitly, in all my intentional activities. Despite the vissititudes of existing, I find a fundamental good at the heart of existence that holds out against against denial.[49] I characterized this affirmative ideal in two distinct ways already—happiness and the narrative unity of a life. Of this idea, Nabert stated:

> The movement of reflection does not direct itself toward primary affirmation so that it may settle down in it. It does this so that the existence of the self, as it produces itself out of desire at all levels of action, will imitate and verify as much as possible this primary certitude. . . . What reflection grasps and affirms as pure consciousness of self the self appropriates as value to the extent that it creates itself and becomes really for itself. This means that value appears in view of existence and for existence when pure consciousness of self has turned toward the world and become the principle or rule of action and at the same time, the measure of satisfaction in a concrete consciousness.[50]

As much as one may want to question the notion of a "pure consciousness of self," and Ricoeur certainly did this by assigning to understanding a hermeneutical task, the claim that reflection directs one toward self-appropriation in the world is squarely within Ricoeur's understanding of human existence. Most broadly considered, primary affirmation represents the individual's desire to be a self. This desire arises within the consciousness of an ideal toward which the self aims, an ideal that confronts the self in reflection as an absolute value.

Primary affirmation confronts the self in the form of desire because it is the recognition of a value that exists solely in an image or sign of the ideal. Primary affirmation is an affirmation of the self that one wishes to become but is not yet. Thus, the affirmation of a value in the self is at the same time the experience of a lack of identity in the self. What the self recognizes in primary affirmation is both its possible ideal and its present inadequacy in light of this ideal. The lack of identity between present existence and future possibility is never completely overcome; identity is approached but not achieved. Subsequently, the affirmation of selfhood both draws individual activity forward in desire and continually reinvests the individual with the experience of lack of identity: "[F]or a self which aspires to produce itself, action becomes the unique way to verify both that it draws closer to its being and that at the same time it always remains distant from that being."[51]

However, what represents a structural feature of existence at the level of abstract reflection, becomes an internal *conflict* at the level of experience. Why is this the case? To coincide in actuality with the ideal that I form is what I desire; yet, my active appropriation of the means toward this ideal reveals that the ideal itself recedes in the midst of my attempts to achieve it. This feature of existence is a source of affective conflict because my fundamental desire is thwarted by the partial constitution that I am. The lack of identity with the ideal takes on the affective overtones of existential disproportion and anxiety, what Ricoeur called the *pathétique of misery*. This account of existential conflict is the ground upon which Ricoeur's account of moral fault is built. Existential conflict gives rise to affective fragility, the path of least resistance for the entrance of moral evil.

The fragility of my existence as a mediation between actuality and possibility, between partial constitution and total demand, becomes a constant source of temptation to overstep the limits of my finitude and establish myself as an immediate totality: In the quest for material security I succumb to acquisitiveness. In the attempt to actualize myself through the power of initiative I resort to violence and domination. In the desire for self-esteem and esteem in the eyes of others I fall into pride and vanity. The fragility of my situation contantly tempts me to overstep my bounds:

> There is something like a dizziness that leads from weakness to temptation and from temptation to fall. Thus, evil, in the very moment when "I admit" that I posit it, seems to arise from man's very limitation through the unbroken transition from dizziness. It is this transition from innocence to fault, discovered in the very positing of evil that gives the concept of fallibility all its equivocal profundity. Fragility is not merely the "locus," the point of insertion of evil, nor even the "origin" starting from which man falls; it is the "capacity" for evil. To say that man is fallible is to say that the limitation peculiar to a being who does not coincide with himself is the primordial weakness from which evil arises. *And yet evil arises from this weakness only because it is posited.*[52]

This claim that evil arises out of weakness and fragility only because it is posited, points to the profound paradox of moral evil.

Ricoeur addressed the "fall" into moral evil in three stages: a *semantics of the experience of moral evil*, passing through the internalization of moral evil in *the experience of guilt*, to the paradoxical notion of *the bound will*. He asserted that the semanitics of evil is, first and formost, a "phenomenology of confession": "a description of meanings, and of signified intentions, present *in a certain activity of language*, namely, *confession*."[53] At its highest point, the confession of evil takes form in the expression of guilt. Guilt represents the extreme interiorization of the experience of evil, the taking upon oneself of the origin of evil in the subjective realization that one is responsible for it. Evil is no longer represented as something "out there," as some "thing" in the world that afflicts me. The experience of guilt brings the recognition that evil is done by me; evil comes about through my decisions and my actions. This recognition of *responsibility-*

for evil at the same time links the genesis of evil to the whole problematic of freedom. My freedom is implicated in evil because I have chosen evil rather than good. Philosophically, this implication introduces a profound paradox: freedom is the condition of possibility for both morality and evil, and it seems that evil finally wins out. To plumb the depths of this paradox, Ricoeur turned to Kant's notion of radical evil.

For Kant the choice of an evil action resides in allowing freedom to be determined by a maxim other than the moral maxim. The proclivity toward determination of freedom by evil maxims gives morality the feeling of obligation; if this proclivity did not exist, morality would be natural and not obligatory. To paraphrase Kant, the perfectly good will knows no obligation because it simply chooses in accord with the right maxims. This idea already points to a deeper level of human evil; evil does not reside, finally, in discrete actions, but in a foundation that already disorients discrete actions. Evil is *radical* because it resides in a maxim that serves as the foundation for all immoral actions. Kant conceived this evil foundation as *self-preference* which tempts one to make oneself the exception to the moral rule.

What makes radical evil so paradoxical is the fact that it resides in the foundation of freedom. Any particular evil choice finds its ultimate foundation in a choice that precedes any discrete determination of freedom. In other words, freedom is already fallen. This signals the ultimate incapacity of freedom to extricate itself from the dilemma of radical evil: "This evil is *radical*, because it corrupts the ground of all maxims; it is, moreover, as a natural propensity, *inextirpable* by human powers, since extirpation could only occur through good maxims, and cannot take place when the ultimate subjective ground of all maxims is postulated as corrupt; yet at the same time it must be possible to *overcome* it, since it is found in man, a being whose actions are free."[54] If the only thing that is good without qualification is a good will, this ideal becomes an impossible possibility; freedom despairs over its incapacity and lack of goodness.

And yet, despair is not the last word. Rather, despair itself opens onto hope, and this opening onto freedom's hope is at once an opening onto the question of religion. Addressing the crisis of freedom, Ricoeur stated:

> Now, evil is a problem for the philosopher only inasmuch as it belongs to the problematic of the actualization of freedom; evil makes of freedom an impossible possibility. . . . A real liberty can be hoped, beyond this speculative and practical Good Friday. We are nowhere so close as here to the Christian kerygma: hope is hope of resurrection, of resurrection from among the dead. In philosophical terms: evil requires a nonethical and nonpolitical transformation of our will, which Kant calls regeneration; it is the task of "religion within the

> limits of reason alone" to elaborate the condition of possibility of this regeneration, without alienating freedom either to a magical conception of grace and salvation or to an authoritarian organization of the religious community.[55]

In other words, the despair of freedom marks the point of entrance into the philosophy of religion and the configuration of hope in freedom's possibility.

At this point, the first real crossing into the realm of religion reveals itself. In the next section, I will explore in more depth the manner in which Ricoeur's theological sensibilities affected the direction of his philosophical anthropology.

Biblical Worlds: The End and the Origin

The problem of moral evil signals a gap in the purely philosophical account of meaningful existence that necessitates a turn toward decidedly religious themes. In the previous chapter, I showed that Ricoeur's account of the self is fundamentally an account of agency: his anthropology is an anthropology of human capability. In this chapter, that agency is configured as meaningful existence through the mediation of figurative texts. Ricoeur turned to figurative texts again in order to counter the impasse of moral evil in the meaning of the self. But the turn to the biblical texts was different from his account of the configuring capacities of narrative in general. Biblical sources had a privileged status in Ricoeur's philosophical project.

His account of biblical witness proceeded in two distinct directions. With regard to the question of evil, biblical witness served to articulate a proposed end that poetically reconfigures the paradox of moral evil. Following in the footsteps of theologians as diverse as Karl Barth, Rudolf Bültmann, and Jürgen Moltmann, he interpreted the gospel kerygma along the trajectory of a *theology of redemption*; biblical witness offered the promise of a restoration of freedom and goodness beyond the presence of evil. However, Ricoeur began to address the possibility of a *theology of creation*, which pointed to a recognition of the fundamental value of the created order. Following Franz Rosenzweig in particular, he relocated the process of redemption itself within an account of an origin that grounded the recognition of value in creation in the power of a benevolent God. Along this twofold path of a theology of redemption and a theology of creation, of the end and origin of human possibility, I will explore what Ricoeur's account of the world the biblical witness presents to the configuration of meaningful existence.

In addressing Ricoeur's adoption of the theology of redemption, I want to focus on the basic structure of hope and its relation to philosophy and theology. Ricoeur claimed that the orientation of hope requires a change in the organization of philosophical systems. Hope presents a reorientation in the structure of philosophical discourse as such: "In the same way as there is the problem of the starting point in philosophy, as was emphasized by Descartes and Husserl, there is also the problem of the closing point, or better, of the *horizon of philosophical discourse*."[56] The theology of redemption stakes its claim at the horizon of philosophical discourse: if contemplation on the origin of evil reveals the fundamental incapacity of freedom, the contemplation of the end offers the possibility of freedom's deliverance, configured in biblical terms by the "Kingdom of God."

The Kingdom of God is addressed in terms of what Ricoeur designated the "logic of superabundance," poetically related by the promise of deliverance, reconciliation, resurrection. The logic of superabundance functions as an answer to philosophy's despair over freedom's incapacity; this logic proposes to the philosophy of freedom a *passion for the possible* which represents the final reconciliation of happiness and duty within the will and the defeat of evil and violence outside the self. Ricoeur argued, "The 'in spite of' [that is, the affirmation of freedom *in spite of* evil] which keeps us in readiness for the denial is only the inverse, the shadow side, of this joyous 'how much more' by which freedom feels itself, knows itself, and wills itself to belong to this economy of superabundance."[57] Under the category of promise, one encounters the possibility of the regeneration of the will and the restoration of freedom's power to choose good. This idea of the passion for the possible spurred Ricoeur to follow Moltmann's interpretation of biblical witness in terms of the eschatological reestablishment of the Kingdom of God. The Kingdom of God is not directed solely to individual freedom. The promise of resurrection concerns the regeneration of all things; it is a claim about the good as such. But this raises the fundamental problem of where to "place" the good. The theology of hope is unable to affirm the good of creation because it places the good outside of creation. How is this the case?

One must first analyze the antithesis that the theology of hope establishes between a religion of promise and a religion of presence:

> The God who is witnessed to is not . . . the God who *is* but the God who *is coming*. The "already" of his Resurrection orients the "not yet" of the final recapitulation. But the meaning reaches us disguised by the Greek Christologies, which have made the Incarnation the temporal manifestation of eternal being and the eternal present, thus hiding the principal meaning, namely, that the God of promise, the God of Abraham, Isaac, and Jacob, has approached, has been revealed as He who is coming for all.

In this way, the theology of hope opposes a religion of promise to one of presence; it emphasizes the proclamation of the eschatological new Jerusalem at the expense of any notion of the manifestation of the sacred in creation. The God it preaches, the ultimate reality to which it points, is "not yet," not present but coming. The kerygma is one of a reality not yet a reality. The theology of hope is the proclamation of a nonpresence. Ricoeur continued, "It is then not only the Name that must be opposed to the idol, but the 'He is coming' of Scripture must be opposed to the 'It is' of the *Proem* of Parmenides. This dividing line is henceforth going to separate two conceptions of time and, through them, two conceptions of freedom."[58] On this reading, the core of the kerygma is the issuance of a promise by a God who recedes from the world, who in effect disclaims the existing creation.

Now, why is this antithesis important for an understanding of the good? Recall that the theology of hope takes the recognition of the reality and radicality of evil as its starting point. Despair over evil calls for a final reconciliation. Yet this reconciliation is "not yet." It is promised at the eschaton. It is important to recognize the *utopian* aspirations of this eschatology of hope; the restoration of the good, configured poetically as universal resurrection, is *non*-historical, *atemporal.* Indeed, it signals the *end* of history. This is an important claim about the relationship of the good to creation. To the degree that the good resides at the end of history, to the degree that it signals the conclusion of creation, the good is fundamentally outside of creation; it is "not yet." Given this "not yet" of the good, the only response open to freedom is hope in the proclaimed promise. This is not to say that hope is passive. Rather, this is a hope that wills itself into an economy of superabundance. It is a hope that engenders a freedom. But this superabundance takes the "not yet" of the promise as its principle theme. In this case, freedom in light of hope results from a negation of the present. Paradoxically, hope wills itself into a nontemporal time; freedom becomes the denial of a creation already characterized as fallen and in need of eschatological redemption.

There was a subtle shift in perspective in Ricoeur's later work, however. There, he adopted the very Greek christologies that he had criticized earlier to establish a mediation between the proclamation of hope and the manifestation of the sacred: "That word and manifestation can be reconciled is the central affirmation of the Prologue to John's Gospel. . . . This identification of word and manifestation was the basis for the concept of revelation that from the Greek fathers to Hegel constituted the central category in terms of which thought about Christianity was organized." Once the word is reconciled with the manifest, once proclamation is a proclamation of the sacred, then the kerygma becomes an affirmation of the present:

> A word that is addressed to us rather than our speaking it, a word that constitutes us rather than our articulating it—a word that speaks—

> does not such a word reaffirm the sacred just as much as abolish it? It does so if hearing this word is impossible without a transvaluation of the values *tremendum* and *fascinosum* into obedience and fervor. For my part, I cannot conceive a religious attitude that did not proceed from "a feeling of absolute dependence." And is this not the essential relation of humankind to the sacred, transmuted into speech and, in this way, reaffirmed at the same time it is surpassed?[59]

The recognition of absolute dependence places the good within time. The feeling of absolute dependence is an affirmation of creation as that which precedes and sustains life, and a testimony to a divine creative intention, which directs that creation.

This reworking of the kerygma has radical implications for an understanding of freedom within the context of Christian witness. If the kerygma was no longer for Ricoeur simply the proclamation of promise and fulfillment, but also the testimony to a word spoken within creation which is fundamentally constitutive of the self, then freedom's orientation is not only hope in a final resurrection, but also response to that word. This discussion points to the idea of a second trajectory in Ricoeur's account of biblical witness. I believe that Ricoeur's continuing interest in the work of the Jewish philosopher Franz Rosenzweig pointed decisively in this direction.

Ricoeur's principal interest in Rosenzweig was the distinction he drew between commandment and law. But, there are two factors involved here that force one to draw broader consequences from Ricoeur's reliance on Rosenzweig. The first concerns the character of commandment itself. Rosenzweig argued that a commandment is a word issued immediately from the divine to the self, a word that confronts the self in the moment of decision. He concluded that there is only one commandment—"Love me!" God confronts the soul with the commandment of love; all other commandments, all laws, and every ethical orientation find their ultimate source in this one commandment. With this single commandment, God addresses an individual self, an individual freedom. More than this, however, the commandment is constitutive of selfhood and of freedom, in that freedom is constituted by the response to the commandment. The self comes to itself in the recognition of being before God.[60]

A second factor is the place that the commandment holds in the complex structure of *The Star of Redemption*. This work is a philosophical-theological treatise on the interconnection of the ideas of creation, revelation, and redemption. Revelation mediates creation and redemption, and the commandment is *the* figure of revelation. Redemption is made possible by the command "love me!"; it resides in love actualizing itself in love of creation, and the self is given form through this process of redemption.[61] Thus, a space is opened for a second trajectory in Ricoeur's understanding of the significance of biblical witness. I address this turn to a theology of creation via two guiding ideas: the recognition of a *fundamental value* that resides at the heart of the created order, and the *experience of dependence* on a divine power that arises out of the confrontation with the divine in the advent of the love command.

The recognition of a fundamental value within the created order is encompassed by the positing of moral evil in the experience of guilt. It is precisely from the perspective of an originally innocent will that the experience of guilt takes on all of its affective weight as a *fall.* What the theology of redemption banished from the created order in its focus on hope for the deliverance from evil is this experience of value that the torn conscience attests to as its fundamental origin. Thus, the proclamation of the kerygmatic promise hinges on some understanding of a value that the guilty self recognizes but from which it feels itself cut off.

This feeling of separation points in the direction of the second orienting theme of dependence. In guilt, the self recognizes itself as bound, that is, unfree, through a choice that it has nonetheless made. In this sense, the possibility of redemption rests in the assistance of a divine power that can restore freedom. This dependence on a transcendent power is poetically construed through biblical narratives of the liberation from Egypt and, in a more existential sense, in St. Paul's account of salvation through grace. But this dependence in light of the end of human existence, that is, redemption, points in the direction of a more primordial dependence with regard to the origin, a dependence that comes to the fore in a theology of creation.[62]

With these two orienting themes in mind, I turn to Ricoeur's dialogue with Franz Rosenzweig. Rosenzweig became profoundly important for Ricoeur's articulation of the relation of the transcendent to the temporal by virtue of his configuration of the triad of creation-revelation-redemption. Within the *Star of Redemption*, creation serves as an enduring origin within which revelation and redemption configure their own particular temporality. In this account, creation, revelation, and redemption represent three fundamental, intersecting modes of temporality: creation is the ever-enduring origin of existence; revelation is the ever-renewed birth of the soul to its relationship with the divine and with the world; redemption is the eternally approaching future possibility of the kingdom of God. Creation signals dependence with respect to the origin of existence. Redemption signals responsibility with regard to the reconciliation of the world. Revelation signals the birth of the self's recognition of this twofold relationship. Thus, a theology of redemption and a theology of creation are not competing strategies. Neither are they trajectories that can be collapsed into each other. Ricoeur argued that "we can affirm that the theology of Creation constitutes neither an appendix to the theology of Redemption nor a separate theme. The always-already-there of Creation does not make sense independently of the perpetual futurity of Redemption. Between these two is intercalated the eternal now of the 'you, love me!'"[63] In the obverse direction, it can be argued that the theology of redemption cannot exist without the theology of creation because it constantly loses sight of the value within creation that redemption seeks to increase.

Therefore, Ricoeur's understanding of the biblical configuration of meaningful existence was twofold. With respect to the end of existence, individuals are oriented by a theology of redemption, which seeks final reconciliation of the self with itself, with the divine, and with the world. With respect to the origin, individuals are oriented by a fundamental value within the created order through which they are sustained in existence and to which they are responsible. These two orientations meet in the moment where the divine manifests itself to the individual soul. But, in turning attention to the moment of the commandment, analysis is turned toward a final dimension of affirmation in which the self appropriates itself in relation to this privileged source of meaning. I will conclude this chapter with an exploration of Ricoeur's understanding of the hermeneutics of testimony as the process in which the self does just this.

The Theological Orientation of Meaningful Existence

While narrative texts in general contribute to self-understanding, in Ricoeur's estimation the biblical texts do this in a special way. As I discussed previously, the engagement with narratives offers some understanding of one's potentiality as a self through the process of imaginative variations of possibility. Biblical texts do this as well. The scope of biblical witness extends beyond the imaginative configuration of human possibility, however. What biblical witness configures poetically, so to speak, is the relationship between a self and the philosophical idea that Ricoeur called a ground of being at once actual and potential. This idea, I suggested, is a philosophical correlate to what is theologically construed as the divine. Biblical witness places one at the horizon of existence, so to speak, in relating existence to a ground of being. Through the use of limit expressions and limit concepts, the biblical texts speak to an experience that exists at the limit of attempts to make sense of existence. The polyphony of the biblical text is, Ricoeur argued, revelatory of one's striving in relation to a ground of being that makes meaningful existence a real possibility. In this way, to engage and appropriate the biblical world hermeneutically is to bear witness, to testify, to a transformation within understanding and self-understanding. I will explore this function of the biblical text in three stages: first, through Ricoeur's presentation of the idea of limit concepts or enigma-expressions, I will trace the manner in which he related the productive capacities of biblical symbols, metaphors, and narratives to the striving for self-understanding. Second, this productive capacity opens onto Ricoeur's understanding of biblical hermeneutics; by examining this understanding, it will be possible to gauge the prestige that Ricoeur granted to the biblical word. Finally, the question of the hermeneutical significance of this word opens the question of the manner in which what is revealed in the text interjects itself into life. At this point *biblical* hermeneutics passes over into a *theological* hermeneutics of the idea of testimony where the individual appropriates his/her self-understanding in relation to the ground of being.

By Ricoeur's account, the biblical word moves thought to the limits of experience through the configuration of the idea of the "unconditioned"—unconditioned freedom of God, unconditional commandment of love, etc. Ricoeur claimed that biblical texts poetically configure the unconditioned through the employment of rhetorical extravagance, for instance, hyperbole, paradox. Through the strategic use of these kinds of extravagant expression, the text opens thought to previously unimaginable possibilities: "It is the extravagance of the narrative that, by bursting out of the mundane meaning of the narrative, attests that 'my kingdom is not of this world,' that is, does not belong to any specific project of human action and remains, in the strong sense of the word, impractical like some utopia. The expression-enigma, under the pressure of the extravagance of the narrative, thus becomes a limit-expression that breaks open the closed representations." In breaking open the closed representations, narrative and symbolic extravagance meaningfully configure experiences of the unconditioned. Thus, Ricoeur concluded, "These limit-expressions . . . would be nothing more than hollow words if, on the one hand, human beings did not have some experience of limit-situations such as evil and death and the strong desire to be freed from them. It is these fundamental experiences that the enigma-expressions come *to configure*."[64] This understanding of the biblical texts as poetic discourse that configures the experience of the unconditioned is centrally important for Ricoeur's understanding of biblical hermeneutics.

The relationship that Ricoeur drew between biblical hermeneutics and a general hermeneutics of texts is a complex one. From one angle, biblical hermeneutics is a species of general hermeneutics, namely, the application of general hermeneutical principles to a particular category of texts. In Ricoeur's estimation, however, the application of general hermeneutical principles to biblical texts tended to invert the relationship; in the end, "theological hermeneutics finally subordinates philosophical hermeneutics to itself as its own organon."[65] To engage in biblical hermeneutics is, in significant ways, to follow the trajectory of this inversion.

Ricoeur's account of biblical hermeneutics was composed of four distinct concerns. In their broadest formulation they can be characterized as such: the biblical text as a *work*, the dialectic of *speech and writing*, *the world of the text*, and the dialectic of *distanciation and appropriation*. The first concern to characterize the Bible as a work seems at first glance to go against the grain of the historical-critical exegetical tradition. Indeed, this tradition claims that the Bible is not *a* work, but a collection of works which, far from offering a common witness, are more frequently at odds in their respective witnesses. This fact is further exacerbated by the recognition of redactional activity within single works. Ricoeur was sympathetic to this criticism, but his understanding of the hermeneutical engagement with the biblical texts relocated the process of engagement from scholarly exegesis, which concerns itself with compositional structures, to the committed critical reading of communities whose self-understandings are mediated through the text. In significant ways, scholarly exegesis is one mode of this committed hermeneutical activity. Ricoeur did not attempt to reduce biblical witness to a singular vision in designating the Bible as a work. Rather, the Bible is a diverse and "polyphonic" witness to the encounter with the divine; it is precisely within the conflict and tension between biblical accounts that individuals in believing communities critically appropriate their self-understandings. Far from presenting a view contrary to historical-critical method, Ricoeur appropriated this method within the larger attempt to address the critical appropriation of understanding.

Ricoeur's second concern was the dialectic of speech and writing. This distinction between speech and writing was encounted above in the discussion of the transposition from the spoken *word* to the written *work*. Here, Ricoeur moved from distinction to dialectic; the dialectic between speaking (preaching) and writing (Bible, exegesis, commentary, etc.) is critical for understanding the process of the formation of tradition. He claimed:

> The upshot of this reflection on the hermeneutical situation of Christianity is that the relation between speech and writing is constitutive of what we term proclamation, kerygma, preaching. What appears to be primary is the series speech-writing-speech, or else writing-speech-writing, in which at times speech mediates two writings, as does the word of Jesus between the two Testaments, and at times writing mediates two forms of speech, as the gospel does between the preaching of the early church and all contemporary preaching. This chain is the condition of the possibility of tradition as such, in the fundamental sense of the transmission of a message.[66]

This continual dialectic between speech and writing, or more appropriately stated, the continued attempt to reactualize the written witness in preaching the word is central to the proclamatory function of biblical witness. But, what does the witness proclaim?

Here, the third of Ricoeur's concerns arises: the world of the text. Recall his claim that the projection of a world is a general feature of written poetic discourse. What one engages in the text is the world of the text. In this sense, the biblical texts function in the same manner as any other poetic text. This understanding has many and profound implications for the notion of what Ricoeur meant by the term *revelation*. Poetic expression, in general, is revelatory. Yet the Bible is revelatory in a particular way because of the scope of the world that it presents: "The biblical world has aspects that are cosmic (it is a creation), communal (it involves a people), historicocultural (it concerns Israel, the kingdom of God), as well as personal. Human beings are implicated in their varied dimensions—cosmological, historical and worldly, as well as anthropological, ethical, and personalist."[67] The world that the biblical text presents is a total one. The biblical world is one that poetically configures experiences of the unconditioned. To appropriate oneself in light of this biblical world is to understand oneself in light of an unconditioned ground that precedes and makes possible any particular project. Poetic discourse in general configures individual possibility; biblical discourse projects this possibility against an unconditioned ground that has historical and cosmic significance. Through the tension of polyphonic discourses, biblical discourse "names God," that is, bears witness to the relation within which individual existence becomes meaningful.

The last of Ricoeur's hermeneutical concerns is the dialectic of distanciation and appropriation. In addressing the manner in which one appropriates the biblical world into self-understanding, biblical hermeneutics, in the narrow sense, inclines toward a more general theological hermeneutics.[68] First, the process of distanciation, central to hermeneutics in general, forces one to realize that there is no direct access to the self; there is no immediate experience or intuition of the *cogito*. Rather, the *I* is always "mediated by a universe of signs." Ricoeur made the powerful claim that, "The first truth . . . that of the 'I think, I am,' remains as abstract and empty as it is invincible; it has to be 'mediated' by the ideas, actions, works, institutions, and monuments that objectify it. It is in these objects, in the widest sense of the word, that the Ego must lose and find itself."[69] Beyond this critical perspective on the nature of the Ego as such, the text offers critical perspective on the illusions that one holds about oneself. Indeed, self-critique is an integral part of understanding oneself before the text.

The critical distance afforded by the confrontation with the world of the text is, however, only one dimension of the encounter. Distanciation itself takes place within a realm of *participation*, of "belonging-to," which surrounds it. Ricoeur asserted, "The ultimate condition of any [critical] enterprise of justification or of grounding is that it is always preceded by a relation that already carries it." That is, critical distance is achieved, is meaningful, only in light of participation in a culture or a tradition that makes it possible. This exchange between distanciation and participation itself opens the way to a final movement, that of appropriation. Ricoeur placed firm bounds around what he intended by the term appropriation:

> By this I mean the very act of understanding oneself before the text. . . . To understand oneself before the text is not to impose one's own finite capacity of understanding on it, but to expose oneself to receive from it a larger self which would be the proposed way of existing that most appropriately responds to the proposed world of the text. Understanding then is the complete opposite of a constitution for which the subject would have the key. It would be better in this regard to say that the self is constituted by the issue of the text.[70]

But this is a feature of hermeneutics in general, a feature we have already encountered several times. What does the passage through biblical hermeneutics lend to the discussion?

Biblical hermeneutics is unique in this respect: the issue of biblical discourse, the "thing" of the biblical texts, is the naming of God through the articulation of the divine/human relationship. Thus, the confrontation with the thing of the text is the confrontation with an absolute power, a power at once actual and potential. The biblical texts testify to this power; thus to engage the text is to engage a testimony to the experience of the absolute or unconditioned. At the same time, to engage this testimony is to allow oneself to be affected, to be interpreted by the text. Testimony to absolute power is at once testimony to radical dependence on a power that precedes my existence, a power that is the possibility for my existence. But what is the status of this testimony? What makes it decisive? Indeed, is it ultimately decisive? The testimony is, after all, delivered by historical beings, fallible beings with a limited perspective. It is delivered from a particular historical viewpoint, a viewpoint that is very different from mine. How can testimony arising in a prescientific, premodern worldview be decisive for *me* at the beginning of the twenty-first century; how can I be "constituted by the issue of the text"? "[D]o we have the right," Ricoeur asked, "to invest a moment of history with an absolute character?"[71]

The engagement with biblical testimony to the existence of absolute power must be a critical engagement. Ricoeur never accepted the option of a naive and uncritical subscription; the paths of literalism and inerrancy he decisively ruled out of bounds. He continued to hold this testimony decisive, but historical and ideological distance from its composition means that appropriation of the truth of testimony is never direct. Engagement with biblical testimony to the absolute must be interpretive, achieved through the enduring symbols that continue to speak from the deposit of testimony: it is a *hermeneutics* of testimony. The hermeneutics of testimony is, Ricoeur explained, "a twofold act, an act of consciousness of itself [that is, self-consciousness] and an act of historical understanding based on the signs that the absolute gives of itself. The signs of the absolute's self-disclosure are at the same time signs in which consciousness recognizes itself."[72] It is a twofold act of a critical engagement with the historically located and conditioned articulations of the exprience of the divine—of the "signs the absolute gives of itself"— and of allowing oneself to be affected by those articulations. I will address each of these acts in its turn.

Testimony is testimony to an experience, to a manifestation that is taken to be the divine. In a very helpful way, Kevin VanHoozer has characterized the relationship between the biblical texts and testimony in Ricoeur's thought as such: "The truth of a certain poetic possibility is determined by its ability to illumine and transform life. 'Testimony' refers to this attestation that a given possibility is no empty passion but gives meaning and power to human existence, that is, to our desire and effort to be."[73] While these testimonies are expressed in historically and culturally localized narratives and discourses, Ricoeur argued that these conditioned expressions could give rise to symbols that convey unconditional meanings. This, he claimed, is the power of the biblical texts. These texts, taken together serve to "name" God, to attach meaning to the experiences of the manifestation of the divine. They are taken to be decisive to the degree that their meanings continue to resonate beyond the historical and cultural location of their production. Biblical symbols continue to speak to contemporary understandings. The two important biblical symbols of creation and redemption were already discussed. The texts that give rise to these symbols serve as testimony to the manifestation of the divine as creator and redeemer, to the experience of absolute power as origin and end of existence.

But the hermeneutics of testimony has a circular effect: to engage biblical testimony is to be engaged by it. To interpret is, at the same time, to be interpeted. To the degree that these symbols remain decisive, self-affirmation, the capacity to recognize and affirm meaningful existence in oneself, remains tied to them. One's own life becomes enmeshed in the drama of creation and redemption that is laid out in the biblical narratives. But allowing oneself to be interpreted by the texts is no less critical than the act of interpreting them. Biblical symbols are not univocal and, Ricoeur always argued, they are never closed to further interpretions. Indeed, there is every possibility that they may cease to be decisive (an idea that Ricoeur rarely addressed, but which is necessarily implied in his approach). The twofold act of a hermeneutics of testimony is also a twofold judgment on the adequacy of the manifestations to which the texts testify. It is both an affirmation—affirmation of meaning in the symbol and in the self—and what Ricoeur, following Jean Nabert, called a "criteriology of the divine" whereby the self critically appropriates its meanings.

In some sense, this twofold movement of a hermeneutics of testimony signals the distinction between *biblical hermeneutics* and *theological hermeneutics* that I indicated above: the critical engagement with biblical testimony encompasses the former, the critical appropriation of testimony the latter. The move to a broadly theological hermeneutics opens this analysis to new dimensions of existence: the configuration of meaningful existence points freedom in concrete directions. It demands that one contemplate action. The following chapters will explore Ricoeur's account of meaningful agency under the practical demands of ethics and morality. This examination will proceed along two interrelated lines, first a philosophical discussion of the practical experience of agency (chapter 4) and then on to the possibilities for understanding Ricoeur's thought that are opened by a theological perspective on practical experience (chapter 5).

Chapter Four

Practice

Practical Experience and Moral Concern

The two previous chapters dealt with agency as the structure of selfhood and meaningful existence configured through narrative. I showed how Ricoeur characterized the basic structure of agency in terms of capability. Capability arose from the reciprocal relationship between voluntary and involuntary structures of action and will. Capability took on a deepened sense through its configuration in terms of the dual designation of the identity of the agent as sameness and selfhood. Finally, this identity rose to the level of experience in self-attestation. Ricoeur characterized attestation as the assurance of being oneself acting and suffering, which I addressed as the experience of an initiative that is traversed by various sorts of passivity.

The bridge that led from this basic structure of agency to the configuration of meaningful existence was the ability of the agent to reflect on his or her existence as a capable self imbued with identity and enmeshed in experience. Within the realm of meaningful existence, capability took its place within a world that presents itself to perception and within ideals that are grounded in inherited meanings and traditions of thought. The twofold identity of the agent was opened, through the fusion of horizons that takes place between the world of the reader and the world of the text; the world of the text presents the agent with a set of possibilities for his/her own identity through the imaginative variations at play between this textual world and human understanding. The attestation to the experience of being a self reached into the realm of affirmation through biblical witness to the ideas of creation and redemption revealed through a hermeneutics of testimony to the absolute. The account of reflective agency was affected and further specified at each level of the analysis.

In this chapter I will discuss practical experience as moral concern. I will argue that practical life is experienced as moral concern due to the fact that practical existence is precisely the realm of actual practices that are carried out in the public sphere shared with others. Practical experience is the place where the self encounters others who make moral demands. A bridge similar to one between the structure of agency and the configuration of meaningful existence can be constructed here. The bridge that leads from meaningful existence to practical experience can be called "public life," the life of communal and political action within institutions that govern society. This conceptual bridge will take more determinate forms as the analysis progresses. In engaging this account of practical experience, I will follow the same itinerary that governs all of these analyses: the argument will move from the structure of practical experience understood as *responsibility*, through its configuration in *ethics*, to the experience of *witness* to moral convictions.

The analysis of responsibility will be a critical reappraisal of ideas that are nascent in Ricoeur's work. He himself used the term sparingly. In articulating the concept of responsibility, I will attempt to offer a broader and more dynamic account that encompasses both the idea of *imputability*, or the sense of being responsible *for* one's actions, and that of *solicitude* where one responds *to* the claim of another. These terms were central to Ricoeur's thought, and they ground a robust understanding of responsibility as the structure of practical experience.

I will address the configuration of practical experience in terms of ethics, that is, ethical aspiration and moral normativity. The narrative configuration of identity encountered in the previous chapter opens onto practical experience through the confrontation with a fundamental sense of value which the self encounters in future possibilities and seeks to achieve through action. This sense of value is configured in a general orientation toward the good life within which the self comes to esteem itself. This is the practical value of the notion of a narrative unity of a life. Self-esteem is the initial basis for an aspiration, an overarching aim, which draws activity. The aim becomes a truly ethical aim in the realization that self-realization is sought within a public realm that is shared with others who have their own aims and governed by institutions intended to preserve that public realm. This aim is subject to the passage through moral norms because my power for self-realization brings with it the ever-present possibility of violence. The ethical sphere, therefore, is the configuration of practical experience in terms of an ethical aim that directs my efforts toward self-realization and a moral norm that demands respect for others.

Finally, I will address the experience of the intractable conflicts that afflict practical experience. The recognition that the moral life is traversed by inescapable conflicts—the good versus the right, happiness versus duty, competing duties, etc.—points to a fundamental dimension of ethical experience that

Ricoeur called "considered convictions." The analysis of testimony, which concluded the previous chapter, opens onto conviction through the experience of tragedy, which stands in the way of the final reconciliation to which biblical testimony points. Tragic experience pervades existence and serves as an impetus for my considered convictions. Tragedy demands my responsible action. What the moral life entails is less a resolution to the enigma of good and evil than a response to the suffering other whom I confront.

Once again, this itinerary follows the threefold path that traverses structure, configuration, and experience. Before proceeding, however, it is necessary to pause and consider the point at which the experience of the other enters into consideration of the self. Indeed, the question of the existence of other persons has not, as yet, really entered my analyses. Nevertheless, it was Ricoeur's contention that the experience of otherness is intrinsic to the constitution of selfhood. I begin by addressing this claim.

Practical Experience

As the first two chapters showed, Ricoeur conceived passivity as a fundamental experience of selfhood. In all cases, a dialectical relationship between dimensions of activity and passivity constituted selfhood. In practical experience, passivity takes on a new significance. Ricoeur argued that the experience of passivity, in its various dimensions, is "the *phenomenological* respondent to the metacategory of otherness." The connection that he drew between the experience of passivity and the encounter with the other is an important one. Otherness is not only a dimension of existence outside of the self; otherness "belongs instead to the tenor of meaning and to the ontological constitution of selfhood. . . ."[1] The other is not simply one who exists alongside the self. The confrontation with the experience of otherness is also constitutive of the meaning and experience of being a self.

The two thinkers whom Ricoeur set in dialogue to address this encounter with otherness were Edmund Husserl and Emmanuel Levinas. The attempt to construct a dialectic between these two thinkers' ideas is a controversial one, to say the least. Levinas's starting point was precisely a criticism of Husserl's phenomenological reduction of the other to an alter-ego, that is, another self. In Levinas's estimation, this is not an encounter with the other, but rather, an occlusion of the other: by reducing the other to an alter-ego, I do not encounter the other but my projection of him/her. Levinas turned Husserl's idea of constitution around: the self does not "constitute" the other through the reduction to alter-ego. Rather, the self is passively constituted in the confrontation with radical alterity, the fundamental "otherness" of the other. How, then, did Ricoeur attempt to construct this dialectic?

Beginning with Husserl, Ricoeur traced the "reduction to ownness," whereby the objective world is intentionally projected by the ego. Husserl exclaimed:

> Therefore if I, as this ego, reduce my phenomenon, "the Objective world," to what is included in my peculiar ownness and take in addition whatever else I find as peculiarly my *own* (which can no longer contain anything "alien" or "other," after that reduction), then all this ownness of my ego is to be found again, in the reduced world-phenomenon, as the ownness of "*my psyche*." . . . Whatever the transcendental ego constitutes in that *first* stratum, whatever he constitutes as non-other, as his "peculiarly own"—that indeed belongs to him as *a component of his own concrete essence* (as we shall show); it is inseparable from his concrete being. Within and by means of his ownness the transcendental ego constitutes, however, the "Objective" world, as a universe of being that is other than himself—and constitutes, at the first level, the other in the mode: alter ego.[2]

What Husserl meant by "reducing the objective world to my peculiar ownness" is simpler than it first sounds. He argued that the ego "constitutes" the world in intuition on the basis of what it attends to in perception. In other words, what the ego knows of the world is what appears to it; what appears to it is what it pays attention to. Thus, the ego projects or "intends" specific meanings onto the world depending upon how the world is constituted in intuition. Therefore, those meanings are the reduction of the objective world to the sphere of ownness; I project *my* meaning on the world. There are two important outcomes of this reduction to the sphere of ownness. First, the ego or self is presented as a monadic structure that looks out onto the world from complete separation. Second, the objective world, including the existence of other subjective, monadic egos, is reduced to an array of phenomena which the transcendental ego claims as its "own," that is, as its peculiar subjective intending. The "world-phenomenon" is reduced to a projection of "my psyche."

Yet Husserl understood that beside objects in the world, there are also other intentional subjectivities, other egos who encounter the world and for whom I am an object. Indeed, he argued that the reduction of the world to the *non*-other or the *non*-alien presupposes the existence of other egos. In encountering this phenomenal world, which has been reduced to a "component" of my concrete "essence," Husserl argued, I recognize other animate organisms, and I recognize a harmony in their animation that forces me to assume that they are subjectivities who likewise intend a world. This recognition was the basis for Husserl's ideas of *analogical appresentation* and *subjective pairing*: "It is clear that, with the other Ego, there is appresented, in an analogizing modification, everything that belongs to his concretion: first, *his* primordial world, and then his fully concrete ego. In other words, *another monad* becomes constituted appresentatively in mine."[3] Husserl contended that this appresentative intuition proceeds to ever more diverse intermonadic communities resulting in what he called the intersubjective constitution of a "common nature."

This movement of the self toward the other, that is, from the reduction to ownness through pairing and analogical appresentation to the position of a community of intersubjective monads, is precisely what Levinas called into question. He reversed the order of priority in the constitutive relationship that exists between self and other: the other is not constituted through my intentional consciousness, which appresents the other as my alter-ego. Rather, I am constituted as a finite freedom in the confrontation with the "epiphany" of the face of the other, which calls me in the accusative. "The way I appear is a summons," Levinas asserted. "I am put in the passivity of an undeclinable assignation, in the accusative self. Not as a particular case of the universal, an ego belonging to the concept of ego, but as I, said in the first person—I, unique in my genus."[4] Against Husserl, Levinas argued that the self does not exist as an ego. While Husserl conceived the ego as a solitary monad intentionally apprehending its world through the reduction of everything that is not self, Levinas claimed that the condition for the genesis of the self is proximity and communication. The self only exists in the first person of a dialogic summons, as the *I* who answers the call with the response, "Here I am." The self is constituted primordially as an *ethical relationship*, as a responsibility that is called into existence by the other.

There is more at stake than a simple reversal of direction, however. The other does not simply confront me in the accusative voice; the accusative becomes, through Levinas's systematic use of hyperbole, an accusation and an obsession:

> In obsession the accusation effected by the categories turns into an absolute accusative in which the ego proper to free consciousness is caught up. It is an accusation without foundation, to be sure, prior to any movement of the will, an obsessional and persecuting accusation. It strips the ego of its pride and the dominating imperialism characteristic of it. . . . To undergo from the other is an absolute patience only if by this from-the-other [*par autrui*] is already for-the-other [*pour autrui*]. This transfer, other than interested, "otherwise than essence," is subjectivity. . . . The subjectivity of a subject is responsibility of being-in-question in the form of the total exposure to offense in the cheek offered to the smiter.[5]

The accusative becomes accusation. Responsibility becomes obsession, persecution, substitution. Subjectivity becomes subjection.

Ricoeur found Levinas's systematic use of hyperbole as a philosophical method both captivating and troubling. He remained sympathetic to Levinas's suspicion of the transcendental ego; indeed, this is a fundamental theme of his philosophical project. However, Levinas's account of the ego prior to the accusation seems to succumb to the same abstraction as Husserl's intentional monad, but in a reverse direction. If the ego is not simply a monad that constitutes a world out of its own monologic intentionality, neither is the self nonexistent prior to the call.

I have already shown how Ricoeur placed the self within a sociocultural environment of shared meanings. But, more importantly for the issue of ethical experience, how can the self discern in the call the difference between the "master of justice" and the executioner? Levinas's hyperbolic accusation teeters on the edge of a demand that would turn the decentering of the ego into a call for self-destruction. More importantly still, *how* is it that the self who heeds the call recognizes that call as a demand for responsibility? Ricoeur concluded, "Must not the voice of the Other who says to me: 'Thou shalt not kill,' become my own, to the point of becoming my conviction, a conviction to equal the accusative of 'It's me here!' with the nominative of 'Here I stand'?"[6] Ricoeur attempted to mediate these two accounts of the relationship between self and other. At the far end of the following analyses resides the idea of considered convictions and, more especially, in that of fidelity. The first step on this itinerary to conviction passes through the structure of responsibility.

Responsibility: Imputation and Solicitude

I will argue that responsibility is the structure of Ricoeur's account of practical life. Having made this claim, let me state that I am using the term *responsibility* in a much broader sense than Ricoeur typically did. While his explicit use of the term was extremely limited, this idea is centrally important to his account once experience is turned toward public life lived with others.

The idea of responsibility arises from two directions. First, the structure of meaningful existence is related to the structure of practical experience once attention is directed toward persons. The introduction of practical experience marks a crossing point whereby the reflective agent is confronted not by objects, ideals, or shared meanings, but by other persons who advance moral demands. Just as the analysis of capability was opened to meaning through reflection on existence in a world, so the analysis of meaning is opened to responsibility through the recognition of life with other persons. Second, the exploration of the manner in which the self experiences the other forces one to give some account of the manner in which this constitutive relationship is structured. Responsibility structures this relationship by virtue of the ability to assimilate both *imputability*, that is, the ascription of responsibility for actions, and *solicitude*, recognition of the other as a being to whom I am responsible. Responsibility is not only responsibility *for* my actions, but also responsibility *to* other persons who confront me in the present.

I will engage this analysis in two stages. First, I will address Ricoeur's limited use of the term *responsibility*. Ricoeur attached responsibility to the problematic of identity as it is configured by the dialectic of sameness and selfhood. With regard to this problematic, responsibility becomes the moral capacity by which selfhood disengages itself in its ethical dimensions from sameness, a capacity most readily manifest in keeping one's promises. In a second pass, I will expand this reading of responsibility to encompass imputability and solicitude. Imputing is the act of ascribing an action to an agent. A sense of responsibility resides at the heart of this ascription because to ascribe an action to an agent is to assign responsibility for the action and its consequences. There is a dimension of otherness within this ascription which Ricoeur seemed to miss, however. In imputing an action to me, someone holds me responsible: my responsibility *for* an action is also responsibility *to* another who counts on me. More pointedly, responsibility inclines solicitude toward the other's moral claim. Solicitude toward another is not simply the recognition of another agent like me, but the recognition of a person who makes a moral demand on me, the recognition of another to whom I am responsible. In this broad sense, therefore, responsibility lays the structural groundwork for the configuration of practical experience through ethics.

Responsibility and Selfhood

The concept of responsibility was centrally important in Ricoeur's account of selfhood: "Let us start from what was at stake in the study on narrative identity namely that component of identity that has to do with time, under the guise of permanence in time. We saw two acceptations of this category confront one another on the plane of narrative, depending on whether self-constancy or empirical perseverance overlapped or were separate. It is the same dialectic that the notion of responsibility assumes and carries one step further."[7] Ricoeur's analysis of responsibility had profound implications for his understanding of the temporality of the self. Responsibility leaves its mark on all dimensions of the experience of time—past, present, and future—and he attempted to address its specific influence in each temporal direction.

The influence of responsibility is most easily readable in the self's orientation toward the future. Recall that the paradigmatic test case for the kind of initiative that distinguishes selfhood from sameness is the ability to keep one's promises. In offering a promise, I commit myself in the present to a future action; I *assume responsibility* for a future possibility that is dependent on me. Thus, self-constancy is fundamentally directed toward the future, toward a future possibility in which a self makes itself beholden to another in the form of a promise. Ricoeur's idea of narrative identity revealed that meaningful existence is lived in this kind of commitment to possibility.

However, the question of responsibility becomes clouded once situations arise where the bounds of responsibility are themselves in dispute, for instance, when the consequences of my actions extend beyond my intentions. To address this problem, Ricoeur resorted to legal reasoning. "[R]esponsibility implies that someone assumes the consequences of her actions despite the fact that they have not been expressly foreseen and intended. . . . This meaning has taken shape, on the one hand within the framework of civil law, with respect to the obligation to repair the damages that one has caused by one's fault . . . and on the other hand, within the framework of penal law, with respect to the obligation to suffer punishment."[8] A fundamental function of jurisprudence is precisely to determine the scope of responsibility in light of these unintended consequences. In willfully choosing to drive while intoxicated, for example, I surely do not *intend* to put my fellow passengers and other drivers at risk; however, I am legally *responsible* for any damage, injury, or death that results from my decision.

But there is an even more profound way that Ricoeur traced responsibility in its future orientation. Following Hans Jonas, Ricoeur sought to address responsibility as a moral imperative directed to a future that is beyond the bounds of individual actions and intentions.

> Hans Jonas attempted to reconstruct the "principle of responsibility" by taking into consideration the long term consequences of the decisions of public powers and of citizens in the age of technology. He thinks . . . he can cause a revolution in our concept of responsibility, by raising it to the rank of a new categorical imperative, that of acting in such a way that a future humanity will still exist after us, in the environment of a habitable earth. This is indeed a revolution, inasmuch as, by emphasizing the consequences of our actions, the moralist directs our gaze in the opposite direction from that of the search for the most deeply hidden intentions, as the notion of imputability prompts us to do.[9]

In this temporal extension of the imperative, my responsibility is extended to a future that is fundamentally beyond the bearing of my actions; it gives a new hue to responsibility. I am not only responsible *for* my actions, but also responsible *to* the future generations that my actions or my complicity in the actions of others may affect.

Somewhat oddly at first glance, Ricoeur also argued that responsibility extends to the past as well. Particularly in his last major work, *Memory, History, Forgetting*, he tied this responsibility to the work of memory. Memory has a duty to justice that falls along three principal axes. "Interrogating" these three axes, Ricoeur wrote:

> First element of a response: it must be recalled, first, that among all the virtues, the virtue of justice is the one that, par excellence and by its very constitution, is turned toward others. . . . The duty of memory is the duty to do justice, through memories, to an other than the self.
>
> Second element of a response: the time has come to introduce a new concept—debt, which must not be limited to the concept of guilt. This idea of debt is inseparable from the notion of heritage. We are indebted to those who have gone before us for part of what we are. The duty of memory is not restricted to preserving the material trace, whether scriptural or other, of past events, but maintains the feeling of being obligated with respect to these others. . . . Pay the debt, I shall say, but also inventory the heritage.
>
> Third element of a response: among those others to whom we are indebted, the moral priority belongs to the victims. . . . The victim at issue here is the other victim, other than ourselves.[10]

Thus, through the work of memory, responsibility is opened to the past. My debt to the past is not due on account of any action I have performed; rather, I am responsible to the past for my very capacity to act, for my ability to distinguish myself in action.

Finally, Ricoeur argued that these "acceptations of responsibility" cross paths in the present. This crossing of prospective responsibility and retrospective responsibility, of imperative toward the future and work of memory in the service of justice, delineate self-constancy as responsible selfhood in the present. To be responsible is to *hold oneself* responsible in the present. However, there may be a more profound sense in which the present is opened to, or better stated, opened *by* responsibility, namely, in the confrontation with another who makes a moral demand upon me.

Ricoeur approached the issue of responsibility to another who can make a moral claim on me in a rather elliptical fashion, through the extension of responsibility in a future imperative of responsibility and in the sense of being indebted to the past. The sense of being responsible *to* another person becomes more explicit the more that Ricoeur's discussions of imputability and solicitude are drawn into the analysis of responsibility.

Imputability and Solicitude

The concept of imputability functions not only in linking an action to an agent, but also in linking together two broad categories of ethical judgment: the criterion of *permissible-impermissible* actions, and the designation of *culpable-inculpable* agents. "Imputing would not only be placing an action under someone's responsibility but would moreover be placing an *action*, as that which can come under the category permissible-impermissible, under the responsibility of *someone* who can be deemed culpable-inculpable." Imputation serves to link a particular action, with all its ethical weight, to a particular agent. Ricoeur's account of imputability arises out of his account of narrative identity. Recall that the configuration of the plot serves, among other things, to configure the relationship between action and agent. The imaginative domain opened by the engagement with narratives lends to reflection the same kind of relationship. Imputation rides on the possibility of establishing the relationship between the agent who acts and the effect of the action. Ricoeur concluded, "To whom then is an action imputable? To the self, as capable of passing through the entire course of the ethicomoral determinations of action, a course at the end of which self-esteem becomes conviction."[11] Imputation assigns responsibility for action to an agent. Thus, responsibility already enters into the very definition of imputation.

However, there is more to the analysis of imputability than the simple ascription of action to agent; imputation concerns not only the location of an agent who is then deemed responsible for the action. There is also the question of the other who imputes actions to me and, in so doing, holds me responsible, a question not frequently addressed by Ricoeur. Imputation is not an abstract assignment of action to agent; imputation is accusation, even if the accusation does not bring with it the sense of moral condemnation that is so frequently associated with accusation. In this way, the premium that Levinas placed on responsibility enters the concept of imputation.

Contact with the idea of responsibility gives moral weight to solicitude, too. Ricoeur unfolded this complex concept through the notion of an "exchange of *giving* and *receiving*." This understanding stemmed from Ricoeur's interest in Aristotle's analysis of friendship. Within a friendship among equals, the only true kind of friendship, Aristotle argued, this exchange is mutual: friendship amounts to the reciprocity of giving and receiving between equal partners. Thus, giving and receiving represent two fundamental orientations to the other, two modes of recognizing the other who confronts me. But solicitude becomes problematic once this situation of reciprocity is canceled out by differences of position, ability, etc.

Ricoeur first addressed the problematic aspects of solicitude under the idea of receptivity to the moral injunction that comes from the other. Under the guise of the moral injunction, the other confronts me as one who levels a moral claim, that is, as a face who commands my responsibility. Turning explicitly to Levinas, Ricoeur stated:

> [T]he "appearing" of the Other in the *face* of the Other eludes vision, seeing forms, and even eludes hearing, apprehending voices. In truth the face does not appear; it is not a phenomenon; it is an epiphany. But whose face is it? I do not think I am unduly limiting the scope of Levinas's *Totality and Infinity*, to say nothing here of his *Otherwise than Being*, by saying that this face is that of a master of justice, of a master who *instructs* and who does so only in the ethical mode: this face forbids murder and commands justice. . . . To be sure, the self is "summoned to responsibility" by the other. It is in the *accusative* mode alone that the self is enjoined. And the summons to responsibility has opposite it simply the passivity of an "I" who has been called upon.[12]

And yet, as Ricoeur correctly pointed out, if the appearance of the face is not to fall on blind eyes, if the call to responsibility is not to fall on deaf ears, then there must be a self who sees, hears, and responds; there must first be a self who is invested with the ability to be open to the other who calls. By the same token, however, the account of responsibility has received a new signification. Responsibility is not simply responsibility *for* the action that is imputed to me; it is also responsibility *to* the other, that is, *ability to respond* to the other who calls me to justice. In responsibility I regard the other person as an irreplaceable individual who has a claim on my moral concern.

This aspect of solicitude as being enjoined by another begs the question of another situation in which the self would be giver and the other receiver. Ricoeur argued that in the self's relation to another who suffers, the roles are reversed: "Here initiative, precisely in terms of being able-to-act, seems to belong exclusively to the self who *gives* his sympathy, his compassion, these terms being taken in the strong sense of the wish to share someone else's pain. Confronting this charity, this benevolence, the other appears to be reduced to the sole condition of *receiving*."[13] On this account, the encounter with the other who suffers is one in which the self is in the position of *giving*, the other in the position of *receiving*. However, is exchange the best way to characterize the dynamic of solicitude?

One might follow Levinas and object to putting the self/other relationship in these terms of exchange. Such would be an economic or political relationship and not an ethical one. The ethical relationship is not based on an ideal reciprocity, he contended, but on a fundamental priority of the other who calls me to responsibility. Additionally, this distinction between the "master of justice" and "suffering other" is illegitimate; the other confronts me as the master of justice *out of* his/her poverty, nakedness, vulnerability, etc.; in short, out of his/her suffering. It is precisely this ability of the suffering other to level a moral injunction to the self that calls into question the supposed sovereignty of the self. The other is a victim who demands that I substitute myself in his/her stead. One need not take this final hyperbolic stance of substitution to recognize the truth in Levinas's critique. The suffering other is not simply the passive beneficiary of my "benevolent spontaneity," but the one who confronts with me with a moral claim. The suffering other demands my responsible action for his/her well-being, and I am solicitous toward the other by responding to his/her need.

This recognition of the other who levels a moral demand, *even in suffering and vulnerability*, signals a broader sense of responsibility than Ricoeur initially assigned. My selfhood is not simply a function of holding myself responsible *for* my actions—past, present, and future. I am also constituted in selfhood in my responsibility *to* another, at once master of justice and the suffering other, who makes demands upon me. This relationship between responsibility *to* and responsibility *for* demands more attention.

Highlighting the distinction, Gabriel Moran argues that historically, "'responsible to' was the usual way of using the term until the latter part of the nineteenth century. Then, 'responsible for,' which played a secondary role, took over to the near exclusion of 'responsible to.' I do not argue that we should go back a century or more, but that the question of 'responsible to' never went away and cannot go away. Failure to notice that 'responsible to' is a question at all vitiates much of the writing on responsibility."[14]

On Moran's account, the two questions are necessarily related: without some answer to the question "To what and to whom am I responsible?" no answer to the question "What am I responsible *for*?" is possible. Without recourse to the former question, any answer to the latter seems selfishly narrow—I am only responsible for myself—or so broad as to be unassumable—I am responsible for everything. The scope of responsibility simply cannot be determined.

In the attempt to provide an answer to the initial question, Moran exclaims, "The simplest answer to the question 'to what and to whom am I responsible?' is: everything and everyone. . . . I can only take up responsibility for my actions as a consequence of what I am responsible to."[15] Quite literally (and quite mundanely) I cannot fail to respond *to* anything and anybody that comes into my "line of sight." I can *choose* not to respond, but, as the adage goes, no response is still a response. Returning to the dialectic between responsibility *to* and responsibility *for*, Moran contends:

> Which actions am I morally responsible for? The answer to that question pushes us to another level of questioning: I am responsible *for* what I am responsible *to*. This principle lies on the side of the "is"

> rather than "ought"; it is not a moral principle stating what should be. Nevertheless, it is a necessary but neglected step in deciding moral responsibility. A person carries out morally responsible actions in relation to what is heard. Moral deficiency is mostly a hearing failure.[16]

To some degree, Moran seems to agree with Levinas's assertion that the self is constituted through response to the injunction of the other, though, like Ricoeur, he is suspicious of Levinas's hyperbolic use of the ideas of substitution and obsession.

These ideas lend an important dimension to my analysis by countering Ricoeur's, somewhat unfortunate, attempt to account for solicitude in terms of an exchange relationship. Doing so risks reducing the other to instrumental value; he/she is valuable in *my* quest for the good life, self-realization, authenticity, etc.. I respond to the solicitations of the suffering other, I *give my attention* to him/her, in the hopes that my response will be rewarded, that my *investment of energy* will be returned, perhaps with interest—the others' gratitude, personal reputation, good karma, entrance into heaven. Basing solicitude instead in a response relation forces me to recognize an intrinsic value in the other who solicits my attention, even if the foundation for that intrinsic value must be sought beyond ethical and moral reasoning. Moral values are not exchange values; the moral life does not revolve around "breaking even" in one's expenditures, or worse, in making a profit.

I believe that these insights are nascent in Ricoeur's thought. This analysis has been an attempt to critically recover a dimension of this. The next section will provide opportunity to test my claims. I will address the manner in which Ricoeur configured this basic structure of responsibility in terms of an ethical relationship. This ethical relationship is configured along the lines of a confrontation between an ethics of the good, in a broadly Aristotelian fashion, and a morality of obligation, in a Kantian vein. Contrary to the frequent tendency to pose these two perspectives as diametrical opposites, Ricoeur claimed that the two perspectives are dialectically necessary complements to each other. While he gave primacy to the overall drift of a teleological striving for the good, he held equally that this guiding intention must pass through the test of moral obligation in order to save it from the ever-present possibility of violence.

Ethics: Power and Violence

This discussion of the configuration of practical experience in terms of ethics opens from two directions. First, the configuration of meaningful existence through narrative opens to the ethical configuration of practical existence through the recognition of a fundamentally evaluative dimension that arises within the narrative configuration of possibility itself. Recall that meaningful existence is lived in the mode of possibility; the self lays claim to its existence meaningfully in terms of a projected future to which it finds access through the expansion of the practical field of action in narrative. Through this expansion, Ricoeur was able to place discrete, basic actions within a larger, nested framework of "levels of praxis," that is, practices, life plans, and the narrative unity of a life. Levels of praxis enter the discourse of ethics once one recognizes that the dialectic between the formation of specific life plans and the projection of a narrative unity constitutes a particular picture of the good life in the Aristotelian sense. What I aim at in a life plan is the total demand of happiness over the course of a lifetime. Aristotle argued that this is what constitutes a sense of a life well lived. Thus, the projected good becomes a guiding ideal by which and against which I evaluate and esteem myself and my actions. I value my existence, in light of the ability to formulate and seek some understanding of the good life and in light of my distance or proximity to that vision.

The notion of power, in various guises, ran throughout Ricoeur's project, from the kind of capability that is open to agents, through the exploration of initiative to which agents attest, to the *conatus* by which selves persist in their particular kind of existence. The possibility of seeking the good life is predicated on this notion of power. I am capable because I can conceive of a good life, which becomes my all-encompassing aim, and I esteem myself in my power to seek and achieve that aim. But, this power that characterizes the quest for selfhood becomes a moral issue because it all too frequently devolves into violence. Ricoeur sought to reclaim a deontological account of obligation within the overall aim of the good life to counter the ever-present possibility of violence. There is reason to assert that the other is an end in him/herself because there is always the possibility that I might reduce the other to a means in my striving for the good life. The ethical aim remains a value that directs my power; the moral norm demands that I recognize the other as a value that I must not violate. Therefore, the idea of responsibility offers a second opening onto ethics in the need for some kind of practical configuration to the self's relation to the other. If responsibility is the basic structure of practical experience, then one must offer some practical configuration of this experience of being responsible to another. This encounter with another in responsibility held a central place in Ricoeur's account of ethics both at the level of concern for the good life and at the level of obligation.

His ethical theory is structured along the lines of a dialect between an ethics of the good and a morality of obligation. This dialectic is characterized by an overall teleological drift, conceived in terms of Aristotelian ethics, which encompasses a Kantian, deontological, moment. At the end of this dialectic lies a conception of considered convictions, which I will treat in the final section of this chapter. Ricoeur used the term *ethics* to indicate the overall teleological direction of an ethical aim toward the good. Conversely, he used the term *morality* to designate the deontological moment of obligation that exists within the quest for the good life. He described the relationship between these two dimensions of ethics as such:

> I propose to establish . . . (1) the primacy of ethics over morality, (2) the necessity for the ethical aim to pass through the sieve of the norm, and (3) the legitimacy of recourse by the norm to the aim whenever the norm leads to impasses in practice. . . . In other words, according to the working hypothesis I am proposing, morality is held to constitute only a limited, although legitimate and even indispensable, actualization of the ethical aim, and ethics in this sense would then encompass morality.[17]

This relationship entails both the subordination of moral duty to an ethics of the good and the complementarity between them.

In addition to this dialectical relationship, the progress of Ricoeur's discussions of both the ethical aim and the moral norm were guided by a threefold structure that began with the individual plane and moved through interpersonal and institutional realms. He defined the ethical aim "as seeking the good life with and for others in just institutions." He traced the moral norm through the Kantian categories of unity of the will, plurality of persons, and total determination of the kingdom of ends, as these were manifest in the three formulations of Kant's categorical imperative. I will address the aim and the norm each in its turn.

The Ethical Aim

Ricoeur defined the ethical aim, or ethical "intention," as "*aiming at the good life with and for others in just institutions*."[18] This aim crosses the three dimensions of individual life, interpersonal interaction, and institutional participation that organize Ricoeur's account of both the ethics of the good and of moral obligation. Broadly speaking, my actions and desires are directed toward a vision of the good life. But seeking this good life is not a solitary endeavor; I have need of the assistance of others. Indeed, the mere existence of some others itself contributes to my good. Finally, this quest for the good life is carried out within a public realm governed by institutions upon which I depend in my endeavors.

The first part of the ethical aim, therefore, concerns the quest for the good life. Ricoeur set this discussion within Aristotle's account of *phronesis* or practical wisdom. In book 6 of the *Nicomachean Ethics*, Aristotle stated: "Practical wisdom . . . is concerned with things human and things about which it is possible to deliberate. . . . The man who is without qualification good at deliberating is the man who is capable of aiming in accordance with calculation at the best for man of things attainable by action."[19] Aristotle argued that the "best for man of things attainable by action" resided in a unitary principle of the good. He suggested that there is general agreement about the nature of this unitary principle, "for both the general run of men and people of superior refinement say that it is happiness, and identify living well and doing well with being happy."[20] While there was general confusion about what happiness is, most agreed that good life is the happy life judged not by discrete moments, but over the course of an entire lifetime.

Ricoeur argued that the quest for the good life is engaged through the construction of life plans. Deliberation over life plans is an exercise in practical wisdom because it becomes a matter of weighing various, vague ideals about the life worth living in light of the practices through which those ideas are actualized. In Ricoeur's words, "The action-configurations that we are calling life plans stem, then, from our moving back and forth between far-off ideals, which have to be made more precise, and the weighing of the advantages and disadvantages of the choice of a given life plan on the level of practices." Under this rubric, the term *life* takes on the connotations of an *ergon*, of a work or a task, to be engaged through practices. Ricoeur's idea of "narrative unity" offers some clarification to the idea of life as a work. Seeking the good life is like constructing a narrative. More profoundly, because life becomes understandable through the stories one tells about it, the narrative projection of possibility offers much with regard to seeking the good life. There exists between the total demand for happiness, for the good life, and discrete actions a horizon-act structure; actions are directed by and take on meaning against a horizon that can be anticipated by way of narrative. Existence becomes a project, a work of narrating, directed toward the fulfillment of a destiny residing in the ideal of the good life.

Ricoeur argued, secondly, that the good life is lived with and for others. How is it that the quest for the good life can extend to a concern for the good of others? His purpose was to show that self-esteem is inscribed within solicitude, to show that "self-esteem and solicitude cannot be experienced or reflected upon one without the other." Indeed, it is in relationship to others that I take hold of and attest to myself. Others are necessary for and sometimes constitutive of my happiness. Ricoeur addressed the problematic of solicitude through Aristotle's treatment of friendship in the *Nicomachean Ethics*. The concern for friendship marks the search for the good life with an aspect of need; the happy man needs friends. The search for the good life is marked by a lacuna, which friendship comes to fill. Friendship is characterized by mutuality; the good one wishes for oneself, one wishes for the friend as well. Likewise, the good one loves in oneself, one's best self, is that which is loved in the other. Ricoeur argued, therefore, that this suffusion of friendship by a sense of goodness is constitutive of mutuality that interrupts egoism in the search for the good. I esteem myself as I esteem the other, in my esteem for the other. Mutuality, achieved in the familiarity of a shared life, undoes the apparent conflict between concern for self and concern for other. "With need and lack, the otherness of the 'other self' . . . moves to the forefront. The friend, inasmuch as he is that other self, has the role of providing what one is incapable of procuring by oneself."[21]

Recall that Ricoeur characterized the solicitous mutuality of friendship in terms of an exchange relation, a relationship of equal exchange between giving and receiving. Aristotle argued that there can only be true friendship among equals, and Ricoeur argued that it is this equality of exchange that Aristotle had in mind in articulating the mutual character of friendship. The effect of solicitude on self-esteem forces the self to recognize itself as "another among others." This recognition of otherness at the heart of selfhood reaches its most immediate configuration, therefore, in the mutuality achieved in the intimacy of friendship. Friendship brands the ethical concern for the good life with a dimension of lack and need, which can only be filled by others. My quest for the good, and the esteem of self gained by this quest, takes place within the mutual recognition of the good of those most intimately related to me; I gain from friendship as I give to it. But what of cases in which my relation to the other is not bound by the intimacy of friendship? Do others who are not my intimates hold any sway in my quest for the good life?

Ricoeur moved from the mutuality of exchange characteristic of friendship to expand solicitude into realms other than friendship—the injunction coming from the master of justice and the recognition of the suffering other. I suggested that the approach to other persons from the direction of exchange is not the best way to address the problem because it threatens to reduce them to purely instrumental values: the other is only valuable to my quest for the good life. To some degree, at the level of aims this is inevitable. Within the trajectory of friendship as Aristotle conceived it, however, the relationship is protected from the fall into instrumentality by the value placed on friendship for the sake of the *good* over friendship for the sake of pleasure or utility: "[T]hose who love for the sake of utility love for the sake of what is good for *themselves*, and those who love for the sake of pleasure do so for the sake of what is pleasant to *themselves*, and not in so far as the other is the person loved but in so far as he is useful or pleasant. And thus these friendships are only incidental; for it is not as being the man he is that the loved person is loved, but as providing some good or pleasure."[22] Only friendship for the sake of the good is characterized as loving the other *for being the man he is*. In this type of friendship, I wish the good for my friend as I wish it for myself. Friendship for the sake of the good is truly mutual friendship. But could mutuality be just as easily characterized by responsibility as by exchange? Indeed, it is peculiar that Ricoeur spoke of it in terms of exchange in the first place. In friendship, I respond to the value of my friend; I am responsible to him/her to seek his/her good and I am responsible for my actions in the service of that good. S/he is equally responsible. Such solicitous responsibility could be extended to nonmutual relations, too. The issue is not one of exchange, therefore, but one of the scope of responsibility. Basing solicitude on a *response* relation, rather than an *exchange* relation, goes some distance toward securing the intrinsic value of the other from a fall into a purely instrumental value. In a profound sense, this tendency to reduce the other to an instrumental value was be an impetus for Ricoeur's turn to Kant's imperative of respect; this is the thrust of the demand to treat others as ends in themselves and never solely as means. I will address this in more detail shortly.

Beyond the question of the claim of immediate others who are not my friends, there is a need to extend the compass of the ethical aim even farther to include those who will never confront me as individuals. At some level, I must realize that my quest is dependent not only on my friends and immediate acquaintances, but on others whom I do not, never will, and in some cases simply cannot know. I am beholden to past generations and, perhaps, to future ones. More directly, my endeavors are dependent upon a stable public realm that I share with fellow citizens. The realization that not all relations are encompassed by the immediacy of the face to face encounter led Ricoeur to place the quest for the good life within a third, broader institutional context. Thus, the good life itself is bound to the question of justice. All benefit from the stability of a just public order. Ricoeur, therefore, sought to show that a *sense of justice* is implicit within the concern for the good, that the good life extends beyond esteem and solicitude to encompass the "faceless other," the other outside the realm of immediacy, in the life of institutions. His principle concern was the relation between power and violence. At stake is the possibility of a power exercised in common by those participating in the life of social institutions, which stands as a barrier to political violence.

The principal player in Ricoeur's discussion of a sense of justice was the political philosopher Hannah Arendt. Arendt proposed that power exists as action pursued in a public space in which individuals appear to each other as partners in a common endeavor:

> What first undermines and then kills political communities is loss of power and final impotence; and power cannot be stored up and kept in reserve for emergencies, like the instruments of violence, but exists only in its actualization. . . . Power is actualized only where word and deed have not parted company, where words are not empty and deeds

> not brutal, where words are not used to veil intentions but to disclose realities, and deeds are not used to violate and destroy but to establish relations and create new realities.[23]

Power exists only in its actualization, an actualization made possible by a public realm characterized by true speaking and acting.

Arendt explored the actualization of power through the related ideas of *plurality* and *action in concert*. She considered plurality to be the basic condition of action and speech. Plurality gives public life the character of a web of relationships in which individuals take on the roles of enacted stories. This web of relationships can only come about in the preservation of a public realm where acting and speaking individuals appear to each other and solicit each other's recognition. Power, exercised in concert, preserves the public realm that makes possible the genesis of the individual:

> Power is always, as we would say, a power potential and not an unchangeable, measurable, and reliable entity like force or strength. While strength is a natural quality of an individual seen in isolation, power springs up between men when they act together and vanishes the moment they disperse. . . . And whoever, for whatever reasons, isolates himself and does not partake in such being together, forfeits power and becomes impotent, no matter how great his strength and how valid his reasons.[24]

Power represents both the power of being oneself and the power that preserves the public realm. Indeed, power is the power of being oneself in the preservation of the public space of appearance.

Violence destroys the public realm by interrupting interactions that preserve power. Violence is a threat to the very power of being a self. Power, on the other hand, "preserves the public realm and the space of appearance, and as such it is also the lifeblood of the human artifice, which, unless it is the scene of action and speech, of the web of human affairs and the relationship and the stories engendered by them, lacks its ultimate *raison d'être*."[25]

The possibility for the good life is tied to the preservation of the public realm. My search for the good can only be secured within an environment of justice, itself secured by institutions that preserve plurality. Indeed, the preservation of the public realm in just institutions is of a piece with my good. The need to preserve this public realm forces one to recognize a fundamental *mutual indebtedness* in practical experience. As self-esteem was inscribed within solicitude to the other, my possibilities for the good are inscribed within the life in institutions with others beyond the immediacy of the face to face relationship.

The question of justice is the place where an ethics of the good most closely approaches the morality of obligation. The institution of principles of justice at the level of moral obligation seeks to preserve this public realm. Thus, it is to the moral norm that I now turn.

The Moral Norm

Given the breadth and that substance of the preceding discussion, why make the move to a deontological moment in ethical deliberation? Ricoeur suggested that there is "a basic and massive answer: there is *morality*, in the sense of moral obligation, because there is *violence*. Morality has to be prescriptive and not merely evaluative, because our moral judgment about violence implies more than saying that it is not desirable, less preferable, less advisable; because violence is evil, and evil is what *is* and what *ought not* to be."[26] This ever-present possibility of violence, encountered several times at the level of ethical aims, demands a level of deliberation beyond the evaluative dimensions of the search for the good life. This demand for another level of deliberation constitutes the need for the aim to "pass through the sieve" of norms of obligation.

Typically, moral norms are characterized by a kind of formalism that abstracts from particular situations in order to seek a standard of universal normativity, a rule that is applicable in all cases. However, Ricoeur's interest was not to pose a moral formalism that stands on its own, but one that stands within the overall drift of a teleological ethics of the good. His recourse to formal norms was, in each case, a critical perspective on and an attempted correction of the problems encountered at the level of the aim. Therefore, his analysis of the norm progresses in a way parallel to that of the aim; this progression can be expressed, in Kantian terms, in the *unity* of the will in autonomy, the *plurality* of persons as ends in themselves, and the *totality* of the kingdom of ends.[27] At each level, moral reason will present a formal norm to which the aim must answer. At the individual level, the good will determined by moral duty corresponds to the aim of the good life. At the interpersonal level, respect for persons as ends in themselves and its attendant norm of reciprocity, corresponds to the dialogical structure of solicitude. Finally, the sense of justice, understood in terms of the will to live and act together, is subjected to a rule of justice designed to ensure a just public realm. As Aristotle was the principal voice for Ricoeur's treatment of the aim, Kantian deontology was the principal lens for addressing the norm.

To Aristotle's understanding of the good life as the happy life, Ricoeur posed Kant's understanding of the will determined by moral duty. The notion of a supreme good that characterizes correct action appears to offer a direct path between the Aristotelian and Kantian orientations in ethics, but this appearance is misleading. Aristotle and Kant attached radically different meanings to the terms *goodness* and *the good life*. Recall that happiness represented the unitary principle of the good for Aristotle; the good life is the happy life judged over the course of an entire lifetime. Kant, on the other hand, asserted that the will that is determined by moral duty is the supreme principle of goodness. He argued that good will is the only thing that can be conceived as "good without qualification."[28] All other things are good relative to something else; they are sought in order to secure something else and not for their own sakes. Only the good will is good in and of itself.

Kant contended that the capacity for moral self-legislation and the ability to formulate universalizable maxims to govern action are the paramount characteristics of the good will. The good will is the *autonomous* will, the self-governing will that acts only on principles that it chooses for itself. In Kantian terms, the good will is "self-caused" and not caused by some other force that would determine its actions. And, the only way that a will could be truly self-caused is to determine its actions on the basis of moral duty. That is to say, what makes the good will "good" is the fact that it acts solely on the basis of moral duties, moral duties that it chooses for itself and imposes on itself.

At face value, these ideas do not seem terribly revolutionary, nor do they seem to be at odds with Aristotle's notion of the good life. However, Kant argued that will is only autonomous if it determines its duties without reference to affection or desire. If desires enter into the calculation, the decision is not an autonomous one; it is not caused by the will itself, but by the desire. Additionally, moral duties are "duties" only if they are chosen for themselves and not for something else. If a course of action is chosen to achieve some particular end, then it is not chosen for itself; it is not a perfect duty but an instrumental calculation designed to achieve a desired result. Given this character of the good will and the determination of action on the sole basis of duty, Kant ruled out happiness as a motive: if happiness is what I desire, then I am no longer motivated by the principle of moral duty.

Were it possible, Aristotle might have responded that he did not ground the good life in just any kind of happiness. True happiness resides in virtue, and virtue *is* sought for itself and not for something else, in which case it *is* unqualifiedly good. But what if virtue does not secure happiness? What if a virtuous action, rather than resulting in happiness, causes me pain? One can at least conceive this possibility; Kant suggested that it is the human condition. He contended that in this mortal life, moral duty and happiness are more likely opposed than coincident. This would not be the case if humans were perfectly good wills, for the truly good will naturally chooses the proper course of action and is pleased, satisfied, and happy with the outcome. This is a characteristic of the good will because it is itself unqualifiedly good; its natural inclination is to act in accord with moral duty. Humans, unfortunately, are not perfectly good. Humans are not naturally inclined to act in accord with moral duty but with their desires and passions. Moral duty therefore demands that one act contrary to his/her natural inclinations; this is why it appears as a duty, that is, as a constraint. Thus, Kant concluded, virtue and happiness do not necessarily correspond, and more than likely they are at odds.

There is more to the argument, however. The fact that humans are naturally inclined to desire and passion also meant for Kant that they are not truly free. Remember that autonomy means perfect self-legislation; but, to be motivated by desires is to be caused to act by something other than the will. This imperfect freedom is the ground for the possibility of moral evil, Kant argued. A good life, if it is to be truly good, must be governed by the principle of moral duty. Thus, it is here that I can begin to address Ricoeur's assertion that the aim of the good life must take recourse to the moral norm.

Recall that Ricoeur gave priority to the aim over the norm: the overarching theme of his ethics was the quest for the good life. To some degree, this was due to his understanding of the structure of selfhood. Selfhood is lived in the mode of possibility; the possible narrative unity of a life represents a vision of happiness that I wish to bring about. To this degree, Ricoeur positively valued desire: desire does not cripple freedom but empowers it.[29] Yet, he was also sympathetic to the notion that virtue and happiness might not correspond. The potential lack of correspondence offers the possibility for moral evil in the form of violence. Thus, there is always the possibility that I might seek my happiness by violent means rather than virtuous ones. Because of this, there is need for recourse to moral duties to govern my quest. This need becomes more apparent in questions of my duty to others.

I showed above that Ricoeur understood solicitude not as an external structure that is appended to self-esteem, but rather as the dialogical realm of relationships within which self-esteem arises. I require the assistance of others to find happiness. Some others, my friends, are themselves constitutive of my happiness. My quest for the good life and my self-esteem in this quest are dependent upon my solicitude of others. But this understanding of the importance of others *for me* leans drastically in the direction of utility: others are reduced to instruments in my quest for happiness. While Aristotle's account of friendship for the sake of the good secured this relationship from such a reduction, there seems little security for others. Surely, those others ought be valuable in and of themselves and not only as instruments in my quest. This is where the ideal of solicitude benefits from contact with the norm.

To solicitude, Ricoeur posed the norm of *reciprocity* revealed by Kant's second formulation of the categorical imperative. Of persons in general, Kant exclaimed:

> Persons are . . . not merely subjective ends, whose existence as an effect of our actions has a value for us; but such beings are objective ends, that is, exist as ends in themselves. Such an end is one for which there can be substituted no other end to which such beings should serve merely as means, for otherwise nothing of absolute value would be found anywhere. But if all value were conditioned and hence contingent, then no supreme practical principle [that is, moral imperative] could be found for reason at all. . . . The practical imperative will therefore be the following: Act in such a way that you treat humanity, whether in your own person or in the person of another, always at the same time as an end and never simply as a means.[30]

Humans, Kant argued, must be regarded as ends in themselves because they are capable of establishing their own purposes, that is to say, their own ends. This is simply to restate that humans are free. Therefore, as free beings capable of forming their own ends, humans must be respected as ends in and of themselves and never regarded solely as means. Morality demands that I respect the humanity of others as I respect it in myself, that I never reduce others to means in the search for my own ends, that I reciprocally respect others in their aims as I respect myself in mine. Not surprisingly, Ricoeur took the golden rule to be the principle that practically grounds this kind of reciprocity.

The golden rule itself takes two forms, one negative—"Do not do unto your neighbor what you would hate him to do to you"—the other positive—"Treat others as you would like them to treat you." While he asserts a rough parity between the negative and positive formulations, Ricoeur privileged the negative formulation in his treatment of the golden rule as intermediary between ethics and morality.[31] The most important reason for this is the positing of evil as that which makes necessary the imposition of norms of obligation: "In each case, morality replies to violence. And if the commandment cannot do otherwise than to take the form of a prohibition, this is precisely because of evil: to all the figures of evil responds the *no* of morality."[32] The golden rule establishes a norm of reciprocity which responds to the asymmetry between agent and patient fundamental to the structure of action. Action is, by nature, social: all endeavors are interactive. I act in a social environment, which means that my actions effect others; all actions involve both an agent and a patient, one who acts and one who undergoes that action. The golden rule replies to this asymmetry even at the level of its grammatical structure: do not *do* what you would hate to *have done* to you. It addresses both the active and passive dimensions of action, both the agent and the patient, and establishes a demand for reciprocity that stands against the violent possibilities at the heart of this asymmetry.

This asymmetrical structure of action is insidious because it provides the occasion for violence. The power that I exercise over another in action, the manner in which the other is subjected to my action, offers the opportunity for the entrance of evil in the diverse forms of violence. Without the demand of reciprocity, the exercise of my power brings with it the threat of violence, which diminishes the other in his or her agency. In this way, the moral norm confronts me in the negative form of a prohibition: to the ever-present possibility of violence, morality says "No!" Ricoeur argued: "It is, indeed, the golden rule that imposes from the start the new ground upon which formalism will attempt to impose itself. What Kant termed *matter* or *plurality* is quite precisely this field of interaction where one will exerts a power over another and where the rule of reciprocity replies to the initial dissymmetry between agent and patient."[33] Conceived in this way, Kant's formulation—to treat humanity never only as a means but also always as an end—is a formalization of the golden rule.

The final dimension of the moral norm takes up the issue of principles of justice. There is need for recourse to principles of justice because, as I indicated above, I can only seek my good within a public realm governed by institutions that secure public peace. However, these institutions must answer to the moral demand of respect for humanity. That is to say, public life needs to be governed by institutions that, as broadly as possible, treat humans as ends and never solely as means. The political theory that has exercised the most influence in modern accounts of justice is social contract theory, and this is the place that Ricoeur looked to formulate general principles of justice to govern the quest for the good life. Contract theory postulates an imaginative situation in which individuals meet prior to the establishment of any society and establish principles, that is, a social contract, upon which the society will be organized. The concept rests on the idea that in a contract situation free and equal bargaining partners will choose principles that work to everyone's advantage: "The aim and the function of the fiction of a contract is to separate the *just* from the *good*, by substituting the procedure of an imaginary deliberation for any prior commitment to an alleged common good. According to this hypothesis, it is the contractual procedure that is assumed to engender the principle or principles of justice."[34] In the imagined deliberation, contractarians argue, participants would agree upon, and hence freely choose, a set of principles that are not tied to any particular conception of the good, but which benefit each one's own individual conception of and search for the good. The purpose of posing this imaginary situation is to discover what participants in such a situation would choose; these then would represent principles that would benefit everyone.

Perhaps the most notable contemporary proponent of social contract theory is the political philosopher John Rawls, and he was the thinker to whom Ricoeur turned. Rawls suggested that in the original position of a contract situation, participants would likely choose two broad principles of justice: "First: each person is to have an equal right to the most extensive basic liberty compatible with a similar liberty for others. Second: social and economic inequalities are to be arranged so that they are both (a) reasonably expected to be to everyone's advantage, and (b) attached to positions and offices open to all."[35] These principles aim to answer directly to a conflict at the heart of the question of fair distribution, that between arithmetic equality and proportional equality. Rawls was willing to permit an unequal distribution of goods and privileges, but he added the caveat that any unequal distribution must finally be to the benefit of all. Thus, as a general formulation of the theory of justice, he offered the following: "All social values—liberty and opportunity, income and wealth, and the bases of self-respect—are to be distributed equally unless an unequal distribution of any, or all, of these values is to everyone's advantage."[36] Rawls believed that these principles would be chosen in the situation of an original contractual deliberation. There is need for recourse to this founding fiction, he argued, because society is both a cooperative and a conflictual enterprise. There is an identity of interests on the part of the members of society due to the realization that cooperation presents the promise of a better life than each could achieve on his/her own. There is a conflict of interests, however, "since men are not indifferent as to how the greater benefits produced by their collaboration are distributed, for in order to pursue their ends they each prefer a larger to a lesser share."[37] While Ricoeur was never completely satisfied with Rawls's findings, it is important to recognize his reasons for pursuing this line of reasoning. There is need to erect principles of justice to ensure the continued existence of a public realm that secures everyone's quest for the good life. Contract theory attempts to do this.

In all cases, Ricoeur addressed this recourse to moral rules and principles as a moment within the overall trajectory of a quest for the good life. I experience life practically as a quest for the good life, a quest that takes place in the presence others both immediate and distant to me. At the same time, I experience those others as a source of value that must be preserved. My search for the good, therefore must be delimited by rules that remind me that others need to be treated as ends and not merely as means, and which perhaps coerce me into obedience. But what does it actually mean to seek the good within the bounds of moral respect? What would such a life look like? Here we move beyond the configuration of ethics to address practical experience as witness to considered conviction in actual situations.

Witness: Conviction and Fidelity

Ricoeur argued that there is need to address moral norms within the overall trajectory of the ethical aim due to the ever-present possibility of violence; the test of moral obligation is crucial within the quest for the good life because of the constant temptation to violence toward others within the search for self-actualization. Ideally, then, the good life would readily present itself within the bounds of moral respect for others, but experience reveals a different case. Practical experience is assailed by impasses that adversely affect the search for the good life within the bounds of morality. For one, the possibilities for conflict between happiness and duty do not simply evaporate in light of the realization that my quest for happiness should not come at the expense of others. For example, my commitment to my family responsibilities forecloses many avenues to happiness that could be legitimate otherwise. But beyond this conflict, the quest for the good life within the bounds of morality is affected by other, perhaps more insidious, vicissitudes.

For instance, I confront limitations to my abilities and my knowledge that complicate my quest. Provided that I am able to formulate a plan for the good life, there is no promise that I will be able to achieve it. Nor can I know if I am able or if this plan will actually result in happiness before I try. This lack of certitude concerning future possibility lends an air of trepidation to decision because to embark on one path necessarily closes off others; the actualization of one set of possibilities bars access to others. In addition to these limitations on ability and knowledge, there are real conflicts within the moral life besides the possible conflicts between happiness and duty. I confront situations in which I face a genuine conflict of duties, times when I am confronted with a decision between seemingly equally binding obligations with no clear choice. Likewise, I am confronted with a conflict of how to apply a moral principle in this or that particular situation. These vicissitudes reach monumental proportions once I move from questions about my happiness and moral responsibility to a more global level; here I am confronted with the tragedies of injustice, warfare, and evil in general. How am I to respond to these tragedies? What would be the proper response were I even able to affect the situation? This is by no means an exhaustive list, but a brief outline of some of the more apparent afflictions of practical experience.

Practical experience is often not harmonious; there are impasses that do not admit of solution. In this final section, I will not attempt to offer any final resolutions. Rather, I will follow Ricoeur in trying to offer practical responses to the undeniable vicissitudes of life. These practical responses lie in the concepts of *conviction* and *fidelity*. The limitations, conflicts, and tragedy that affect practical experience force one to admit that the quest for the good life within the bounds of moral respect is more often witnessed to in conviction and fidelity than actually achieved once and for all. Conviction and fidelity were well-represented topics in Ricoeur's corpus, though his own analysis focused on philosophical aporias—autonomy versus actual freedom, the distinction between the abstract categories of humanity and actual persons, the conflict between disinterest and mutuality in institutional life. However, these philosophical aporias steer attention away from practical experience, or so I am arguing. Thus, I am attempting to be faithful to Ricoeur's ideas, but to move them in a slightly different direction.

This final examination is suggested from two directions. The first arises from the conjunction of the aim and the norm and impasses that arise out of it. The second direction is suggested by the last section of the previous chapter. There, I discussed the experience of meaningful existence under the idea of biblical testimony to the origin and end of existence. With regard to the origin of existence, life becomes meaningful within the designation of a fundamental value that inhabits the created order through the act of creation itself. With regard to the end of existence, biblical testimony holds out the promise of final reconciliation, conceived philosophically as the reconciliation of happiness and duty, and biblically as the redemption from evil. However, the gift of creation and the promise of reconciliation introduce their own aporias due to the recognition of evil in the present. While the idea of creation turns our attention to the fundamental value of the created order, experience is hounded by the tragic visions of human degradation and environmental devastation that deform that value. While hope is buttressed by the promise of future deliverance, the present is inhabited by the tragic realization that evil is still pervasive. That is to say, the biblical testimony that grounds one's sense of possibility is confronted by the experience of tragedy to which s/he must respond. This experience of the tragic serves as a further specification of the idea of public life that bridges the movement from meaningful existence to practical experience.

Considered convictions witness to one's responsibility in light of these basic experiences of moral conflict and tragedy. Convictions seek to direct attention back to the other to whom one is responsible and to faithful responsibility in light of the tragedy that afflicts practical experience. More to the point, Ricoeur's account of conviction and fidelity seek to direct attention toward moral judgment in the actual situations in which I confront others who make demands on me. Yet, if conviction serves to redirect my gaze, it does not offer a final solution. It provides an angle of approach to a more comprehensive vision, which will be the subject of the next chapter.

The limitations intrinsic to human action give the quest for the good life within the bounds of moral respect the character of conviction. Even if I am capable of engaging my quest for the good life in line with a particular life plan, there is no promise that my quest will end in happiness. This fact of life becomes apparent in the risky proposition of choosing a profession. I, for instance, devoted a substantial amount of time and resources to education in the hopes of becoming a college professor. It was my conviction that this was the life that would make me happy (and happily, this turned out to be the case), but there was no promise that this would be the outcome. (Indeed, there was no promise that there would be a job in my chosen profession waiting for me.) Additionally, the time and resources that I devoted to this quest closed off many other possibilities that might have issued in happiness. My choice came with sacrifices, many of which I didn't even know I was making.

This lack of prospective knowledge is precisely the issue at hand, however. I cannot know what the future brings. I am forced to strive for a life plan that forecloses other possible life plans; not to choose is still a choice. I am condemned to freely determine my own way, as Jean Paul Sartre so eloquently pointed out.[38] I am forced to live in the conviction that my choices are the correct ones and live with the consequences if I am wrong. There is the constant threat of crushing regrets for missed opportunities or poor choices. My only solace in the face of such threats is the conviction that I could not or would not have done otherwise. *C'est la vie*!

A similar lack of knowledge extends to the effects my actions will have on others. I cannot know for sure if or how my actions will affect others, but I can anticipate. I can commit myself to certain moral values and to certain duties in the service of those values. But this possibility opens even deeper conflicts. Even if I could produce for myself a comprehensive set of moral duties to govern my quest, I am sure to come upon situations where my duty is not clear. Experience is rife with situations where no clear course of action presents itself, indeed where more than one incompatible possibility seem to open up. These are situations where one is faced with a genuine conflict of duties. One famous example of such an apparent conflict was offered by Immanuel Kant: Kant related a hypothetical situation in which one is harboring a friend from a homicidal maniac. Suppose that this maniac knocks on the door and inquires about the whereabouts of the friend. What is the proper response? Should s/he tell the maniac that the friend hides within or should s/he lie to protect the innocent friend? There appears to be a conflict between two equally laudatory, equally binding duties: (1) tell the truth, (2) protect the innocent.

Somewhat counterintuitively, Kant argued that there was not in fact a conflict of duties; the duty to tell the truth must surely win out because it is a perfect duty that must be absolutely universalized to protect the continuation of society. Indeed, without respect for the truth, it would be impossible to discern innocence from guilt; hence one must sacrifice the innocent friend in order to protect the respect for honesty.[39] This example raises a deeper problem within a morality of duty. The possibility of a conflict within the imperative of respect did not arise for Kant because, he argued, the test for the adequacy of any particular maxim of action proceeds only in one direction, what Ricoeur called the "ascending route" of universalization. A maxim qualifies as a moral rule if it can pass the test of universalization. As Ricoeur pointed out, along this first path, "the moral character of maxims is verified in a two-step test: first the maxim is stated in terms such that one can later ask whether, formulated in this way, it successfully passes the test of universalization. As for the second stage, that of actual testing, it is strictly limited to the test of contradiction internal to the maxim."[40] A maxim qualifies as a moral rule so long as it can consistently be willed to be a universal law without contradictions. However, Ricoeur argued that it is along a second, "descending," route of application to specific situations that conflicts arise. So long as the test for the moral validity of maxims travels only in the direction of universality, the question of moral commitment concerns only commitment to the rule; an action is moral so long as it is faithful to the rule of universality. Even more problematic, however, this moral concern seems directed not toward others who are deserving of my respect, but toward one's own personal integrity as the one who gives the moral law to him/herself. So long as I act from duty, I am assured of my freedom as a moral agent, regardless of the effect of my action on another. Taking Kant's condemnation of false promises as an example, Ricoeur questioned, "are others really taken into consideration here?"

> This is doubtful. It is striking that the condemnation of suicide and that of false promising, although belonging to two different classes of duties toward others, tend to be confused to the extent that it is humanity that is treated merely as a means, first in one's own person and a second time in the person of others. Perhaps one should go even further: is it not actually personal integrity that is at stake in the so-called duties toward others? Is it not oneself that one despises in giving a false oath? The wrong done to others as other than myself could perhaps not appear along the first path moving from action to maxims and from maxims to the criterion that tests their moral tenor.[41]

The wrong done to others can only be addressed along the second path of application of rules to situations.

Ricoeur's focus on Kant's prohibition of false promises is telling; recall that the ability to keep one's promises was the principle characteristic of Ricoeur's account of selfhood as self-constancy. Keeping one's promises marked human initiative in its orientation toward the future. But, the notion of keeping promises comes upon a fundamental problem so long as promising represents a commitment to one's own integrity. Citing Gabriel Marcel, Ricoeur commented:

> "In a sense," [Marcel] wrote in *Being and Having*, "I cannot be faithful except to my own commitments, that is, it would seem, to myself."

> But here arises the alternative; 'At the moment of my commitment, I either (1) arbitrarily assume a constancy in my feelings which is not in my power to establish, or (2) I accept in advance that I shall have to carry out, at a given moment, an action which will in no way reflects my state of mind when I do carry it out. In the first case I am lying to myself, in the second I consent in advance to lie to someone else." How can one escape this double bind of self-constancy?[42]

The only way out of this double bind is the recognition that my commitments to myself are tied to my fidelity to another who holds me responsible for those commitments. Moral conviction without fidelity becomes scruple, rigidity, perhaps violence. That is to say, commitment to moral conviction is, at the same time, fidelity to another who *counts on me*, to whom I am available in my commitments. Ricoeur concluded, "This *counting on* connects self-constancy, in its moral tenor, to the principle of reciprocity founded in solicitude. . . . If fidelity consists in responding to the expectation of another who is counting on me, I must take this expectation as the measure for applying the rule."[43] The foundations of my very selfhood rely on my availability *to* another; solicitude becomes responsibility to another in my responsibility for my actions.

Thus, the primary distinction between responsibility *to* and responsibility *for* arises again. Recall Gabriel Moran's argument that one cannot adequately assess his/her responsibility *for* actions without the corresponding assessment of responsibility *to* others. With the introduction of the notion of fidelity, Ricoeur seemed to have come to a nearly identical conclusion. The self-constancy of selfhood and the moral dimensions of selfhood that enter through the central theme of the promise are oriented by openness, that is, by responsibility *to* the one who confronts me with a moral claim.[44]

This practical negotiation of the question of my duty to another, fragile on its own, does not banish affliction from practical experience. Evil in the broad sense of the term—injustice, violence, warfare—continues to exist. Biblical testimony witnessed to fundamental value and a possible deliverance from evil that made sense of existence in the world, but the experience of the tragic within history distorts this value and brands this possibility with an ineluctable sense of the "not yet." Our collective memories of the tragic episodes of history stand as a stumbling block to any easy assumption that evil and violence have been overcome, or even could be overcome once and for all. However, this collective memory is itself a witness to the value, despite vulnerability, of human life, and the moral outrage that seethes out of this collective memory even more so. To call attention to the suffering of history's victims, to proclaim that violence is a scourge that must be eradicated is, at the same time, to bear witness to the value within the created order that violence attempts to negate. By holding the conviction that evil "is what is and what ought not to be," one witnesses equally to the conviction that there is a purpose, despite the lessons of history, that holds attention, directs existence, and demands fidelity.

I have argued that Ricoeur's project necessarily opens onto theological ideas. It is in the face of the tragic that this theological dimension becomes most apparent. Religious witness stands as a fundamental response to tragic experience. In the next chapter, I will turn directly to this topic.

Chapter Five

Conscience

Conviction and Fidelity in Theological Perspectice

In this chapter, I will have opportunity to test the central claim of this project, namely, that Ricoeur's writings on religion lend important perspective on his philosophy. This theological dimension of his work creatively juxtaposes the ideals of love and justice, which appear to be fundamentally at odds. However, Ricoeur argued in numerous articles that a creative tension exists between the respective demands of love and of justice which allows for a mutual reinterpretation that yields a deeper understanding of both. He never offered any systematic account of of these ideas, but dealt with them in a series of occasional articles that address more specific topics. My principal aim in this chapter is to present a possible reading that is faithful to Ricoeur's thought.

At the conlusion of the last chapter, I argued that conviction witnesses to an affirmation of value and a hope for possibility. Theological perspectives give content to this affirmation and hope. They articulate a dimension of value to which conviction and fidelity respond.[1] If the bridge that led from the basic structures of agency to the configuration of meaningful existence was the recognition of reflective existence in a world that presents itself to experience, and if the bridge that led from configuration to practical experience was the recognition of public life with others, then the bridge that leads from experience to a properly theological conviction and fidelity is the recognition of existence within a realm inhabited by value that demands my moral response. This demand takes the form of the love command, or what I will eventually call the *poetic imperative*.

The love command can be thought in terms of a poetic imperative because of the imperative sense that it imparts; love, biblically construed, is a commandment. The idea of a "poetic use" of the imperative arose from Ricoeur's engagement with the thought of Franz Rosenzweig. In *The Star of Redemption*, Rosenzweig spoke of the love command as a ground for all other commandments, all laws, every ethical orientation. In this way, the love command holds a place analogous to the categorical imperative in Kant's moral philosophy. Yet, Ricoeur correctly argued that the love command cannot be reduced to a moral imperative, especially in Kant's sense of the term. For Kant, in order for an imperative to be moral, that is, categorically binding, it must be purely formal, that is, devoid of specific content. In order for the moral imperative to function adequately as a test for any particular maxim of action, it must represent a pure, formal requirement, universality; a maxim of action can be considered moral if it conforms to this test of universality. Thus, the categorical imperative provides a purely formal structure into which any content, that is, any maxim of action, can be plugged. As I noted in the last chapter, this raises the fundamental problem of application: Kant orients the test for moral validity solely along the "ascending route" of the test for universality. But what of situations in which one is confronted with a choice between two equally valid, yet conflicting courses of action? For instance, is one permitted to lie in order to protect another from needless harm? The categorical imperative, as a purely formal requirement, is ill equipped to adjudicate these kinds of moral conflict.

In distinction, the love command, as Ricoeur conceived it, draws its imperative form *as a commandment* from the biblical symbols, metaphors, and narratives that surround it. This is what makes it a *poetic* imperative. Therefore, the commandment to love God and the neighbor is both morally revelatory and morally productive. The love command is not a purely formal imperative, but a content-rich source for reflection upon obligations to others in particular situations. To put things in terms more amenable to the distinction with Kant's categorical imperative, the love command is universal in scope, but not purely formal in character. It gains its motive force from particular situations of interaction with specific others. As such, it holds a centrally important place in the proposal for conviction and fidelity in theological perspective.

Within this perspective, however, the love command does not stand alone. Ricoeur placed this commandment opposite another, the golden rule. He held the golden rule to be the most general practical characterization of an ideal of justice. Setting the problem in these terms, Ricoeur suggested, "What is called 'Christian ethics,' or, as I would prefer to say, 'communal ethics in a religious perspective,' consists, I believe, in the tension between unilateral love and bilateral justice, and in the interpretation of each in terms of the other."[2] The tension between love and justice can be explored in three stages, which mirror the structure that has directed my entire project: basic structure, configuration, experience. The first stage explores the confrontation between two opposing logics: a *logic of superabundance* and a *logic of equivalence* corresponding to love and justice, respectively. These two logics provide basic structure for the confrontation between the ideals of love and justice. They issue in differing principles of behavior, or more accurately, in differing orientations to the other located at a second stage of analysis. These differing orientations, which serve to configure this theological perspective, are the *golden rule*, that is, the principle grounding the reciprocity demanded by justice, and the *love command*, which demands generosity to the point of forgoing the concern for reciprocity. Finally, these differing orientations find their foundation in experience in the creative tension that Ricoeur established between the ideas of *autonomy* and *theonomy*.[3] This relationship is both tensive and creative; theonomy does not negate autonomy, but establishes it, invests it with its ownmost possibilities. Theonomy establishes autonomy as *human* freedom, as capability. Ricoeur called for an endeavor of mutual interpretation between ideals of love and justice. The point was not to pose the relation in terms of a static opposition; the final move of interpreting each in terms of the other gives a deeper understanding of both, Ricoeur argued.

The introduction of religious themes has broader ramifications than a deepened understanding of the ideal of justice and its relationship to love, however. I have claimed that Ricoeur's religious writings provide an important interpretive key to the overall coherence of his philosophical project, and this becomes most pronounced at the level of moral responsibility to others. One significant dimension of this function of clarification comes to recognition in the idea of moral conscience, in both its philosophical and theological interpretations, that emerged in Ricoeur's thought near the end of his life. I will allow his understanding of the voice of conscience to be informed by Rosenzweig's presentation of the love command. While the two ideas cannot be collapsed into each other, there is, nonetheless, a fruitful dialectic that can be established between them that will help broaden the idea of moral conscience into areas that Ricoeur himself did not explore in any detail. It is necessary, therefore, to pause and examine the place that conscience played in his work.

The Testimony of Conscience

Ricoeur held a professionally ambivalent relationship with the field of theology throughout his career, claiming not to be a theologian, but a philosopher who listens seriously to the Christian witness. His moral philosophy was a particular point at which the influence of religious ideas became most pronounced. I showed in chapters 2 and 3 that theological concepts entered Ricoeur's thought in the face of despair over the existence of violence and evil; the religious confronts me with the option of hope in spite of the existence of evil. Hope points to a still deeper affirmation. This affirmative stance is a discerning affirmation that sees in violence a negation, a violation, of the valuable. As Ricoeur, in a slightly different context, claimed, "[T]he soul of refusal, of recrimination, of contestation, and lastly, of interrogation and doubt, is fundamentally affirmation . . . denegration is never but the reverse of a more primordial affirmation, only half an act."[4] Faced with evil, hope takes up the position of recrimination and contestation. But, hope points to an underlying affirmation, which I addressed in chapter 4 through the ideas of conviction and fidelity. I contend that the ability to witness to value lies in the faculty of conscience, more specifically, in moral conscience. The first stop, therefore, is a brief exploration of the connections between the idea of moral conscience and conviction.

Conscience, Conviction, and Value

In one of the places that he discussed conscience, Ricoeur stated, "It belongs to human beings . . . to have a conscience, that is, a self-knowledge that includes the minimal relational aspect of relating oneself to some instance qualified by the difference between good and evil."[5] Conscience is the human capacity to relate oneself to some instance qualified by value; or, perhaps more adequately stated, conscience is that which compels human beings to a recognition of instances of value.

Ricoeur approached the idea of conscience through the central metaphor of the voice. Because conscience confronts experience in the form of a call that compels, Ricoeur addressed conscience in the form of passivity within selfhood: I am the passive reciever of the call of conscience. Yet, while one gets some sense of the experience of conscience via this metaphor, analysis of the structure of conscience itself is exceedingly difficult and much disputed. For his part, Ricoeur sought to offer an account of this structure by answering a set of challenges, or what might be called reductions, that have been leveled at the idea of conscience: (1) suspicions leveled by Hegel and Nietzsche with regard to the distinction between good and bad conscience, which serve to reduce conscience to the hypocritical "bad" conscience, (2) Heidegger's association of the call of conscience with the call of authenticity, which serves to reduce conscience to self-attestation, and (3) Levinas's tendency to reduce the otherness of conscience to the otherness of other persons. In providing answer to these challenges, Ricoeur hoped to carve out a space within which to assign conscience its own particular moral ground.

However, his account of conscience tended to raise as many questions as it answered. He may have been successful in assigning to conscience its own particular form of otherness, but in his role as philosopher he was reduced to silence in the face of the question of where the call comes from. He concluded:

> Perhaps the philosopher as philosopher has to admit that one does not know and cannot say whether this Other, the source of the injunction [of conscience], is another person whom I can look in the face or who can stare at me, or my ancestors for whom there is no representation, to so great an extent does my debt to them constitute my very self, or God—living God, absent God—or an empty place. With this aporia of the Other, philosophical discourse comes to an end.[6]

It is my intent to press the issue of the source of the injunction because the incapacity of philosophical discourse to answer this question provides an opening onto religious discourse, or what might be called considered religious convictions.

The first challenge to the idea of conscience that Ricoeur addressed was the criticism of good and bad conscience leveled first by Hegel and later radicalized by Nietzsche. Hegel launched his attack on Kant's ethics on the basis of three postulates that Ricoeur characterized as such:

> The first postulate . . . is that morality, while requiring that duty be done—hence, become real—dismisses the whole of nature as insignificant, through its condemnation of desire, which is nature in us. The second postulate maintains that, unable to produce any harmony between the ought and the is, morality postpones indefinitely the moment of satisfaction which the agent nonetheless seeks in the effectivity of action. Finally, the third postulate concerns the fact that since this agreement between form and content is never given here below, it is cast into another consciousness, that of a holy legislator situated outside the world.[7]

Hegel attempted to show that the idea of conscience that arises on the basis of the moral view of the world suffers from an insurmountable hypocrisy that manifests itself in the distinction between bad conscience and good conscience.

Bad conscience is subject to hypocrisy due to the unfathomable schism between the universal, that is, pure duty, and the particular, that is, self-determined action. The idea of conscience itself throws a wrench into any final reconciliation of these two. Hegel asserted:

> To make the deed a reality does not mean here translating its content from the form of *purpose* or *being-for-self* into the form of an *abstract*

> reality [that is, pure duty]: it means translating it from the form of immediate self-*certainty*, which knows its knowledge or being-for-self to be essential being, into the form of an *assurance* that consciousness is convinced of its duty and, as conscience, knows *in its own mind* what duty is. . . . To ask whether the assurance is true would presuppose that what the individual self wills can be separated from duty, from the will of the universal and pure consciousness. . . . But this distinction between the universal consciousness and the individual self is just what has been superseded, and the supersession of it *as* conscience.[8]

In actualizing the imperative of duty, conscience sets itself up as the universal, though still particular; conscience is the brute assertion of its own moral absolute, and in this lies the very nature of evil. Conscience is capable of choosing its principle in conformity with the universal law, thereby negating itself, or out of the arbitrariness of its own particularity. However, it cannot do both at the same time.

Yet how does the capacity for evil lead to the charge of hypocrisy? Hypocrisy enters the moral vision of the world in the individual's attempts to justify his or her actions. "To act in an evil manner and with an evil conscience does not amount to *hypocrisy*," Hegel argued:

> Hypocrisy includes in addition the formal determination of untruthfulness, whereby *evil* is in the first place represented *for others* as *good* and the evildoer pretends in all external respects to be good, conscientious, pious, etc.—which in this case is merely a trick to deceive *others*. But secondly, the evil person may find in the good he does at other times, or in his piety, or in *good reasons* of any kind, a means of justifying *for himself* the evil he does, in that he can use these reasons to distort it into something he considers good.[9]

Thus, hypocrisy results from seeking to make oneself *appear* good both to others and to oneself.

If Hegel cast an initial suspicion on the idea of moral conscience, a suspicion that is overcome in the supersession of the moral viewpoint in the movement to ethical existence, Nietzsche's criticism brought on the near collapse of the idea. Nietzsche described bad conscience as "the serious illness that man was bound to contract under the stress of the most fundamental change he ever experienced—that change which occurred when he found himself finally enclosed within the walls of society and peace."[10] Bad conscience is an affliction that results from the turning inward of aggressive "instincts," an internalization that peaceful society demands. Nietzsche asserted that there is no escape once the human animal is subjected to conscience. With the radicalization of bad conscience comes an equally devastating radicalization of hypocrisy. The claims to *good* conscience are nothing but the *ressentiment* of the "weak" directed at the strong who forswear the claims of conscience. The afflicted become the persecutors of those noble souls whom they resent and fear.

What is centrally important in the attention that Ricoeur paid to these attacks is the tendency on the part of both Hegel and Nietzsche to presuppose the existence of *bad* conscience and to place any reclamation of good conscience out of bounds: "This reversal of pro and con would remain captive to the same circular problematic, justification and judgements of indignation simply being replaced by self-justification and self-glorification."[11] Thus, any reclamation of the idea of moral conscience must be mounted from outside of the "poisoned circle" that reduces conscience to hypocritical and/or disfiguring guilty conscience, and which sees in good conscience an even worse form of hypocrisy. At this point, the second challenge arises regarding conscience, what Ricoeur called the "demoralizing of conscience" in the ideas of Martin Heidegger.

Ricoeur claimed that the separation of the idea of conscience from the "false alternative of 'good' and 'bad' conscience" reached its most radical formulation in Heidegger's *Being and Time*. Indeed, for Heidegger, bad conscience and, even more so, good conscience are inauthentic interpretations of the phenomenon of conscience; they are the result of concernful being-with-others, distractions that keep one tied to the "they-self." The authentic function of the call of conscience is to wrench Dasein out of its "lostness in the they." Heidegger exclaimed:

> The sort of Dasein which is understood after the manner of the world both for Others and for itself, gets *passed over* in this appeal; this is something which the call to the Self takes not the slightest cognizance. And because only the *Self* of the they-self gets appealed to and brought to hear, the "*they*" collapses. . . . Precisely *in passing over* the "they" (keen as it is for public repute) the call pushes it into insignificance. But the Self, which the appeal has robbed of this lodgement and hiding-place, gets brought to itself by the call.[12]

For Heidegger, this appeal of conscience arises out of the uncanniness of the fact that the self is thrown into an existence not of its own choosing. It is precisely this character of uncanniness that marks the peculiar sense that Heidegger gave to conscience.

This peculiar nature of conscience becomes particularly apparent in Heidegger's explanation of the "whence" of the appeal; if Dasein is appealed to, who calls? Paradoxically, it is Dasein that calls *itself* out of its lostness. And yet, the call is not something that the self voluntarily chooses; rather, the call comes to Dasein, though Dasein is nonetheless the source of the call: "Ontologically . . . it is not enough to answer that Dasein is *at the same time* both the caller and the one to whom the appeal is made. . . . The call comes *from* me and yet *from beyond me and over me*."[13] More paradoxical still is Heidegger's discussion of what conscience gives to understanding. Conscience confronts the self with an accusation, with the charge of "Guilty (*Schuldig*)!" "All experiences and interpretations of the conscience," Heidegger asserted, "are at one in that they make the 'voice' of conscience speak somehow of 'guilt.'"[14]

This charge of guilt seems to draw conscience back into the very moralism and hypocrisy of the good and bad conscience that Hegel and Nietzsche went to such lengths to undermine. Yet Heidegger separated the kind of existential guilt to which conscience leads from the "everyday understanding" of guilt that consigns conscience to the dichotomy between good and bad conscience.[15] Existential guilt cannot be split up into moral categories by virtue of the fact that morality itself must first presuppose it; the "Guilty!" is more primordial than morality. Heidegger concluded that the appeal of conscience is self-attestation:

> Hearing the appeal correctly is thus tantamount to having an understanding of oneself in one's ownmost potentiality-for-Being—that is, to projecting oneself upon one's *ownmost* authentic potentiality for becoming guilty. When Dasein understandingly lets itself be called forth to this possibility, this includes its *becoming free* for the call—its readiness for the potentiality of getting appealed to. In understanding the call, Dasein is *in thrall to* [*hörig*] *its ownmost possibility of existence*. It has chosen itself.[16]

Conscience calls the self to responsibility for itself, not in the sense of responsibility for its actions, but rather, in the sense of its responsibility for its very potentiality for being a self. In this sense, the self called to account by conscience for its own possibility is a presupposition of morality; there must be an authentic self capable of responsibility before responsibility can be assigned.

This priority of authentic selfhood over ethical determinations and moral deliberations is sealed by Heidegger's idea of resoluteness: "Only by authentically Being-their-Selves in resoluteness can people authentically be with others—not by ambiguous and jealous stipulations and talkative fraternizing in the 'they' and in what 'they' want to undertake." It would be an oversight not to recognize dimensions of what Ricoeur called considered convictions within this account of resoluteness, dimensions that will be explored in more detail in a moment. Indeed, Heidegger continued, "What one resolves upon in resoluteness has been prescribed ontologically in the existentiality of Dasein in general as the potentiality-for-Being in the manner of concernful solicitude."[17] Yet, if he seemed to have laid the groundwork for a return from fundamental ontology to ethics, he never made the return. With the introduction of resoluteness, conscience has been reduced to the attestation of the self's possibility for being a self and lost all of its moral flavor. While Heidegger posited an authentic way of being-with others, the shape of this authentic being-with remained indeterminate.[18]

Ricoeur objected to this "demoralized" account of conscience and sought to attach to the idea of attestation what he took to be the closely associated idea of injunction: "Listening to the voice of conscience would signify being-enjoined by the Other. In this way, the rightful place of the notion of debt would be acknowledged, a notion that was too hastily ontologized by Heidegger at the expense of the ethical dimension of indebtedness." With the introduction of the idea of injunction, the attestation of conscience meets up again, in a more content laden sense, with the idea of conviction whereby the self declares itself responsible; in turn, conviction returns one to the ethical aim. Ricoeur concluded, "To find oneself called upon in the second person at the very core of the optative of living well, then of the prohibition to kill, then of the search for the choice appropriate to the situation, is to recognize oneself as being enjoined to *live well with and for others in just institutions and to esteem oneself as the bearer of this wish*."[19] However, relocating the voice of conscience within the realm of the other who calls and placing the self in the position of the second person who answers to the injunction raises the question of where the voice comes from. Who is this other who summons me? At this point, a third challenge to the idea of conscience is encountered.

If Heidegger equated the voice of conscience with self-attestation, thereby reducing conscience to Dasein's calling itself to authenticity, there is an equally strong temptation, Ricoeur suggested, "to compare, by contrast, the otherness of the injunction to that of other people." I showed the priority Emmanuel Levinas gave to the other in the constitution of the self in the last chapter. Levinas turned the tables on Heidegger's account of conscience as Dasein's self-summoning out of lostness, claiming instead that selfhood is constituted through the encounter with the epiphany of the face. In this sense, Levinas reduced all otherness to alterity, to other persons outside the self. As I suggested, Ricoeur wanted to account for conscience in a way that succumbs to neither of these reductions:

> To these two alternatives—either Heidegger's strange(r)ness or Levinas' externality—I shall stubbornly oppose the original and originary character of what appears to me to constitute the third modality of otherness, namely *being enjoined as the structure of selfhood*. . . . On the one hand, if the injunction coming from the other is not part and parcel of self-attestation, it loses its character of injunction, for lack of the existence of a being-enjoined standing before it as respondent. If one

> eliminates this dimension of auto-affection, one ultimately renders the metacategory of conscience superfluous; the category of the other suffices. To Heidegger, I objected that attestation is primordially injunction, or attestation risks losing all ethical or moral significance. To Levinas, I shall object that the injunction is primordially attestation, or the injunction risks not being heard and the self not being affected in the mode of being-enjoined.[20]

Conscience is neither completely anxiety/authenticity nor complete alterity. The injunction can be reduced neither to the voice of Dasein to itself nor to the other commanding the self to moral concern. But, this reveals more about what conscience is not than what it is. From where does the voice of conscience confront me? Who is the Other who enjoins me? Ricoeur claimed that philosophical discourse is reduced to silence on this point.

I want to push the discussion in a slightly different direction. I have shown that Ricoeur followed Heidegger in exploring conscience through the metaphor of the voice; conscience is the silent voice that comes from me, yet from beyond me. He then expanded upon this idea to include the voice of injunction to the self which comes from elsewhere. Therefore, the voice of conscience becomes a mediating structure between self-attestation and moral injunction. His reliance on this metaphor gives opportunity to explore the symbolic potency of the image of the voice in order to give some more determinate character to the phenomenon of conscience. However, this exploration takes us in a decidedly different direction, into the realm of theological discourse.

Conscience, Commandment, and Love

Ricoeur made forays in the direction of a theological interpretation of conscience. In at least one place, he traced the metaphor of the voice from the biblical narratives of the prophetic call, through the progressive internalization of the voice in Augustine's figure of the inner teacher and the Christian doctrine of the *imitatio Christi*, to a decidedly theological interpretation of the "testimony of conscience." Following Gerhard Ebeling, Ricoeur described the structure of conscience within this theological context as a "word-event" which announces the "unconditional character of the judgement of conscience." Ebeling's account was indebted to Heidegger, as Ricoeur pointed out. Conscience is fundamentally an aspect of attestation and individuation:

> Ebeling does not go as far as Heidegger does in his interpretation of *Schuld* (guilt) beyond good and evil, if we may put it this way. Instead, he proposes to situate this phenomenon at the point of articulation

> between dogmatics (for him essentially soteriology) and ethics. . . . And in this way he thinks he can reconcile Paul's and Heidegger's analyses inasmuch as for both of them the call of conscience is a call of the self to itself where the identity belonging to ipseity proceeds from a cleavage, a *Distanz*, rather than from an *Instanz*, more radical than any "bad" conscience. Conscience reveals the problematic character of personal identity at the very moment when this identity is recalled to its condition of "ultimate concern." "Bad" conscience is, before any moral characterization, the painful sense of nonidentity from which ipseity emerges; "good" conscience is the joy that stems from the coming to expression of the self beyond the "pangs of conscience."[21]

While this theological interpretation goes some way to circumventing the conundrum of good and bad conscience, it seems to lose its character of moral injunction. Rather, in conscience, the soul is concerned in sealing its own joy "beyond the pangs of conscience." Is there a possible perspective from which one can recapture a theological account of conscience that still contains the dimension of moral injunction? There is a return path from what might be called a demoralized theological interpretation of conscience. This path reverses the direction of the one that leads from alterity, or the prophetic call, to interiority, that is, testimony of conscience. This reverse path leads from the interiority of conscience, through the hermeneutics of testimony, to the notion of the love command, both of which were encountered in chapter 3. There is room within Ricoeur's work to make this return path, even if the path itself must be pieced together from seemingly disconnected fragments.

I have just addressed Ricoeur's attempt to carve out a space for conscience by juxtaposing the dual reductions of Heidegger and Levinas. While philosophical discourse was reduced to silence at the end of this endeavor, there are other places where he launched similar efforts that include reference to theological discourse. These offer more constructive accounts of conscience, even if they confront conscience in a roundabout fashion. In one article, Ricoeur posed the thought of Jean Nabert as an intermediate position between Heidegger and Levinas. The focus of this essay is the topic of testimony (*témoignage*), rather than conscience. Ricoeur's analysis of the topic of testimony in Nabert was built onto an analysis of Heidegger's interpretation of conscience as the call of Dasein to itself, and Ricoeur leveled a nearly identical critique of Heidegger's demoralized account. In Nabert's thought, conscience entered the realm of moral concern, first and foremost, in response to the "unjustifiable," that is, to the radicality of evil and to the ubiquity of suffering and violence. The protest with which conscience rages against the unjustifiable moves conscience out of the concern with either moral rectitude or the care over authenticity. I remain concerned about the state of my soul, so to speak. But, in the confrontation with the unjustifiable nature of evil, conscience directs the me outside of myself in recognition of and protest against cruelty and violence the depths of which my individual consciousness is unable to plumb. Ricoeur argued, "The unjustifiable is what cannot be measured by the mere violation of those norms to which the moral conscience equates itself. . . . Thus to the very extent that the unjustifiable surpasses the invalid, the demand for justification surpasses the resources of the good will least satisfied with itself."[22] In the face of the unjustifiable, the false dichotomy of good and bad conscience collapses upon itself; I can neither blame myself nor rest assured in the rectitude of my nature.

The crushing experience of impotence in the face of the unjustifiable initiates the turn toward the hermeneutics of testimony. I have already followed Ricoeur in linking the hermeneutics of testimony with the idea of primary affirmation in which the self testifies to its desire to be. In this sense, primary affirmation is among the constellation of ideas that includes attestation and conviction, understood as the self's witness to itself in moral commitment and responsibility. If primary affirmation opens onto the hermeneutics of testimony, it is because reflection is unable to achieve a coincidence between what it perceives and what it affirms as having ultimate value. However, the hermeneutics of testimony is inseparable from what Nabert called a "criteriology of the divine," or the effort of reflection to witness to the decisive images of divine action.

It is important to point out that, within this understanding of testimony, reflection does not, cannot, arbitrarily choose its images. This would amount to idolatry, both for Nabert and for Ricoeur. Rather, testimony testifies to the decisive events of divine self-disclosure, and in the exegesis of this testimony, the self gains a greater understanding of itself. What testimony calls for is a divestment (*dépouillement*) of the "idols" by which the self defines itself, the pretention to absolute self-foundation being perhaps the most pronounced of these idols.[23] But this criterion complicates the idea of testimony. Indeed, testimony does not travel in a single direction, but "divides itself, outside of reflection." At a first order level, testimony takes the form of the immediate witnesses to the event of divine action. This first order testimony is then taken up into the second order testimony of the witnesses to this witness. Ricoeur followed Nabert in designating this second order testimony "absolute testimony to the absolute." "What, in fact, is it to interpret testimony?" Ricoeur asks:

> It is a twofold act, an act of consciousness of itself and an act of historical understanding based on the signs that the absolute gives of itself. The signs of the absolute's self-disclosure are at the same time signs in which consciousness recognizes itself. . . . By being extended in a criteriology of the divine, original affirmation [*l'affirmation origi-*

> *naire*] is led to encounter the crisis of idols that testimony calls forth. Thus the hermeneutics of testimony arises in the confluence of two exegeses—the exegesis of historic testimony to the absolute and the exegesis of the self in the criteriology of the divine.[24]

Thus, the hermeneutics of testimony becomes an interpretation of divine activity that offers the possibility of greater self-understanding. In this way, the hermeneutics of testimony reattaches itself to the idea of conscience.

More importantly, the hermeneutics of testimony places conscience at the crossroads of interiority and alterity where philosophical discourse found its stumbling block. If testimony calls forth a self-divestment of the pretension to self-sufficiency, it nonetheless arises out of the protests against the unjustifiable character of evil: "The moral conscience is first of all the protest against the unjustifiable. Its height lies in the demand for justification apart from which evil cannot be taken as unjustifiable. Its exteriority lies in the testimony of those acts whose ethical signification results from the position on the trajectory of 'approaches to justification.'"[25] But this exteriority of absolute testimony to the absolute demands some answer to the whence of testimony itself, and this demand marks the return to biblical witness, understood as the textual deposit of absolute testimony, which is constantly open to engagement.

Is there a decisive trajectory within biblical witness that calls conscience to its responsibility and which conscience affirms at the same time? I intend to argue that, for Ricoeur, there was such a decisive trajectory that found its most adequate formulation in the love command. More adequately put, the trajectory of love, in its creative tension with the philosophical ideal of justice, is the poetic presentation of the whence of the call of conscience. This creative tension between love and justice is the backbone for what I have designated the theological and ethical endpoint of Ricoeur's project.

From Conscience to Theological Witness

Conscience, in both its philosophical and theological interpretations, links up with the creative tension between love and justice through the idea of value. Recall that Ricoeur defined conscience in terms of a relation to instances qualified by moral value. In moving from this recognition of value within instances that command moral concern, I want to suggest that the recognition of value represents a sort of philosophical approach to the theological understanding of love of creation.

Ricoeur's work relied in important places on philosophical "approximations" of theological ideas. One of these philosophical approximations that has occupied a significant portion of my analysis concerns the problem of moral fault. Recall that Ricoeur followed Kant in the assertion that moral fault is radical, it lies in a disposition of the will, in the adoption of an evil maxim that directs all choice. This account becomes paradoxical, however, in that moral evil results from a free choice of the will that makes the will unfree; remember that for Kant freedom is autonomy, that is, self-governing will, which is the source of the moral law. The incapacitation of the will in moral fault in no way relieves the will of its responsibility before the moral law. The will is still bound by moral obligation, but the moral law now confronts the will with a feeling of constraint. Morality is a constraint on the will because the will does not automatically choose the moral good. That is to say, the will is not perfectly good, hence not perfectly free, but is corrupted by self-interest. The best that can be hoped for in this case is a future reconciliation of happiness and duty, that is, that the will might someday act from duty of its own accord and not out of constraint.

Now, on Ricoeur's understanding, the Kantian idea of radical evil represented a philosophical approximation of the Christian notion of sinfulness. By the same token, hope for the future reconciliation of happiness and duty represented a philosophical approximation of the Christian hope for redemption through grace.[26] There is little dispute about the influence that this set of ideas exercised on Ricoeur's thought. I want to suggest, however, that there is another parallel and equally influential philosophical approximation that emerged within Ricoeur's later writings on love; glimmers of this were revealed in his return to a theology of creation. I indicated that the conceptual bridge that leads from practical moral experience to theological perspective is the recognition of existence within a realm inhabited by value. I suggest that the recognition and affirmation of moral value is a philosophical approximation for the theological idea of love of creation. Just as the ideas of sin and redemption lend meaning, in a *poetic* fashion, to the paradox of the bound will, love of creation lends meaning to the moral value that moral philosophy affirms but cannot grasp.

The articulation of this religious trajectory is nothing less than an exercise in biblical hermeneutics. The examination of the creative tension between love and justice is undertaken via the passage through scriptural sources. I will explore these scriptural sources along three intersecting levels: the basic structures of the logic of equivalence and the logic of superabundance, the orienting configurations of the golden rule and the love command, and experiential dimensions of autonomy and theonomy.

Basic Structures: The Logic of Equivalence and the Logic of Superabundance

The basic structure of this theological perspective takes the form of a confrontation between the logic of equivalence and the logic of superabundance. I will explore this basic structure in two stages. First, I will address the basic logics themselves; this discussion yields two ideas that can be called the economy of reciprocity and the economy of the gift. Second, I will show how these ideas are funded poetically by the biblical symbols of creation, revelation, and redemption.

Basic Logics: Reciprocity and Gift

Two seemingly opposed logics of *equivalence* and *superabundance* ground the basic structure of the confrontation between love and justice. The logic of equivalence was the inchoate force at the heart of the exploration of justice in the previous chapter. This logic has two dimensions. The first is a punitive dimension characterized most immediately by the *lex talionis*: an eye for an eye, and a tooth for a tooth. Though this dictum seems barbaric, it nevertheless represents the first imposition of law, of a measure of justice, within the spiraling escalation of vengeance; it is the first measuring of penalty to crime. Second, and more important for these meditations, the logic of equivalence concerns commutative justice. The whole point of commutative justice is to establish an equality between participants in a system of distribution.

What is remarkable about the logic of equivalence, Ricoeur contended, is that it is most profoundly a human logic: "The ideal, according to the spirit of the law, would be that the penalty equal the mistake. In this admirable effort is summarized human logic; human logic is the logic of equality, of equivalence."[27] What is equally remarkable is that biblical witness conceives a logic in nearly direct opposition to this logic of equivalence. The logic of biblical witness is one of excess and superabundance. Ricoeur took as the paradigmatic case of this logic of excess the extreme sayings of Jesus in the Sermon on the Mount: "Do not resist an evildoer. But if anyone strikes you on the right cheek, turn the other also; and if any one wants to sue you and take your coat, give your cloak as well; and if anyone forces you to go one mile, go the second mile. Give to everyone who begs from you, and do not refuse anyone who wants to borrow from you" (Matt. 5:39b–42, NRSV). It is not difficult to see how the logic of these sayings flies in the face of the logic of equivalence. The lines that precede these statements intensify their excessive nature: "You have heard that it was said, 'An eye for an eye and a tooth for a tooth.' But I say to you. . ." Relying on the work of biblical scholar Robert C. Tannehill, Ricoeur claimed that the strategy employed in these and other extreme statements is nothing less than that of commanding the opposite of the expected response; the commands simply reverse our natural tendencies in such situations. The natural tendency when hit is to hit back; here, the reader is commanded to offer the other cheek to be slapped as well.

It may seem foolhardy to take these statements literally; but if they are not to be taken literally, how should they be taken? Tannehill argued that such extreme commands function as "focal instances" which direct attention toward patterns of behavior. As such, they are characterized by both specificity and extremity. First, these sayings do not propose general principles to guide behavior, but focus attention on specific, rather unusual situations. To casuistically derive general moral principles from these specific instances, he claimed, is to miss their power for reorienting attention. Second, the extremity of the sayings causes a radical disorientation with regard to general modes of behavior and judgments about the correct response given the situation. It is precisely in the tension between the extremity of the command and the typical response that the command takes on meaning and functions to reorient imagination toward a different way of being. As Ricoeur explained:

> Parables, paradoxes, hyperboles, and extreme commandments all *dis*-orient only in order to *re*orient us. But what is reoriented in us? and in what direction? I would say that what is reoriented by these extreme sayings is less our will than our imagination. Our will is our capacity to follow without hesitation the once-chosen way, to obey without resistance the once-known law. Our imagination is the power to open us to new possibilities, to discover another way of seeing, or acceding to a new rule in receiving the instruction of the exception. . . . [W]hile the will is the intention to a specific project, the imagination is the intention of a dominate direction. It is at the level of dominate direction that we are overtaken by the disorienting logic of Jesus.[28]

It is important not to underestimate the significance of this relation between will, in its role in the embarking on a particular course of action, and imagination, as the opening of a dominant direction in the configuration of possibility. I have pointed to this relation in veiled forms in previous chapters—the analysis of the "intention-to" do something, the role of "imaginative variation" in the narrative emplotment of action and identity, the effect of the pair proclamation/revelation in the orientation of imagination, etc.. Most recently I discussed the profound effect of limit expressions and limit experiences. This effect marks the extremity of the commandments in the Sermon on the Mount; the logic of excess places its stamp on the limits of human experience and action.

In what sense, however, is the logic of excess a logic of superabundance? What is put in place here, it seems, is a logic of reversal; the commands dictate that I simply reverse my ordinary pattern of response. But this is not really the case. What these extreme commands press is the demand to *give more* than would reasonably be expected. Ricoeur explained, "Yes, each response *gives more* than that asked by ordinary prudence. . . . Not just this, but even that! It is this *giving more* that appears to me to constitute the point of these extreme commands."[29] The link between the extremity of the command and the logic of superabundance appears within the overall drift of the Sermon on the Mount that carries these extreme sayings. At issue is a promise, but this time within the orbit of love rather than that of hope. Ricoeur did not specifically address the idea of promise in its association with the ideal of love, but it is indicated from the beginning of the Sermon on the Mount. The beatitudes that introduce this passage take precisely the form of promise. The central power of these statements is the tension between an existing state of desperation and deprivation, and a promised future of comfort and abundance. This tension reaches its crescendo in the last of these introductory statements: "Blessed are those who are persecuted for righteousness' sake, for their's is the kingdom of heaven. Blessed are you when people revile you and persecute you and utter all kinds of evil against you falsely on my account. Rejoice and be glad, for your reward is great in heaven. . ." (Matt. 5:10–12). In what sense, however, is this promise a call to action and not simply a promise of future relief from suffering? In what sense does it introduce the demand to give more?

What is ultimately announced here is a realm of superabundance and security assured by the providence of a benevolent God. This announcement of abundance frees action from anxiety and reorients it toward the other whom I confront. This idea reaches its highest point in the analogical connection that Jesus draws between human existence and the birds of the air and the lilies of the field (Matt. 6:25–33). There, Jesus counsels not to be anxious, "But strive first for the kingdom of God and his righteousness and all these things will be given to you as well." Paradoxically, it is in seeking the kingdom of God, which is promised to the suffering, to those who go the second mile, that the promise of succor resides.

One might want to stop and ponder how far to push divine providence as a groundwork for a metaphysics of morals, however. I want to turn, once again, to Robert Tannehill in order to gain some bearing on what is being presented here. He argued that this passage serves to shock the reader out of the concerns that anxiously direct actions toward the garnering of a measure of security:

> [W]e may point out that the birds are also concerned with food; indeed, they spend most of their day seeking it. Even so, the contrast remains between man's elaborate structures of care and the comparatively simple, direct supplying of needs in the life of other creatures, and it is on this contrast that the text wishes us to meditate. . . . We experience a heightened awareness and the disturbing impingement of another reality. This opens a new possibility for life, a possibility which the text describes as seeking the Kingdom.[30]

Again, through the employment of limit expressions as a strategy of disorientation and reorientation, this time in the mode of extravagance, imagination is redirected. In what sense is this reorientation a redirection of action toward others? In what way does the announced superabundance invest the will with the capacity to go the second mile?

In general, theories of justice view the conditions under which justice becomes an issue in terms of moderate scarcity: the perception of moderate scarcity of goods and benefits to be distributed is what inclines individuals toward the formation of rules of justice in the first place. Each prefers a greater to a lesser share of scarce social goods. If one accepts for the moment this assertion of moderate scarcity, then it seems that this condition is precisely what is called into question by the announcement of abundance characterized by the kingdom of God. While moderate scarcity is a condition for the formation of rules of justice, a sense of fundamental security becomes the condition for or structure of the love command, if I can put it these terms. This sense of security turns the orientation toward the other away from contestation and competition toward a fundamental concern for his or her good, well-being, and integrity, that affords the extremity of Jesus' commands. In this way, the logic of reversal is implicated in the logic of superabundance.

Moving beyond the level of basic logics, one recognizes the structures at work in each. The structure that justice takes can be called an economy of reciprocity. What justice seeks to establish is an ideal of reciprocity that guides relations and distributions between individuals. Perhaps the most revealing example of this economy of reciprocity was encountered in Ricoeur's discussion of solicitude in situations of inherent inequality encountered in the previous chapter. The movement of solicitude seeks to equalize relations of give and take. The golden rule serves to formalize this economy of reciprocity by placing the desires and the aversions of both actors and those subject to actions in the forefront and on equal footing.

The logic of superabundance places this economy in question. The extreme sayings of Jesus demand that I renounce the concern for reciprocity. This demand inaugurates a radically different economy, which Ricoeur called the economy of the gift.[31] The economy of the gift forces the issue of the good of the other, and takes as its central focus his or her integrity, even if that integrity appears counter to my interests and/or comes at my expense. The gift is not without a demand for reciprocity, but the reciprocity it articulates is placed elsewhere than in the attempt to establish equivalence. Reciprocity arises out of the recognition of a gift already proffered to the self; this sense of the gift is composed out of the symbols of divine activity which present the self's very existence as gift, as a gratuitous act on the part of the divine. The paradox is that this act fundamentally cannot be reciprocated; yet if the initial act is radically nonreciprocal, it is not without strings. The demand that it generates is directed toward others. In this sense, the gift perpetuates gifting; the instantiation of a fundamentally gratuitous act demands that generosity be reciprocated, not from the self toward God, but from the self toward the other. As such, the love command, ordered as it is by the logic of superabundance and structured by the economy of the gift, places love at its limit.

The idea of the economy of the gift needs some further development. I will trace this notion along three related lines of enquiry that can be addressed in the traditional, dogmatic terms of *creation*, *revelation*, and *redemption*.

Biblical Symbols: Creation, Revelation, Redemption

Ricoeur did not couch his discussion in exactly the classic dogmatic terms of creation, revelation, and redemption, but the structure is clearly there. This characterization also pays homage to Rosenzweig's *The Star of Redemption*, to which Ricoeur's later work owed much.

The articulation of the economy of the gift from the angle of creation follows two lines, both of which characterize the hyperethical character of this economy. First, the idea of creation is expressive of the experience of *radical dependence* on a higher power that precedes life, envelops it, and sustains it. For Ricoeur, the symbol that gave meaning and direction to this experience is that of "an original but always ongoing creation."[32] He highlighted the supramoral quality of the experience of radical dependence to which the symbol of creation gives rise:

> No doubt, this symbol sets human beings in the place of honor, but within a cosmos created before them and that continues to shelter them. Each of us is not left face-to-face with another human being, as the principle of morality taken in isolation seems to imply. Rather nature is between us, around us—not just as something to exploit but as an object of solicitude, respect, and admiration. The sense of our radical dependence on a higher power thus may be reflected in a love for the creature, for every creature, in every creature—and the love of neighbor can become an expression of this supramoral love for all creatures.[33]

It is not difficult to understand the manner in which the supramoral character of the sense of radical dependence, which makes the love of neighbor an expression of love for all creatures, compels love to its greatest extreme, even to the enemy.

Yet, if the experience of radical dependence constituted by the symbol of ongoing creation is supramoral in quality, Ricoeur emphasized that "supramoral" does not mean "amoral," because the idea of power is joined with that of goodness. This second aspect of the articulation of the economy of the gift from the angle of creation emphasizes the confirmation of the goodness of the creation, which follows every creative act, culminating in Gen. 1:31: "God saw everything that he had made, and indeed, it was very good." Ricoeur continued: "What is important to emphasize here is that the predicate 'good' is assigned to the state of the creature as such, and not yet to some act of the human will or to some human disposition. At the same time, this highly affirmative qualification extends to every creative activity, inasmuch as God . . . is a creator of creatures."[34] The conjunction of the power of the creative act and the predicate "good," which designates God's ongoing creative project, constitutes the affirmative stance toward a fundamental value secured by the symbol of creation.

However, it may be objected that this characterization of God as loving creator presents only one side of the coin. Is God not also portrayed as harsh judge and, often, as destroyer of the creation that has been made? Is God not also the one who threatens the chosen with destruction, who rewards the unjust and visits suffering on the just? These aspects of the tradition do seem to stand as obstacles to a representation of divine activity solely in terms of its gift-like character. Yet Ricoeur argued that these instances must not be singled out and isolated from the matrix of religious symbolism that surrounds them; God is, after all, the one deemed, or perhaps more accurately, the one *revealed* as being worthy of praise, veneration, and love. This concern opens onto the second line of enquiry in the articulation of the economy of the gift, that of revelation. Ricoeur offered two instances in support: the giving of the Torah and the Christology of Atonement:

> The gift of the Torah is recounted narratively as a founding event, as we read in Exod. 20:1: "I am the Lord your God, who brought you out of the land of Egypt, out of the house of slavery." In this way, the law becomes an integral part of a history of liberation and becomes the expression of a gift. As for the Christian doctrine of "satisfaction," to the extent that it is accepted, it must not eclipse the giftlike character attached to the symbols of the cross. The apostle John opposes to the abuse of this narrow Christology of satisfaction, the sovereign proclamation; "No one can take my life from me, but I lay down my life in order to take it up again" (John 10:18).[35]

Thus, it is under the aspect of revelation—revelation of God as liberator at Sinai, revelation of Jesus as the suffering Christ—that places the symbols of divine legislation back within the economy of the gift.

A final line of enquiry concerning the economy of the gift leads to the idea of redemption. Here analysis links up once again with the idea of theological hope. The introduction of the idea of redemption places the revelation of divine activity, conceived within the compass of the economy of the gift, in the interstices between a beginning characterized by the symbol of creation and an end characterized by final reconciliation, that is, between origin and end of human existence:

> It is preceded . . . by the sense of originary creation. And at the other extremity of the symbolic keyboard is found the eschatological symbol that gives rise to the representation of God as the source of *unknown* possibilities. The symbol of the creator is "repeated," but from the angle of anticipation and not just from that of rememoration. The God of beginnings is the God of hope. And because God is the God of hope, the goodness of creation becomes the sense of direction. The predicate "good" attached to the process of creation returns enriched by the symbols of the gift of the Torah and the gift of the remission of sins. So it is the task, the heavy task, of the hope engendered by the symbol of God of unknown possibilities to preserve the sense of directionality in spite of . . . in spite of evil.[36]

The perseverance in the *sense of directionality*, characterized by the kingdom of God, extends the economy of the gift into future possibility. This end of the symbolic keyboard signals a return to the theology of hope, but this theological hope has itself been regenerated, so speak, by its inclusion within an overall trajectory that takes into account the goodness of creation and the historicity of kerygma. Hope, therefore, becomes the perseverance in a sense of direction characterized by the goodness and value of creation, a sense of direction that is intimately connected with the work of love. Hope will find its primary direction, its primary affirmation, within this work of love.

At this point, exploration opens onto the differing orientations implied in the opposing ideals of justice and love, orientations characterized by the golden rule and the love command, respectively.

Configuration: The Golden Rule and the Love Command

The competing logics of equivalence and superabundance find fruition in two equally competing orientations: the golden rule and the love command. These competing orientations serve to configure what I have called Ricoeur's theological perspective in terms of the creative tension between love and justice. The golden rule is expressive of the ideal of reciprocity characteristic of justice in two senses. First, it highlights the fundamental asymmetry of action, or the fact that action involves both an agent and a patient. This recognition is guaranteed by the tension between "doing unto others" and "as oneself." Opposed to a conception of the situation of action solely in terms of the confrontation between two agents, this presentation of the fundamental asymmetry of action recognizes both an actor and another who is a potential victim. The merit of the golden rule is its acknowledgment, at the level of grammar, of both the one who acts and the one who is acted upon. In addition, the golden rule sets both agent and patient on the same footing relative to the deliberation over action. An equivalence is established in its application to discrete situations; both I and others are potential aggressors or potential victims.

The equivalence established by the golden rule is called into question in significant ways by the love command. How is this the case? Does the command to love one's neighbor as oneself not establish the same equivalence by the qualification *as oneself*? The love command enters a logic of extremity once the question of who the neighbor is enters the calculation. I take as an example Luke 6:27–31, where the compass of love is extended to include even one's enemies. If this command to love one's enemies does not directly contradict the equivalence of the golden rule, it nonetheless radically disorients the manner in which it is applied, and at the same time calls into the question the status of the distinction friend/enemy. Indeed, the tension between the golden rule and the love command is heightened within the Lukan text itself: verses 27–28, which introduce the passage, command the reader to "Love your enemies, do good to those who hate you, bless those who curse you, pray for those who abuse you." Verse 31, which concludes the passage, commands precisely the golden rule: "Do to others as you would have them do to you."

The conjunction of these two ideals is vertiginous, to say the least. First, one is commanded to forgo reciprocity, then to uphold it. Yet, the disorientation does not signal contradiction. Rather, it disorients in order to reorient; what is reoriented is the very understanding of the golden rule. What love demands is that one not reciprocate evil for evil, but exercise a generosity of spirit toward others, even in the advent of evil. At the same time, this generosity of spirit extends to the golden rule. It is inclined away from a reactive interpretation of strict reciprocity, that is, do to others what they do to you, toward a proactive orientation that takes generosity as its keystone.

Ricoeur argued that the love command, placed as it is here within the logic of extremity, introduces, par excellence, the hyperethical orientation of the economy of the gift. The logic of this economy is well expressed farther on in Luke: "Be merciful, just as your Father is merciful" (Luke 6:36). The orientation of love structured by the economy of the gift results in the paradoxical reciprocity of escalating generosity: love as you have been loved, give as you have been given, forgive as you have been forgiven. Love's "mercy for mercy" has already been instituted. The economy of the gift has already been recognized in the experience of radical dependence through the recognition of creatureliness, in the revelation of liberation, in the subsistence of hope in promise.

I have given some outline to the configuring orientations of love and justice and, antecedent to this, the competing logics that structure them. However, I have yet to touch upon their foundations in experience: the relationship between theonomy and autonomy. A basic tension immediately presents itself: How does one hold together the idea of obedience to a principle outside of freedom itself and the self-legislative capacity of the autonomous will?

Experience: Autonomy and Theonomy

The confrontation between autonomy and theonomy represents the point of highest tension between the ideals of justice and love to the degree that principles of justice are predicated on free self-legislation. Ricoeur suggested, "At least at first blush, the idea of a legislation of divine origin must appear as a form of heteronomy, diametrically opposed to the presumed autonomy of moral consciousness."[37] The thinker that Ricoeur had in mind here was Immanuel Kant. Recall that Kant argued that morality and justice reside in the autonomous will and the capacity for pure self-legislation. This capacity is a necessary presupposition of most social contract theories of justice, which argue from principles that free contracting parties would rationally choose in an original contract situation. The tension between love and justice reaches its highest pitch here precisely in the fact that love of neighbor is commanded; its imperative force lies in a divine commandment and not in autonomy. Kant placed the admission of a divine command as the ground for ethics out of bounds by positing the self-legislating capacity of autonomy as moral foundation. The proposition of such a command radically calls into question the self-sufficiency of autonomy as the principle of ethics.

Remember, however, that Kant placed the ability for pure self-legislation outside the capacity of the human will. Only the good will is truly free because only the good will is naturally motivated by the good, the principle that secures autonomy. I, on the other hand, am motived by passion and desire. As such, I am likely to choose something other than the good. That is to say, I am likely to allow my actions to be directed by principles other than the good. When this happens, I fall into evil. I am responsible for evil because I freely choose a maxim to determine my action that is not in accord with the moral principle, the very principle that determines action as free. Because evil, or better, the genesis of an evil principle determining action, arises within freedom itself, freedom conceived in terms of pure autonomy, that is, pure self-legislation, is branded with incapacity. Thus is revealed the need for an agency beyond freedom, which would reestablish the capacity of autonomy, which would make freedom accessible.

The reality of moral fault marked the dividing line for Kant between moral philosophy and the philosophy of religion. The power of religion, insofar as religion is conceived within the limits of reason alone, is its configuration of the possibility of the restoration of the good principle in the determination of action, of the regeneration of the will, the restoration of freedom:

> When it is said, Man is created good, this can mean nothing more than: He is created *for good* and the original *predisposition* in man is good; not that, thereby, he is already actually good, but rather that he brings it about that he becomes good or evil, according to whether he adopts or does not adopt into his maxims the incentives which this predisposition carries with it. . . . Granted that some supernatural cooperation may be necessary to his becoming good . . . yet, whether this cooperation consists merely in the abatement of hindrances or indeed in positive assistance, man must first make himself worthy to receive it, and must *lay hold* of this aid (which is no small matter)—that is, he must adopt this positive increase of power into his maxim. . . . For despite the fall, the injunction that we *ought* to become better men resounds unabatedly in our souls; hence this must be within our power, even though what *we* are able to do is in itself inadequate and though we thereby only render ourselves susceptible of higher, and for us inscrutable, assistance.[38]

To this paradoxical situation, whereby freedom makes itself incapable, the philosophy of religion responds by positing of an inscrutable "higher power" that comes to aid in the restoration of autonomy. This does not relieve the will of its responsibility, for it remains to the will to make itself worthy of and to incorporate this assistance. Yet it is still the positing of divine agency, inscrutable as it may be, that relieves the aporia of a power, for which the will is responsible, which is beyond its power. Autonomy is saved, but at the cost of making itself unintelligible.

The strategy that Ricoeur adopted in juxtaposing the ideas of autonomy and theonomy is decidedly different. Indeed, it is precisely Kant's ideal of a self-sufficient autonomy that is at issue. With the idea of theonomy, Ricoeur sought to articulate a power outside the self which founds freedom, and in doing so he intentionally blurred the line between moral philosophy and theology:

> In that work [*Religion Within the Limits of Reason Alone*], reflection on religion actually starts out with a meditation on radical evil, and continues with an examination of the conditions for the regeneration of a moral subject: Is it on his or her own strength that the subject is regenerated, or is it with help from without? Expelled from moral philosophy, autonomy reappears in the philosophy of religion. The little

> that Kant concedes here to the idea of a gracious assistance suffices to prevent practical philosophy from being forbidden to open itself to the very particular dialectic between autonomy and what is called, on the strict plane of morality, heteronomy. To be sure, the philosophy of religion is not moral philosophy. But how can the dividing wall between, on the one hand, a morality that separates the *principle* of obligation from any taking account of the human *ability* to obey the law, and on the other, religion, which has no other object, according to Kant, than the regeneration of the moral subject—in other words, the restoration, or, better, the inauguration of an *able* moral subject—be kept watertight?[39]

The notion of a power that makes human freedom a possibility was encountered in chapter 3, first in the guise of Spinoza's idea of the life of God—what Ricoeur characterized as a ground of being at once actual and potential—and second in the biblical articulation of divine power as creation and redemption. This point, more than any other, offers the opportunity to test my central thesis that Ricoeur's religious writings are instrumental for understanding his philosophical project. The idea of theonomy represents precisely that articulation of a ground of being which makes human capability possible and human existence meaningful.

Ricoeur conceived the idea of theonomy in two stages. First, by exploring what he called the "scriptural sites of divine legislation," he hoped to indicate the scope of theonomy as it is presented by biblical symbols, metaphors, and narratives. Of course, the narrative of the giving of the decalogue in the revelation at Sinai takes central place in this analysis. However, the notion of divine law gains depth in its relation with the other scriptural sites that ground divine agency in relation with human beings and human history. These other scriptural sites are the creation stories, prophetic texts, and wisdom literature, among others. At a second stage, Ricoeur delineated the character and texture of theonomy that is constituted by these biblical symbols. In addressing these "traits of theonomy," I will follow a trajectory that runs from the relational character of the idea of *covenant*, through the twofold pulsation of unity/complexity within the dynamics of the idea of law itself, to the notion of *loving obedience* which arises out of the idea of the commandment, specifically the commandment to love.

Poetics of Theonomy

The giving of the law at Sinai is surely the principal scriptural site of divine legislation. At this point in the biblical worldview, God decisively enters history as legislator and judge. It is important to recognize the interconnection between this episode and the general narrative framework that surrounds it. This is significant for the juxtaposition of autonomy and theonomy because it is precisely in its entanglement with the narrative of the deliverance from Egypt that the law takes up its central place. What makes this situation remarkable is that, from this point on, the ideas of law and liberation become linked in the biblical imagination: "It is important for us to see that, on one side, the bestowal of the law is linked to an act of deliverance that founds the 'narrative' identity of the people of Israel. . . . The law, then, will be that of a free people, or at least, of a people called to freedom. But the counterpart is also important. Thus restored to its narrative framework, the law is seen to be inseparable from a gift consisting in a memorable event, an event worth recounting."[40] Thus, the ideas of law and freedom are linked, in much the same way as they are for Kant, but a law *and* a freedom that are inclined in a direction that he would surely have considered heteronomous and, hence, not morally valid.

A second linkage places the giving of the law in its interconnection with the trajectory of the Torah as a whole, and specifically in connection with the creation stories in Genesis. As Ricoeur explained, "The essential contribution of the creation stories is the idea of an origin older than all history, the idea of an anteriority antecedent to all memory. In a sense, the law participates in this antecedence of a creation always 'already there.'"[41] This interconnection of legislation and creation reveals the divine not merely entering at a particular point in history, but rather as the active principle that sustains history. In this sense, the law pertains not only to this particular time and place, but is crafted into the cosmos as such. It becomes part of the original and ongoing creative act.

At a third point of interconnection, Ricoeur addressed what he called the dialect of menace and hope that arises out of the voice of the prophets. The revelation at Sinai names God as protector and sustainer, while the prophetic texts name God as judge, as one who punishes and enslaves. Yet he argued that the most remarkable effect of this perspective, at least with regard to the idea of theonomy, "is a qualitative change in the injunction as such, which appears less and less as imposed from without and more and more as carved on hearts instead." This process is clear in the statements of Jeremiah and Ezekiel. It is revealed more clearly in the realization that the prophets of Israel lashed out not only at those who strayed from the law, but also those who misused it, those who interpreted the law such that they compounded injustice in the name of righteousness. As Abraham J. Heschel proclaimed in his seminal work on the Hebrew prophets, "The prophet faces a coalition of callousness and established authority, and undertakes to stop the mighty stream with mere words. . . . [T]he purpose of prophecy is to conquer callousness, to change the inner man as well as to revolutionize history."[42] To the extent that Jesus' ministry is placed within the compass of prophetic discourse, one can see the same effect in such statements as those concerning the interdictions of the Sabbath, for example, "The Sabbath was made for humankind, not humankind for the Sabbath" (Matt. 12:1–14, Mark 2:23–3:6, Luke 6:1–11). At stake here is the spirit as opposed to the letter of the law, to use a rather clichéd expression. Through this progressive questioning of the use of the law, through the progressive internalization of its guiding spirit, the law becomes less an object of legislation, and more the guiding *ethos* that grounds the relations between self and God, and between self and others. The prophetic genre is ethical discourse in its profoundest.

Ricoeur took as the final site of divine legislation the genre of wisdom literature concerning such themes as the origin of evil, justice and retribution, and, above all, the enigma of unjust suffering. He argued that wisdom discourse serves "to bind together *ethos* and *cosmos*, the sphere of human action and the sphere of the world." In significant ways, therefore, wisdom literature recapitulates the dimensions of creation and prophecy precisely by linking them. But, he continued, wisdom literature joins ethos and cosmos not by "demonstrating that this conjunction is given in things, nor by demanding that it be produced through our action. Rather it joins *ethos* and *cosmos* at the very point of their discordance: in suffering and, more precisely, in unjust suffering."[43] In this sense, wisdom literature does not tell one how to avoid suffering, nor how to deny it, but how to "suffer suffering." Take, for example, Job's repentance in the confrontation with the voice from the whirlwind. Ricoeur argued, "His questions about justice are undoubtedly left without answer. But by repenting, though not of sin, for he is righteous, but by repenting for his supposition that existence does not make sense, Job presupposes an unexpected meaning which cannot be transcribed by speech or *logos* a human being may have at his disposal."[44] If one stops to consider this statement, I would suggest that Ricoeur intended a poetics of theonomy, not so much opposed to rational speculation as complementary to it. If this is a valid interpretation, then wisdom literature can be conceived as *poesis*, which responds to the impasses of *logos*. The poetics of theonomy responds to the inscrutability of freedom in light of radical evil.

In a second stage, Ricoeur addressed what he called the "traits of theonomy." He attempted to give a general account of the idea of theonomy that is expressed poetically in biblical symbols, metaphors, and narratives. I turn to this second stage now.

Traits of Theonomy

The first aspect to be emphasized in this second stage of analysis is the relational character of theonomy entailed in the notion of *covenant*. It is not the case that God *imposes* a law on human relations, but rather, seeks to establish a covenant that directs relations with God and among individuals. While it must be admitted that this covenantal relation is not a relation among equals, it nonetheless takes on a remarkable quality of reciprocity in the form of an exchange of promises. Ricoeur explained, "To the *sought* promise of obedience there corresponds the *proffered* promise of succor. Thus is instituted a bond of 'fidelity to fidelity': two 'words given' are welded together. This doubly 'promissory' character of the covenant is essential for an understanding of the notion of theonomy." This double promise of the covenant establishes the two sides of the category "before God." First, God is revealed as the one who follows the chosen through their history of trial and tribulation, the one who offers protection and comfort. At the same time, however, the experience of being before God, the recognition of the promise of support and protection, imposes a responsibility for a promise of obedience. Ricoeur continued, "Here is the other side of the coin of the 'before God' category: free consent is sought within a nonetheless unequal relation."[45] It is in this sense that covenant issues in legislation.

The whole issue of law is not a simple one, however. Ricoeur claimed that the idea of law is subject to a "twofold pulsation": on the one, there is a thrust toward a fundamental level of legislation, which seeks to gather together and unify the various codes toward a common purpose; on the other, there is the tendency toward complexity and multiplication into "ever finer layers of legislation." To some extent, this bifurcation in biblical accounts of the law mimics the process of constitutional law: while it is possible to conceive of a constitution in terms of a single entity, there is nonetheless a distinction to be made between what might be called general principles of law and constitutional rules. Constitutional law functions in the tension between these general principles, which are open to argument and interpretation, and rules that more closely approach the ideal of univocity. A comparable tension is at work in the legislation of the Torah. One sees the unifying impulse most profoundly at work in the commandments to love God and neighbor, the impulse to complexity in the Deuteronomic and Levitical codes. While the former compose the core content of the law, the latter interpret what this core content means and how it is to be achieved, how the principle is to be applied.

This core content of the law—love of God, love of neighbor—establishes the idea of theonomy in its crowning glory. With the commandment to love, both the depths and heights of theonomy are reached. However, there is reason to pause and contemplate the paradoxical nature of this commandment. Indeed, can love be commanded? Does it even make sense to command love? Is love not rather an affection that is either present or not present, fundamentally beyond the dictates of law? In addressing this enigma, Ricoeur turned to Franz Rosenzweig's *The Star of Redemption*; at the conceptual and compositional center of this monumental work resides the revelatory character of the love command.[46] Indeed, for Rosenzweig, the command to love, issuing from the mouth of God, is the core of revelation. Addressing the enigma of the love command directly, Rosenzweig exclaimed:

> Yes of course, love cannot be commanded. No third party can command it or extort it. No third party can, but the One can. The commandment to love can only proceed from the mouth of the lover. Only the lover can and does say: love me!—and he really does so. In his mouth the commandment to love is not a strange commandment; it is none other than the voice of love itself. The love of the lover has, in fact, no word to express itself other than the commandment. Everything else is no longer direct expression but already declaration—declaration of love. A declaration of love is a very poor thing; like every declaration it always comes behindhand and thus, since the love of the lover is present time, the declaration of love is in reality always too late.[47]

God directly addresses the individual in the immediacy of the moment. In this direct address, the command takes on its imperative overtones.

Ricoeur argued that what Rosenzweig was employing here was a "poetic use of the imperative." As such the love command makes use of the whole poetic matrix of the biblical text, most immediately poetic praise. Ricoeur explained that "[t]hanks to this kinship between the command 'Love me!' and the song of praise, the commandment of love is revealed as being irreducible, in its ethical overtones, to the moral imperative, so legitimately equated by Kant to obligation, or duty, with reference to the recalcitrance of human inclinations."[48] This irreducibility of the poetic imperative to the imperative of duty raises another issue, that of the relationship between the commandment and the idea of law. There is a distinction to be made here, Rosenzweig asserted, due to the fact that the love command exists only in the present. Laws, on the other hand, are concerned to set a standard by which to dictate future actions. He claimed, "Law reckons with times, with a future, with duration. The commandment knows only the moment; it awaits the result in the very instant of its promulgation. And if it possesses the magic of the true voice of command, it will truly never be disappointed in this expectation."[49] Indeed, it is from this one command that all commandments and laws issue.

This is most profoundly the case with the commandment that has taken up so much space in these final analyses, the love of neighbor. Rosenzweig argued that it is only in light of the command "love me!," which paradoxically secures the soul as beloved of God beyond any declaration of love, that love of neighbor is possible. The clarity of purpose in the love of neighbor, outstripping any willing "in general" proposed by the idea of autonomy, is fundamentally directed by the commandment that proceeds from the lover: "This love [of neighbor] originates in the directed freedom of the character, and this commandment needs a presupposition beyond freedom. *Fac quod jubes et jube quod vis* means that God's 'ordaining what he will' must, since the content of the present ordinance is to love, be preceded by God's 'already having done' what he ordains. Only the soul beloved of God can receive the commandment to love its neighbor and fulfill it."[50] Who is the neighbor? This concept has been placed within the logic of extremity by extending love even to the enemy. Rosenzweig extended this logic even farther: "Love goes out to whatever is nighest to it as a representative, in the fleeting moment of its presentness, and thereby in truth to the all-inclusive concept of all men and all things which could ever assume this place of being its nighest neighbor. In the final analysis it goes out to everything, to the world."[51] In this extreme case, the one I see is life as such, life conceived in its broadest possible sense—the "coming into being" of the world.

What, then, is the outcome of this disorienting logic that takes us from the commandment, to the love of neighbor, extending the designation of neighbor even to enemies and, finally, to life? Ricoeur offered a deceptively simple formula: "Love obliges." "Only sundered from its source—the commandment to love—is there any scandal in an interhuman love (a 'horizontal' love, so to speak); that the lover's love obliges is a surprise, but not a scandal."[52] But, to what does love oblige? Again the deceptively simple response: to *loving obedience*. Loving obedience to what? Oddly, to love itself. The outcome seems to have opened more questions than it has provided answers. What does loving obedience to love mean? And, more importantly, what does it tell us about Ricoeur's philosophical project? I will explore these questions in the final chapter by analyzing the kind of critical rapproachment between ideals of love and justice that Ricoeur sought.

Chapter Six

The Economy of the Gift and the Poetic Imperative

I have argued throughout that Ricoeur's religious writings provide an important interpretive key to the overall coherence of his thought. I have charted several key places where his thought opens onto theological matters, revealing the degree to which Ricoeur's philosophical project made an approach to religious discourse possible. These places tend to revolve around dimensions of his moral philosophy. Speculation over the radical nature of evil was the point of initiation for many "philosophical approximations" of religious themes and symbols. Ricoeur's early appropriation of the theology of hope was spurred by this concern over radical evil. But these forays into theological matters always appeared somewhat peripheral to his central philosophical concerns. In advancing my argument, I have attempted to press these theological matters more to the center of Ricoeur's philosophy. I have uncovered the degree to which biblical discourse lends itself to meaningful existence. This borrowing from religious discourse becomes even more pronounced at the level of ethics. Biblical symbols, metaphors, and narratives provide poetic resolutions to problems as diverse as the enigma of moral evil and philosophy's self-imposed silence with regard to the source of moral conscience.

In concluding, I want to explore these aspects of Ricoeur's thought in a more focused and more creative manner. I will remain faithful to his ideas, but I want to explore aspects of those ideas in ways that Ricoeur himself did not. These concluding reflections will proceed in three stages. First, I will return to the peculiar notion of an economy of the gift that appeared in the last chapter. Second, I will expand upon the critical rapproachment that Ricoeur sought to articulate between the ideals of love and justice. This exploration opens onto a third, about which Ricoeur did not go into detail, concerning the idea of a "poetic use of the imperative" that arose out of his engagement with Franz Rosenzweig's ideas. This final stage will allow me to make some tentative conclusions about the importance of theological orientations in Ricoeur's philosophy.

The Economy of the Gift

Addressing the now-familiar relationship between the golden rule and the love command, Ricoeur wrote:

> It is this commandment [to love one's enemies], not the golden rule, that seems to constitute the expression closest, on the ethical plane, to what I have called the economy of the gift. This expression approximating the economy of the gift can be placed under the title of a logic of superabundance, which is opposed as an opposite pole to the logic of equivalence that governs everyday morality. . . . Detached from the golden rule, the commandment to love one's enemies is not ethical but supraethical, as is the whole economy of the gift to which it belongs. If it is not to swerve over to the nonmoral, or even the immoral, the commandment to love must reinterpret the golden rule and, in so doing, be itself reinterpreted by this rule.[1]

This passage offers the reader a number of enigmatic expressions, but the most enigmatic of all is the notion of an "economy of the gift."[2] What could Ricoeur have meant by *economy of the gift*? At the level of general reflection, it is at least difficult to think the ideas of "economy"and "gift" together. In a passage that has now become iconic, Adam Smith explained economic transactions as such: "It is not from the benevolence of the butcher, the brewer, or the baker, that we expect our dinner, but from their regard to their own interest. We address ourselves not to their humanity but to their self-love, and never talk to them of our necessities but of their advantages."[3] A gift, on the other hand, is something quite different. A gift is something that is given to another out of generosity, without an interest in return. Ideally, it is precisely out of the benevolence of the giver that the gift is proffered. Intuitively, economy and gift have little in common and, in fact, seem diametrically opposed.

However, while we intuitively oppose gift and economy, this intuition is misleading. At least since the publication of Marcel Mauss's anthropological study *The Gift*, it has become difficult, if not impossible, to think the terms *economy* and *gift* apart from each other. Mauss argued that it is not the case that gift and economy are diametrically opposed, as one might suppose. He claimed, in fact, that exchange systems based on mutual gift giving precede and are the basis for modern, abstract, market economic systems.[4] Still others, following in Mauss's footsteps, state the relationship more pointedly. Claude Lévi-Strauss, for instance, credited Mauss for recognizing that gifting is not a completely altruistic, disinterested activity, but he criticized Mauss for failing to recognize the true nature of gifting: to initiate, in a veiled fashion, a relationship of exchange. The gift disguises the true motives of those engaged in economic exchange.[5] More pointedly still, Pierre Bourdieu suggests that gift and economy are both examples of social practices through which systems of domination/authority are established and maintained. In other words, both gift exchange and free market exchange are economic practices, broadly construed. Both are employed to garner a share of the material and/or symbolic capital that improves one's lot in the given social hierarchy.[6]

At the other end of the spectrum are those who oppose the connection made between gift and economy. Jacques Derrida was among the most vocal critics of Mauss and others in this regard. Derrida did not claim that the gift is unrelated to exchange; Mauss's great insight stands: gift and economy are related. But, he argued, they are related only as mutually exclusive concepts. "One cannot treat the gift, this goes without saying, without treating this relation to economy, even to money economy. But is not the gift, if there is any, also that which interrupts economy?"[7] The advent of the gift, if such exists, interrupts the very possibility for a calculation of return, hence the possibility of economy. Gift stands as the irreducible (and impossible) other of economy, fundamentally an *aneconomic* phenomenon.

Like Derrida, Jean-Luc Marion seeks to preserve the gift from falling into economy, but without reducing it to the impossible other of economy. Marion argues that the gift can be disconnected from the horizon of economic relations once it is reduced to pure *givenness*, that is, through the triple phenomenological bracketing of givee, giver, and given object. Through this bracketing, the gift reveals itself, *shows* itself, as that which *gives itself* as gift. Once the gift is so understood within a phenomenology of pure givenness, it becomes the principle mode of the appearance of all phenomena: "The exclusion of exchange and the reduction of transcendencies finally define the gift as purely immanent. Givenness characterizes it intrinsically, no longer extrinsically. . . . This being done, we will observe a decisive point: the way in which the gift gives itself coincides exactly with the way in which the phenomenon shows itself."[8] Elsewhere, Marion places the advent of the gift in explicitly theological terms, arguing that the gift is a fundamental act of charity extending from the divine that is most especially manifest in a eucharistic hermeneutic. The eucharist reveals the divine gift of the Christ by manifesting the true meaning of the biblical word: "It alone allows the text to pass to its referent, recognized as the Word of the words. . . . The Word intervenes in the Eucharist (in person, because only in this way does he manifest and perform his filiation) to accomplish in this way the hermeneutic."[9] In a similar way, Calvin O.

Schrag argues that gift is other than economy. However, Schrag attempts to set gift and economy in a relationship of "transversality," which "exhibits the interrelated sense of lying across, extending over, contact without absorption, convergence without coincidence, and unity without strict identity."[10] The gift is the transcendent other of economy which breaks in, disrupts, and reorients it. As transcendent other, the gift is also associated with the divine, Schrag argues.

Given the complexity of these viewpoints, what could Ricoeur possibly have meant by the phrase *economy of the gift*? He was hardly unaware of the history of scholarship on the idea of the gift. Either the gift is of a piece with economy and "economy of the gift" borders on tautology, or the gift is radically (impossibly) *aneconomic* and "economy of the gift" is absurd. The fact that Ricoeur presented the idea with little explanation, as if it were unproblematic and unencumbered, makes its presence all the more jarring. There are, however, resources in Ricoeur's thought that lend some perspective to this odd predication of an economy of the gift.

The first place to look in uncovering the meaning of Ricoeur's strange turn of phrase is his theory of metaphor. On Ricoeur's understanding, metaphor functions on the basis of an "impertinent predication." The metaphor presents the hearer/reader with an absurdity at the literal level of the statement; it therefore requires a suspension of the literal meaning so that a figurative, and truly novel, meaning can emerge. Ricoeur argued that metaphor is "a semantic event that takes place at the point where several semantic fields intersect. It is because of this construction that all the words, taken together, make sense."[11] The use of metaphor is a literary/rhetorical strategy that plays on predicative impertinence in order to produce new meaning.

This theory of metaphor gives some initial purchase on the meaning of the phrase "economy of the gift." It is possible to think of gift and economy as two distinct conceptual realities that function, or become meaningful, on the basis of two different semantic fields. Unlike Bourdieu, Ricoeur was reticent about consigning the gift to the field of economic practices. There is reason to preserve the difference even if it is not clear-cut in practice. The gift has a linguistic, conceptual, and semantic context that is distinct from economic relations. Thus, two disparate semantic fields exist that cannot be thought together except as distinct realities, or perhaps more accurately, cannot be thought except together as distinct realities. In lumping gift and economy together, perhaps Ricoeur was playing on the intersection of semantic fields to see what gifts of meaning arise. But if this is so, one must consider what, if any, meanings one is gifted with. In answering this question I look to Ricoeur's understanding of the referential economy of narrative.

The move from metaphor to narrative is a natural one in Ricoeur's *oeuvre*. The two function as partners, so to speak, in the production of *semantic innovation*, the one dealing at the level of rhetorical tropes and figures of discourse, the other at the level of literary genres and the synthesis of plots. I have shown that narratives function on the basis of a conflictual encounter similar to the one that drives metaphor: the exchange of narrative discord and concord in the synthesis of the plot. The plot transforms discordant events into a concordant whole at the end of the narrative. Just as the metaphor gives new meaning *through* the impertinence of attributes at the literal level of the statement, narrative offers new possibilities for consideration *through* the introduction of discordant events, which are brought into concord through the narrative economy of the plot. The narrative therefore functions like an extended metaphor.

The narrative plot is, then, a configuration of events engaged in the act of reading. The reader becomes "contemporaneous" with the narrative; that is to say, the reader is invited to inhabit the story. This understanding led Ricoeur to propose the threefold mimetic structure of narrative engagement that I addressed in chapter 3. Through this threefold *mimesis*, the narrative "produces" reality. Put differently, the narrative is genuinely productive of meanings by virtue of the refiguration of possibilities and the invitation to the reader to inhabit and/or adopt those possibilities. This, Ricoeur argued, is a function of poetic texts in general, poetic understood in the broad sense of imaginative literary constructions:

> To understand these texts is to interpolate among the predicates of our situation all those meanings that, from a simple environment (*Umwelt*), make a world (*Welt*). Indeed, we owe a large part of the enlarging of our horizon of existence to poetic works. Far from producing only weakened images of reality . . . literary works depict reality by augmenting it with meanings that themselves depend upon the virtues of abbreviation, saturation, and culmination, so strikingly illustrated by emplotment. . . . For some years now I have maintained that what is interpreted in a text is the proposing of a world that I might inhabit and into which I might project my ownmost powers. In the *Rule of Metaphor*, I held that poetry, through its *muthos*, redescribes the world. In the same way, in this work I will say that making a narrative [*le faire narratif*] resignifies the world in its temporal dimension, to the extent that narrating, telling, reciting is to remake action following the poem's invitation.[12]

This understanding of the function of poetic literary constructs offers the path of least resistance to an understanding of what Ricoeur meant by economy of the gift.

The approach to the idea of an economy of the gift from the angle of poetic narrative is telling because of the point at which this idea entered Ricoeur's conceptual vocabulary: in his account of the theological (and primarily Christian) narrative of salvation history. As a hermeneutical thinker, Ricoeur was always interested in the primary texts of this tradition, and he typically approached them as special cases of poetic literary construction. That Ricoeur saw a profound connection between poetic expression and religious discourse is without question. In his writings on the issue of religion, Ricoeur always privileged religious *discourse* over religious *experience*. This is not to say that the religious is more a linguistic phenomenon than an experiential one; he withheld judgment on this question: "What is said is only this: whatever may be the nature of the so-called religious experience, it comes to language, it is articulated in a language, and the most appropriate place to interpret it on its own terms is to inquire into its linguistic expression."[13] He also privileged written discourse over spoken discourse because interpretation is less an issue in the situation of speech. If there is a question of meaning, I am free to ask my interlocutor what s/he intends. The speaker has, among other things, the benefit of ostensive reference to make the point clear. Such is not the case for written discourse, most especially when the writer is no longer available for questioning. This is quintessentially the case for Ricoeur's example of the originary expressions of the encounter with the holy, the Jewish and Christian biblical texts. The claim that the engagement with the text requires the detour through interpretation because of lack of direct referential markers to ground meaning does not, however, entail the stronger claim that the text lacks all referential markers. In fact, Ricoeur argued that texts do employ reference in revolutionary ways that make them fundamentally important carriers of meaning. They do this by suspending the ostensive reference of the face to face encounter and the author's original intention in composing the text—the author's intention may be relevant, but it is no longer decisive. Through this double suspension of immediate reference and authorial intention, the written discourse becomes an autonomous entity that projects a world of possibilities "in front of itself." Through the confluence of literary structures—plot, literary and rhetorical figures, intertextual reference, etc.—the text appeals to the reader. As I showed in chapter 3, the narrative presents the reader with a world of possibilities and invites him/her to inhabit that world. What the reader engages, then, through the hermeneutical interaction with the text is what Ricoeur called the "world of the text" or the "issue of the text."

The Christian narrative of salvation history, as Ricoeur conceived it, is a "secondary" theological discourse that is constructed over the foundation of what he called "originary expressions" of religious experience found principally scattered throughout the biblical texts. I addressed this set of ideas in chapter 3 in terms of the hermeneutics of testimony. These originary expressions form a "polyphonous" discourse that functions to "name" God. In other words, the biblical texts are a collection of literary genres and theological traditions from a range of different time periods that attempt to give expression to the experience of the holy. These texts are not univocal in their expressions. The narrative texts name God differently than the prophetic texts, which in turn name God differently than the wisdom literature. Nonetheless, they together serve to name God in the fundamental attributes of creator and redeemer. The issue of the texts is God as creator and redeemer, attributes that have appeared at key places throughout these analyses.

Ricoeur's ultimate interest was what the poetic texts engender *in the imagination* through the act of reading, and here one comes upon some of the more revolutionary aspects of his thought. He wished to unfold the hermeneutical aspects of what Immanuel Kant called the "productive imagination." Kant discussed the productive imagination as a form of norm-governed invention (that is, the imagination functions on the basis of schemata that determine the bounds of imaginative variation) and as a power that gives form to human experience (that is, the productive imagination takes the "raw data" of experience and synthesizes them into a meaningful structure).[14] Ricoeur paraphrased Kant to mean by the productive imagination, among other things, "the power of redescribing reality." The writing and the reading of fiction manifests, in Ricoeur's estimation, the hermeneutical dimension of the productive imagination: "Fiction is my name for the imagination considered under this double point of view of rule-governed invention and a power of redescription."[15]

Ricoeur saw this work of redescription of the productive imagination to be closely linked to the originary expressions of the experience of the holy at work in the biblical texts. These biblical texts then function as a powerful redescription of reality; when the reader engages these texts in a serious manner s/he is asked to consider reality from the perspective of this redescription and to participate in the power of redescription:

> I would like to consider the act of reading as a dynamic activity that is not confined to repeating significations fixed forever, but which takes place as a prolonging of the itineraries of meaning opened up by the work of interpretation. Through this first trait, the act of reading accords with the idea of a norm-governed productivity to the extent that it may be said to be guided by a productive imagination at work in the text itself. Beyond this, I would like to see in the reading of a text such as the Bible a creative operation unceasingly employed in decontextualizing its meaning and recontextualizing it in today's *Sitz-im-Leben*. Through this second trait, the act of reading realizes the union of fiction and redescription that characterizes the imagination in the most pregnant sense of this term.[16]

To read the biblical texts is to participate in the redescription of reality initiated by the text and completed in the reader. What the texts offer to the imagination is, among other things, a *moral* redescription of reality brought about through the interaction of the ideal of the golden rule and that of the love command.

Most important for my purposes here, a notion of the *giftedness of existence* takes shape against the backdrop of the naming of God. In the previous chapter I highlighted the supramoral quality that Ricoeur located in the giftedness of existence that rises out of the biblical symbols of creation and redemption. This supramoral quality becomes more manifest as the gift is exposed to the idea of moral reciprocity, that is, as it comes into contact with economic rationality in its moral manifestation of justice. If one takes the golden rule as the most general practical expression of moral justice, one recognizes in this rule a dimension of economic rationality broadly conceived as reasoning that functions on the basis of a calculation of returns, reciprocation, or, as I referred to it in the last chapter, a logic of *equivalence*. At its most basic, the golden rule asserts that I ought to perform the good for others that I would like for myself. One might suggest that, implicit in this statement, is a hope that the good I perform might be reciprocated by the other, though this is not explicit. The supramoral quality of the biblical symbols of creation and redemption is manifest in the fact that they reveal existence as a gift that cannot be reciprocated. The God who is poetically named in the narratives of creation and redemption is the God with whom humans cannot hold relations of equivalence; the gift of existence, original and redeemed, cannot be returned to the giver. These two ideas, supramoral gift of existence and moral economy of the golden rule, operate as the two semantic fields that Ricoeur sought to bring together in the notion of an economy of the gift. This notion ultimately finds expression, therefore, in the exchange between the two seemingly opposed biblical ideals that I addressed in the previous chapter. Thus, it is to the rapprochement of love and justice that I now turn.

Love and Justice

The first point to be made in the critical rapprochement of the ideals of love and justice is that love requires *more*, and not less, than justice. This character of love to demand more than justice marks it as supramoral. At the same time, it is this character that preserves the hypermoral from devolving into the amoral, or worse, the immoral. Because love demands more than justice, love often demands a dimension of self-sacrifice, most notably in the form of renouncing a strict reciprocity. Nonetheless, this demand for self-sacrifice is not equivalent to a demand for complacency in the face of injustice nor to a demand for self-negation and self-denigration. Indeed, I have suggested, following Rosenzweig, that the love command is constitutive of the self as such, a suggestion I will explore in more detail shortly. This alone ought to preserve the character of love from its perverse interpretations. Beyond this, however, the *more-than-justice* of love marks out the intersection of the two ideals in its depth. Ricoeur argued:

> The tension we have discerned in place of our initial antinomy is not equivalent to the suppression of the contrast between our two logics. Nevertheless, it does make justice the necessary medium of love; precisely because love is hypermoral, it enters the practical and ethical sphere only under the aegis of justice. . . . In one sense, the commandment to love, as hyperethical, is a way of suspending the ethical, which is reoriented only at the price of a reprise and a rectification of the rule of justice that runs counter to its utilitarian tendency.[17]

In other words, the supramoral ideal of love is drawn in the direction of an authentic interpretation only so long as it remains within the compass of its relationship with the ideal of justice. What, then, is the character of the *more-than-justice* that love demands?

Recall that a general feature of many theories of justice is the tendency to characterize the goods with which justice is concerned as scarce. John Rawls, for instance, argued that a just society is both a cooperative and a competitive venture. Citizens are led to cooperate because they realize that life is better in society with others. But, they also compete over the manner in which the goods society offers are to be distributed. Each wants the greatest possible share s/he can get. The fact that justice is a form of economic rationality intensifies this fact. Remember that Adam Smith based economic activity on competition and rational self-interest. The circumstances of justice, namely, competition over moderately scarce goods, tend to portray others as competitors with whom I must bargain, or worse, as obstacles I must overcome, to get what I want. Ricoeur argued that the rule of justice, "given over to itself, tends to subordinate cooperation to competition, or rather to expect from the equilibrium of rival interests the simulacrum of cooperation."

The proximity of the golden rule and the command to love one's enemies in the gospel of Luke exposes this situation. I addressed the perverse interpretations to which the golden rule, left to its own, is not immune. These take two principal forms. First, the golden rule might be interpreted in terms of what I have called a reactive reciprocity: do to others what they do to you. It is this orientation that links the golden rule to the "eye for an eye" of the law of retribution. Second, and perhaps more insidious, the golden rule can be interpreted in terms of a kind of instrumental reciprocity: I give so that you will give. This interpretation, which inclines the golden rule in the direction of a refined form of utilitarian calculation, was Ricoeur's principle concern. He argued that posing the golden rule and love command along the lines of dynamic encounter, rather than static opposition, offers a profound solution to these dual tendencies:

> In this relation of living tension between the logic of superabundance and the logic of equivalence, the latter receives from its confrontation with the former the capacity of raising itself above its perverse interpretations. Without the corrective of the commandment to love, the golden rule would be constantly drawn in the direction of a utilitarian maxim whose formulation is *do ut des* (I give *in order that* you will give). The rule "Give *because* it has been given you" corrects the "in order that" of the utilitarian maxim and saves the golden rule from an always possible perverse interpretation. It is in this sense that we may interpret the harsh words of Luke 6:32–39, just after the reaffirmation of the golden rule in 6:31 and just before the reaffirmation of the new commandment in 6:35. In these intermediary verses the critical point of the logic of superabundance is directed not so much at the logic of equivalence of the golden rule as against its perverse interpretations.[18]

Thus, the supramoral category of love, paradoxically, preserves the moral from a fall into the immoral and saves reciprocity from its perversion into utility or retribution.

This creative tension strikes justice at its foundations because it is precisely out of the *more-than-justice*, the demand of loving obedience, that love calls for justice. But this is a call for justice, as Ricoeur stated, "reared" in the economy of gift, "for a justice that would frankly place the sense of mutual indebtedness above the confrontation between disinterested interests."[19] With the introduction of loving obedience the integrity of the other moves to the fore. At this critical juncture, moral concern becomes focused on responsibility to another who makes a claim on me: "In this sense, theonomy, understood as the call to a loving obedience, generates autonomy, understood as call to responsibility. Here we touch on a delicate point, where a certain *foundational passivity* joins with an active acceptance of responsibility."[20] Love comes to me as a call in the face of which I am passive. The call demands a response; response to the word is realized in responsibility to, responsibility *for*, the world. Theonomy is, therefore, generative of freedom. Response to the word issues in responsible spontaneity on behalf of the world. Love has an imperative structure, but this structure is funded by the poetry from which the call issues. As Ricoeur claimed, the love command offers a poetic use of the imperative. A deeper analysis of this idea will conclude my reflections.

The Poetic Imperative

Idea of conscience is perhaps the place in Ricoeur's thought where moral philosophy and theology stand in closest proximity. Recall Ricoeur's attempt to negotiate a path between Heidegger's "demoralized" account of conscience, which risks evacuating self-attestation of any ethical and moral concern, and Levinas's "deontologized" account, which risks reducing the phenomenon of conscience to the otherness of other persons. By setting the otherness of conscience in this context, Ricoeur conceived of conscience as a mediating structure between self-attestation and moral injunction. Yet, in attempting to carve out a space between these two reductions, Ricoeur claimed that philosophical discourse is reduced to silence with regard to the "Other" who confronts the self in conscience. This self-imposed silence on the part of philosophy offered an initial path for a theological construal of moral conscience.

As I pointed out, Ricoeur mounted a theological interpretation of moral conscience. This account centered on the idea of the summoned self, moving from the narratives of the prophetic call, through progressive internalizations, to the voice of conscience. He claimed that this summoned subject is "constituted and defined by its position as respondent to propositions of meaning issuing from the symbolic network I have previously described [that is, the polyphonous manner in which the bible *names* God]."[21] However, as enlightening as this interpretation might be, it seemed to turn into a theological interpretation of Heidegger's *strange(r)ness*: conscience was once again deflected away from the moral injunction. There is one avenue, however, that Ricoeur did not explore in the journey that leads from the prophetic call to the voice of conscience: Rosenzweig's account of the love command.[22] This is not overly surprising; Rosenzweig rarely, if ever, touched on the topic of conscience, and the idea of a direct address is problematic from Ricoeur's perspective. Still, the possibilities that Rosenzweig's account offers to the idea of "*being-enjoined as the structure of selfhood*" are tantalizing to say the least.

It will be useful to pause and examine what this notion entails. I argued in chapter 1 that there are two themes that underwent a parallel development in Ricoeur's philosophical anthropology: the creative tension between activity and passivity, which serves as a kind of ontic characteristic of selfhood in general, and the idea of promising, which grounds the moral dimensions of the self considered as a capable agent. In important ways, the idea of being-enjoined as the structure of selfhood, which most adequately characterized conscience in Ricoeur estimation, yokes these two themes together. One can trace the development of activity/passivity and promising across the studies that compose my treatment of Ricoeur's thought.

In chapter 2, I argued that Ricoeur's account of agency is structured by the idea of capability, configured in identity, and experienced as attestation. The basic structure of capability focused on the reciprocity between the voluntary and involuntary structures of action and will. The configuration of identity addressed the dual designation of *idem* and *ipse*. The experience of attestation explored the idea of an initiative traversed by forms of passivity. This initial analysis gave rise to the themes of activity/passivity and promising in their most general forms, and each took on more determinate characteristics as I progressed.

In chapter 3, I dealt with the idea of meaningful existence that is structured by understanding, configured in terms of possibility, and experienced as affirmation. The explication of understanding dealt with the active receptive synthesis of meaning in imagination through the confrontation with a world that presents itself to perception. Meaningful existence is configured, I argued, in terms of possibility through the synthetic operation of emplotment. Through the fusion of horizons between the world of the reader and the narrative world, reflection is opened to an ontological ground of being that is both actual and potential. The analysis of the experience of meaningful existence in terms of affirmation took this notion of an ontological ground in a decidedly theological direction. I traced the experience of affirmation from the idea of primary affirmation, through the biblical symbols of creation and redemption, to the hermeneutics of testimony.

At the end of this journey through the configuration of meaningful existence, the two themes of activity/passivity and of the idea of the promise reappeared, but in slightly different forms. In addressing agency, I located the first of these themes in Ricoeur's work in the form of an initiative that is traversed by forms of passivity, broadly construed. In chapter 3, passivity took on a more determinate form of receptivity to objects that present themselves to perception, ideals that lend direction to actions, and inherited meanings that encompass the process of understanding itself. Even more importantly, passivity took the form here of dependence upon a power to which the self is receptive for its very capacities for selfhood. The idea of the promise arose too, but this time from a different direction. Within biblical witness, the promise was conceived as a phenomenon coming to the self. While the discussion of agency addressed the self as the bearer of the promise, the analysis of meaningful existence conceived the self as the receiver of the promise that grounds meaning.

In chapter 4, I took up the idea of practical experience, which I claimed is structured by responsibility, configured by ethics, and experienced as witness. At the first level of basic structure, I sought to offer an expanded account of responsibility in terms of responsibility *to* persons and responsibility *for* actions. In addressing the configuration of ethics, I explored Ricoeur's presentation of the interaction between the ethical aim and the moral norm. Finally, practical experience was directed toward the witness to considered convictions about moral obligations within specific situations.

The theme of activity/passivity took on a more veiled form in the analysis of practical experience, but it arose nonetheless. The expansion of the idea of responsibility into the dual designations of responsibility *to* and responsibility *for* lent a more determinate sense to the ontic characteristic of activity/passivity. This expanded account made responsibility *for*, that is, the active sense of "holding oneself responsible," dependent upon responsibility *to*. My holding my self responsible *for* my actions only becomes meaningful, in a moral sense, within the realm of my responsibility *to* another and his/her moral claim on me, a claim to which I am receptive in moral concern. This account squares nicely with the understanding of fidelity that I addressed at the level of witness to considered convictions. But it should be noted that the idea of fidelity represented a further determination of the theme of promising. Promising is not merely a matter of remaining constant in the future to the word I give in the present; it is also a matter of being open to another's expectation that I will keep the promise that I have given. A promise is a promise because someone has a legitimate claim to my fidelity. As these two themes developed, they approached each other, and this was particularly the case in the theological trajectory of Ricoeur's ethical thought.

In chapter 5, I adopted the idea of conscience as a lens through which to explore a theological perspective in Ricoeur's thought. This analysis followed the same threefold organization of structure (logic of equivalence/logic of superabundance), configuration (golden rule/love command), and experience (autonomy/ theonomy) that has directed my entire project. But there are broader issues that must be addressed here. For one, the idea of conscience presents us with something of an overlapping of the two themes of activity/passivity and promising. The summons/response structure of conscience lends a new dimension of meaning to the relationship between responsibility *to* and responsibility *for*, even if this new dimension is more poetic than philosophical. The theological interpretation of conscience only heightens this factor. But this summons/response structure places the ontic characteristic of activity/passivity itself with the domain of morality because Ricoeur attempted to establish conscience as a mediating term between attestation and injunction. To attest to oneself in conscience *is* to respond to the injunction that comes to one. I attest to myself as an acting and suffering being through the capacity to respond faithfully to the moral claims of another, through the bond of fidelity to another. This overlapping of the ontic and moral characteristics of selfhood, I suggest, captures the profundity of Ricoeur's claim that being-enjoined is the structure of self.

In concluding, I want to begin to articulate what I have called the poetic imperative. I want to suggest that one can locate a line of development that leads from Ricoeur's account of the testimony of conscience to the proposal of a poetic imperative encapsulated in the love command. I argued in chapter 5 that the testimony of conscience opens onto theological ethics through the idea of value. Ricoeur defined conscience as a relation to instances qualified by the difference between good and evil, that is, instances qualified by moral value. I claimed that this recognition of value in particular instances functioned as a sort of philosophical approximation of the theological idea of love of creation. That is to say, the recognition of value in conscience is the approximation of an idea that is expressed figuratively in the biblical notion of the love command.

Ricoeur gave a privileged place to Rosenzweig's account of the love command, and he claimed that Rosenzweig employed a poetic use of the imperative in unfolding the profound nature of the love command. Rosenzweig's understanding of the love command lends itself to Ricoeur's discussion of conscience at two key points. First, it answers to the silence that Ricoeur imposed on philosophical discourse with regard to the otherness of the voice of conscience. While philosophy pulls up short with regard to naming the source of the voice, Rosenzweig, at once a philosophical and a theological thinker, located the summons as the word issued by the divine. Secondly, the love command places the theological interpretation of the voice of conscience back within the realm of moral concern.

I have addressed the particular place that the love command holds in *The Star of Redemption*. It serves as the ground for all ethical orientations and, as such, holds a place analogous to the categorical imperative in Kant's moral philosophy. Yet, Ricoeur argued that the love command cannot be reduced to the moral imperative, but is instead funded in its meaning as an imperative by figurative biblical expressions that revolve around the idea of theonomy. His principal purpose in posing the ideas of autonomy and theonomy was to show how freedom is inhabited by a sense of heteronomy that is not pathological in the Kantian sense, but truly empowering. The articulation of theonomy was funded by the many biblical symbols and themes that organize the relationship between human initiative and divine power, for instance, creatureliness, absolute dependence, deliverance from bondage, redemption. This same force was present in Rosenzweig's account of the love command; the commandment awakens the self to its nature as a part of the unfolding of creation. This awakening into self-recognition prepares the individual for openness to the other, *makes him/her capable* of love of neighbor.

Despite the apparent similarities, however, there is a fundamental incongruity between Rosenzweig's account of the love command and Ricoeur's account of conscience that precludes any easy reduction of one to the other. Rosenzweig's understanding of the command as direct address is extremely problematic for a position such as Ricoeur's, which rested so heavily on the idea of mediation. With regard specifically to the metaphor of the voice,

Ricoeur stated, "Christian faith does not simply consist in saying that it is God who speaks in our conscience. This immediateness professed by Rousseau in his 'The Profession of Faith of a Savoyard Priest' ('conscience! conscience! divine voice . . .') misconstrues the mediation of interpretation between the autonomy of conscience and the obedience of faith."[23] I do not believe, however, that this divergence precludes one from allowing Ricoeur's account to be informed by the love command conceived in terms of a poetic imperative. If one continues to speak of conscience as a voice, s/he must stress the *metaphorical* nature of this characterization. However, this limitation should not be regretted; it should not even be viewed as a limitation. The metaphor of the voice discloses the wealth of meaning surrounding the word *conscience* that cannot be uncovered any other way. And the temptation to equate the summons-like character of the voice of conscience with a direct address from the divine reveals the deep connections that exist between conscience and the poetic imperative structure of the love command.

Such a connection exists in Ricoeur's thought. It becomes more explicit in the link he established between conscience and the scriptural word:

> It is to the extent that the self is capable of judging itself "in conscience" that it can respond in a responsible way to the word that comes to it through scripture. . . . Therefore, it is regarding this articulation that we need to reflect further, between a conscience in which, in the spirit of the Enlightenment, we have discovered autonomy, and a confession of faith in which, in the spirit of hermeneutics, we have discovered a mediate and symbolic structure. . . . The Christian is someone who discerns "conformity to the image of Christ" in the call of conscience. This discernment is an interpretation. And this interpretation is the outcome of a struggle for veracity and intellectual honesty.[24]

Conscience touches faithful obedience in the self's capacity to respond to the word, which arises out of the mediating symbolic structure of scripture, the deposit of absolute testimony to the absolute. The love command affects conscience *through* testimony in all its density and in its connection with the poetic discourse of biblical texts. In this sense, the love command functions as a poetic imperative, indeed *is* a poetic imperative.

The love command has an imperative structure. It is a commandment, after all. But, it also serves as a ground for praxis, at least as Rosenzweig conceived it:

> [T]he sole commandment of love is simply incapable of being law; it can only be commandment. . . . For this reason, as the only pure commandment, it is the highest of all commandments, and where it takes

> the first place as such, there everything else too becomes commandment though otherwise, and viewed from without, it could as well be law. God's first word to the soul that unlocks itself to him is "Love me!" And everything which he may reveal to the soul in the form of law therefore without more ado turns into words which he commands it "today." It turns into execution of the one initial commandment to love him.[25]

The soul awakened by love acts on the basis of love. Love becomes the ground for acting as such. For this reason, the love command partakes of the nature of the imperative.

But the love command functions poetically as well. Recall that the nature of the poetic, as Ricoeur understood it, lies in the power of redescription: poetic works function by virtue of their power to redescribe reality. This poetic function of the love command is revealed in how it affects justice. Remember Ricoeur's claim that loving obedience gives rise to a sense of justice "reared in the economy of the gift." The economy of the gift came to light within the structure that Ricoeur called the logic of superabundance. I addressed this excessive logic first through an analysis of the extreme sayings attributed to Jesus in the gospel of Matthew, and secondly through the discourse of the lilies of the field a few verses on in Matthew. As Robert Tannehill suggested, these extreme and extravagant statements serve to reorient attention toward reality. They reconfigure experience in terms of security and abundance. As Tannehill pointed out, "We experience a heightened awareness and the disturbing impingement of another reality." This other reality, Ricoeur characterized under the title of the economy of the gift. So what is justice reared in this economy?

Again, theories of justice tend to characterize the goods with which justice deals as moderately scarce. Justice functions on a competing logic of equivalence because the question of fair and equitable shares becomes an issue under conditions of moderate scarcity; if the goods in question were not hard to come by, no one would compete to get a "fair share." Thus, justice casts relations in terms of competition: I must compete or bargain with others to get what I want and need. However, if justice is reared in the economy of the gift, then the concern for justice becomes touched by the redescription of reality that the logic of superabundance brings to bear. If the background conditions for calculating justice are characterized by abundance and security rather than moderate scarcity, then the efforts to establish justice have a different tone. Justice is a cooperative venture designed to "spread the wealth," not a competition to secure basic needs. If one is convinced by this treatment, the love command redescribes reality in such a way that justice is afforded a sense of abundance and generosity.

These ideas deserve more attention than I can give them here. One hopes that they are suggestive enough to enter the general discussion that is bound to develop in the aftermath of Ricoeur's recent death. Allow me to conclude with my initial claims that Ricoeur's theological interests affected his philosophical project in profound ways and provide an important interpretive key for that project. His philosophy, I argued, is principally a philosophical anthropology structured by the idea of capable agency, configured in meaningful forms of existence, and experienced through the practical engagement with life. With the idea of conscience, agency, meaning, and practice are introduced to values that draw attention. The world is recognized as a realm of truth that withstands the threat of meaninglessness, a realm of goodness despite the manifold forms of evil, a realm of beauty that outshines moral and ecological degradation. My life is lived within a world of objects and of persons, which is inhabited by moral values that demand my creative response. The fact that these values rise to expression in figurative discourse in no way limits either their validity or their comprehensiveness. Indeed, validity and comprehensiveness are sealed by the poetic expressions in which values confront me. Theonomy as the poetic expression of authentic obligation, and the love command as the poetic expression of the form obligation takes, strike one at an affective level, though this affectivity is not insulated from philosophical interrogation. Through the poetic imperative, I am metaphorically born anew into an original creation newly recognized as valuable and worthy of moral respect.

Does this poetic imperative (indeed, might one call it a poetics of the will?) signal the point at which Ricoeur the philosopher meets up with Ricoeur the faithful listener? Perhaps, but one thing seems certain: this is the place where the faithful reader of Ricoeur finds possibilities for articulating his or her convictions about the moral value of creation.

Notes

Chapter One. Introduction

1. Paul Ricoeur, "Interview: Chateney-Malabry, July 8, 1991," in Charles Reagan, *Paul Ricoeur: His Life and Work* (Chicago: University of Chicago Press, 1996), 125–26. Later in his life, Ricoeur did offer tentative conclusions about the overall shape of his work, but these comments were directed not to speculative structure or methodology, but to prevailing "problematics" in his thought that he characterized in terms of capability (c.f., Paul Ricoeur, "Ethics and Human Capability: A Response," in *Paul Ricoeur and Contemporary Moral Thought*, ed. William Schweiker, John Wall, and W. David Hall [New York: Routledge, 2002], 279–90).

2. Charles E. Reagan, "Words and Deeds: The Semantics of Action," in *The Philosophy of Paul Ricoeur: The Library of Living Philosophers, Vol. XXII*, Lewis E. Hahn (Chicago: Open Court, 1995), 331. Reagan explains: "This, it will be remembered, was to be the third volume of the trilogy announced in the introduction of *Freedom and Nature*. There, Paul Ricoeur laid out a plan to write an *eidetics* of the will, followed by an *empirics*, completed by a *poetics* of the will. The first part of the plan was accomplished in *Freedom and Nature*. The second in the two parts of *Finitude and Culpability*. But he has never published the third part" (ibid).

3. Don Ihde, *Hermeneutic Phenomenology: The Philosophy of Paul Ricoeur* (Evanston: Northwestern University Press, 1971), 6–7.

4. David M. Rasmussen, *Mythic-Symbolic Language and Philosophical Anthropology: A Constructive Interpretation of the Thought of Paul Ricoeur* (The Hague: Martinus Nijhoff, 1971), is a notable exception.

5. Dan R. Stiver, *Theology After Ricoeur: New Directions in Hermeneutical Theology* (Louisville, KY: Westminster John Knox Press, 2001).

6. John Wall, *Moral Creativity: Paul Ricoeur and the Poetics of Possibility* (New York: Oxford University Press, 2005).

7. Cf., James Fodor, *Christian Hermeneutics: Paul Ricoeur and the Refiguring of Theology* (New York: Oxford University Press, 1995); Stiver, *Theology After Ricoeur*; Kevin J. VanHoozer, *Biblical Narrative in the Philosophy of Paul Ricoeur: A Study in Hermeneutics and Theology* (Cambridge: Cambridge University Press, 1990); Henry Isaac Venema, *Identifying Selfhood: Imagination, Narrative, and Hermeneutics in the Thought of Paul Ricoeur* (Albany: State University of New York Press, 2000).

8. Cf., David E. Klemm, *The Hermeneutical Theory of Paul Ricoeur: A Constructive Analysis* (Lewisburg, PA: Bucknell University Press, 1983); Richard Kearney, *On Paul Ricoeur: The Owl of Minerva* (Burlington, VT: Ashgate Publishing, 2004); Wall, *Moral Creativity*; Jean Greisch, *Paul Ricoeur: L'itinerance du sens* (Grenoble: J. Millon: Diffusion Harmonia mundi, 2001).

9. A notable exception is Mark I. Wallace, *The Second Naivete: Barth, Ricoeur, and the New Yale Theology, 2ed., Studies in American Biblical Hermeneutics* (Macon, PA: Mercer University Press, 1995). Wallace, who is more appropriately placed in the opposing camp, suggests that Barth has much in common with early twentieth-century liberal theology, despite his protestations to the contrary. The Yale school theologians, therefore, misinterpret Barth and thus mischaracterize Ricoeur in their criticisms.

10. Hans W. Frei, *The Eclipse of Biblical Narrative: A Study in Eighteenth and Nineteenth Century Hermeneutics* (New Haven: Yale University Press, 1974).

11. VanHoozer, *Biblical Narrative in the Philosophy of Paul Ricoeur*, 256.

12. Fodor, *Christian Hermeneutics*, 302.

13. David E. Klemm and William Schweiker, "Meanings in Texts and Actions: Questioning Paul Ricoeur," in *Meanings in Texts and Actions: Questioning Paul Ricoeur*, ed. David E Klemm and William Schweiker (Charlottesville: University Press of Virginia, 1993), 4.

14. Kearney, *On Paul Ricoeur*, 73.

15. David E. Klemm, "Searching for a Heart of Gold: A Ricoeurian Meditation on Moral Striving and the Power of Religoius Discourse," in *Paul Ricoeur and Contemporary Moral Thought*, ed. John Wall, William Schweiker, and W. David Hall (New York: Routledge, 2002), 113.

Chapter Two. Agency

1. Kathleen Blamey, "From the Ego to the Self: A Philosophical Itinerary," in *The Philosophy of Paul Ricoeur*, ed. Lewis E. Hahn (Chicago: Open Court, 1995), 597.

2. Paul Ricoeur, "Philosophy of Will and Action," in *The Philosoph of Paul Ricoeur: An Anthology of His Work*, ed. Charles E. Reagan and David Stewart (Boston: Beacon Press, 1978), 69.

3. It may appear that Ricoeur fell back into the conundrum of transcendental idealism at this point; one can argue that he continued to presuppose an *I* in shifting the emphasis from reason to will. This is a sticky point at this level of exploration because he never really explained how the capacity for self-reflection, i.e., reason or mind, comes to inhabit a body. In future chapters I will show that Ricoeur did not succumb to the perils of transcendental idealism by virtue of his attempt to locate the capacity for self-reflection in the cultural participation, i.e., at the level of meaning. The capacity for self-reflection is found in the engagement with cultural productions, e.g., traditions of thought, artistic works, social-political institutions. But, this self-reflection is oriented by a philosophy of will that continues to direct Ricoeur's project. Self-understanding is the understanding of one's own possibilities for action won in and through participation in the ongoing development of culture.

4. Paul Ricoeur, *Freedom and Nature: The Voluntary and the Involuntary*, trans. and introd. by Erazim V. Kohák (Evanston: Northwestern University Press, 1966), 4–5.

5. Ibid., 9–10, emphasis added.

6. Ibid., 484.

7. Ibid., 486. The turn to Kant's postulate of divine freedom has often led to accusations that Ricoeur's anthropology was thoroughly Kantian. One commentator who has leveled this criticism is Pamela Anderson. Anderson's criticism centers on what she calls Ricoeur's "dual-aspect account of human willing." On her reading, Ricoeur succumbed to a form of the phenomenal/noumenal dichotomy with which Kant's philosophical anthropology is criticized. Anderson claims: "The import of his philosophy of the will, as becomes evident at each level of his developing project, depends upon a potentially illusory relation of the temporal and the non-temporal in the act of willing. The eidetic level of description of willing already involves assuming the existence of a bond between the non-temporal ideal of the voluntary and the necessary temporal structures of the involuntary" (*Ricoeur and Kant: Philosophy of the Will: American Academy of Religion Studies in Religion, no. 66* [Scholars: Atlanta, 1993], 46–47). One can

and ought to challenge this interpretation of the conditioned and unconditioned aspects of Ricoeur's, admittedly *polemical*, account of the will in terms of temporality/nontemporality. In point of fact, Ricoeur did not present freedom as a nontemporal reality that effects conditioned, temporal nature. Rather, he attempted to plumb the depths of the paradox of an *incarnate freedom* that becomes manifest at the level of the body in the reciprocity of the voluntary and the involuntary. If he presupposed anything, it is not a dualistic account of the will, but rather a fundamental relationship between the objective and subjective conditions of willing. However, he presupposed this relation precisely in order to surpass the kind of dualistic epistemology for which Anderson accuses him. Ricoeur stated: "In effect, if we wish to surpass epistemic dualism deriving solely from the demands of clarity and conceptual distinctness of thought, and if we wish to discover the actual bond of the body as mine to the self which sees it, yields to it, and governs it, we shall discover that this bond is itself *polemic*" (*Freedom and Nature*, 17). This discovery of a bond that is at once polemical reveals the profound significance of Ricoeur's account of the *reciprocity* of the voluntary and the involuntary. Far from an established dualistic account of the will, he sought to establish a reciprocal relation between the apparently opposed notions of the voluntary and the involuntary.

8. In *Oneself as Another*, Ricoeur approached the question of the relation of character and self-constancy via a very long detour through analytic philosophy, specifically the analytic philosophy of language of P. F. Strawson and J. L. Austin and the analytic philosophy of action of Donald Davidson. These positions raise the issue of agency in a roundabout way by asking the question: "What is the nature of the subject who speaks and acts?" Ricoeur argued that Strawson's attempt to account for persons as objects among other objects in the world about which one can speak, though analytically important and significant, is overly reductionistic. Strictly speaking, Strawson's account reduces identity to a third person reference: persons are objects in the world to which we can refer. What is lost is the notion of personhood as the experience of existing in the mode of agency. To this end, Austin's speech-act theory offers a necessary corrective, giving account of persons as the point from which utterances, i.e., intended meanings, emerge into the world. This set of ideas reintroduces first and second person reference into the philosophy of language: persons are beings capable of saying "I" and addressing themselves to a "you".

In a reductionistic move similar to Strawson's, Davidson attempted to explain actions independent of intentions, placing the issue of the agent out of the account altogether. Actions can be described, Davidson argued, as events that take place in the world. As such, an analysis of the intentions of an agent is superfluous. The agent becomes an unnecessary complication. While he recognized the value of Davidson's analytic approach, in Ricoeur's judgment it was misleading by virtue of its portrayal of actions purely in terms of the point at which they spring forth. This is precisely what marks them as events; actions irrupt in the course of things and produce changes. However, this tends to divorce actions from the temporal process in which they occur and out of which they proceed. By placing action back in the process of choosing, in which an agent decides on a course of action, i.e., in which he/she forms an *intention to* do something, the full complexity of the temporality of action enters the picture. Ricoeur addressed the process of choice in terms of three "moments": hesitation, attention, and decision. The benefit of reintroducing the agent, as the one who deliberates about particular courses of action, into analysis (at the expense of making the philosophy of action exceedingly more complex) is to show that action *depends on* an actor. The self is introduced as a necessary part of the equation: "*A principle that is a self, a self that is a principle*—this is the characteristic trait of the relation we are looking for" (*Paul Ricoeur, Oneself as Another*, trans. Kathleen Blamey [Chicago: University of Chicago Press, 1992], 91). Simply put, the relation between action and agent points to the idea of *initiative*, which the reader will encounter in more detail in the next section. The key in establishing the relation between action and agent is showing how the agent is implied, as a principle, in actions, and how agency is displayed in actions through the capability of initiating.

9. Ricoeur, *Oneself as Another*, 122.

10. Ibid., 121.

11. Ibid., 123.

12. In addressing the idea of promising to the problematic to self-constancy Ricoeur's thought converged with a central theme of Nietzsche's. Posing the act of promising in opposition to the active, "positive faculty of repression," i.e., forgetfulness, Nietzsche claimed, "[Promising] involves no mere passive inability to rid oneself of an impression, no mere indigestion through a once-pledged word with which one cannot 'have done,' but an active *desire* not to rid oneself, a desire for the continuance of something desired once, a real *memory of the will*: so that between the original 'I will,' 'I shall do this' and the actual discharge of the will, its *act*, a world of strange new things, circumstances, even acts of will may be interposed without breaking this long chain of will. But how many things this presupposes! To ordain the future in advance in this way, man must first have learned to distinguish necessary events from chance ones, to think causally, to see and anticipate distant eventualities as if they belonged to the present, to decide with certainty what is the goal and what the means to it, and in general be able to calculate and compute" (Friedrich Nietzsche, *On the Genealogy of Morals*, trans. Walter Kaufmann [New York: Vintage, 1989], 58). For Nietzsche, as for Ricoeur, promising is the mode in which the self holds

itself in time. Of course, Nietzsche's evaluation of this capacity ran counter to Ricoeur's; the capacity to keep one's word is most fundamentally the manner in which the self experiences its capacity for initiative.

13. Ricoeur, *Oneself as Another*, 22.

14. Ibid., 15–16.

15. This strategy is outlined in Ricoeur's work as early as *Freud and Philosophy* where he describes the back and forth movement between reductive interpretation and restorative interpretation. See, Paul Ricoeur, *Freud and Philosophy: An Essay on Interpretation*, trans. Denis Savage (New Haven: Yale University Press, 1970).

16. Ricoeur, *Oneself as Another*, 302.

17. Paul Ricoeur, "Initiative," in *From Texts to Actions: Essays in Hermeneutics, II*, ed. Kathleen Blamey and John B. Thompson (Evanston: Northwestern University Press, 1991), 217.

18. Ibid., 215.

19. Ibid., 216.

20. Paul Ricoeur, *Time and Narrative I*, trans. Kathleen McLaughlin and David Pellauer (Chicago: University of Chicago Press, 1984), 135–36. In effect, to posit the "the totality of what is the case" in the first place is already to *make something happen*; to posit the totality is to cause a change within it by wrapping actuality in the cloak of meaning. To theorize, to postulate, is to act. Thus, it is impossible not to adopt the language of action.

21. The inclusion of the idea of promising under the theme of initiative also serves to orient agency toward moral deliberation: "The promise . . . is the ethics of initiative. The heart of this ethics is the promise to keep my promises. Being faithful to one's word thus becomes the guarantee that the beginning will have a sequel, that the initiative will actually inaugurate a new course of things" (Ricoeur, "Initiative," 217).

22. Nietzsche, *On the Genealogy of Morals*, 67. I will trace the development of bad conscience in chapter 5.

23. Ricoeur, *Oneself as Another*, 220.

24. Paul Ricoeur, "Guilt, Ethics, and Religion," in *The Conflict of Interpretations: Essays in Hermeneutics*, ed. Don Ihde (Evanston: Northwestern University Press, 1974), 435–36. Patrick Bourgeois has criticized Ricoeur's anthropology for being too Kantian in its inclusion of moral evil. Bourgeois claims that "it is necessary to criticize Ricoeur for remaining too Kantian in spite of his fundamental opposition to Kant's view of the place of evil in [the sensible nature of] man. In such a critique what emerges is the view that the structures of human existence

are, like the eidetic structures, equally foundational for innocent, fallen, and regenerated existence, for it is precisely existence which is neutral to all of these, and the bracketing of fault, innocence, passion, and transcendence should be maintained in a pure reflection on existence. For existence is not only manifest as fallen, and the conditions which make evil possible are equally the conditions which make the good will possible" (Patrick Bourgeois, "The Limits of Ricoeur's Hermeneutics of Existence," in *The Philosophy of Paul Ricoeur*, ed. Lewis E. Hahn [Chicago: Open Court, 1995], 562–63). I am not sure, however, that this criticism takes into account some of the intricacies of Ricoeur's ideas. For instance, Bourgeois tends to conflate the ideas of *fallibility* and *fault*, which Ricoeur goes to great lengths to keep separate in *Fallible Man*. Fallibility, or fragility, is the anthropological root for *the possibility of evil*. In this sense, Ricoeur's account of the will upholds the kind of neutrality with regard to innocence and fault that Bourgeois claims is missing.

On the basis of this conflation of terminology, Bourgeois seems to ignore the existential/conceptual divide that separates *Fallible Man*, Ricoeur's phenomenological "empirics" of the will, and *The Symbolism of Evil*, his hermeneutical analysis of the primary symbols of the *experience* of evil. Ricoeur did not address the mythics of evil to any "necessary structures" of freedom but to experienced realities which escape philosophical articulation; the primary symbols of evil are expressions of an experience practical philosophy finds inscrutable. As Ricoeur claimed in response to Bourgeois' criticism, "However inseparable freedom and evil, considered historically may be, these two magnitudes are apprehended in accordance with two distinct modes of thought" (Bourgeois, "The Limits of Ricoeur's Hermeneutics of Existence," 569). This assertion substantiates my claim that the passivity associated with moral fault represents a point of crossing between philosophical anthropology and theological concerns.

25. Paul Ricoeur, "Evil, A Challenge to Philosophy and Theology," in *Figuring the Sacred: Religion, Narrative, and Imagination*, ed. Mark I. Wallace, trans. David Pellauer (Minneapolis: Fortress, 1995), 258–59.

26. Ricoeur, *Oneself as Another*, 124.

Chapter Three. Meaning

1. Paul Ricoeur, *Time and Narrative I*, 3.

2. Augustine, *Confessions*, trans. R. S. Pine Coffin (London: Penguin, 1961), 264.

3. Ibid., *Confessions*, 269.

4. Ricoeur, *Time and Narrative I*, 18–19.

5. Ibid., 21–22.

6. Ibid., 33.

7. Hans Robert Jauss, *Toward an Aesthetic of Reception*, trans. Timothy Bahti, introd. Paul de Man, Theory and History of Literature, vol. 2 (Minneapolis: University of Minnesota Press, 1982).

8. In unfolding this basic structure of understanding I will be guided by the first two movements of Ricoeur's self-styled *phenomenological empirics* of the will, *Fallible Man*, trans. Charles A. Kelby (New York: Fordham University, 1986). However, while I will adopt the principal structures of this work, I am attempting to answer a slightly different question.

Fallible Man is composed of three distinct but related examinations that function as a phenomenological approach to Kant's threefold interrogative: What can I know? What must I do? What can I hope for? In each case, Ricoeur conceived of human existence as a point of active mediation between two poles of existence that he called finitude and infinitude. In the first exploration, which Ricoeur labeled the "transcendental synthesis," he attempted to give an account of how it is that consciousness can know its object. At this level of investigation, consciousness is represented by the pure imagination that mediates between the bodily perception and the infinite possibilities of signification. At the second level of the "practical synthesis," Ricoeur attempted to account for the inauguration of the moral feeling of respect in the will. Respect exists as the intermediary between brute facticity of individual existence (which again inclines attention toward the body) and the total demand for happiness toward which actions aim.

I am only interested in these first two movements of *Fallible Man* at this level of analysis. In a final movement, Ricoeur addressed the issue of "affective fragility" in which this intermediary character of human existence is recognized as the point of least resistance for the entrance of moral evil. My concerns are directed toward the idea of understanding as this is reflected at the level of basic structures. Thus, while Ricoeur was interested to show how consciousness comes to know its object, I am interested in exploring how it is that perception rises to the level of meaning. While Ricoeur was concerned to show how moral concern arises in the will, I am concerned to show how the idea of humanity comes to represent, abstractly, the figure of meaningful existence. In other words, I am attempting to show how understanding takes on the structure of active receptivity in Ricoeur's work. My reason for reorienting this discussion is the desire to uncover a set of hermeneutical concerns that reside just beneath the surface of Ricoeur's phenomenological analysis. Ricoeur's project can be viewed as a hermeneutic phenomenology, i.e., a philosophical exploration of the fundamentally interpretive character of human existence that is informed by phenomenological method. Given this claim, the two lines of questioning—

phenomenology and hermeneutics—are clearly related, and this allows me to adopt the phenomenological structures that Ricoeur laid out in the service of a hermeneutics of understanding. To place this synthetic activity revealed in his phenomenological empirics within a hermeneutical framework, understanding is the interpretive mediation between the givenness of bodily existence and the appropriation of interpreted meaning.

9. Ricoeur, *Fallible Man*, 19.

10. Ibid., 20.

11. Ibid., 12.

12. Ibid., 26.

13. Ibid., 29.

14. Ibid., 39.

15. Ibid., 52–53.

16. Ibid., 63, emphasis added.

17. Ibid., 66. The claim that happiness represents a "total demand" and the "termination of a destiny" is a somewhat opaque way of saying, in Aristotelian fashion, that happiness is the final aim of a complete life. Later, we will relate the idea of happiness to the idea of the narrative unity of a life.

18. Ibid., 68. This total demand of a meaningful life in the idea of happiness becomes at the purely affective level the principal point of entrance for moral evil. A disproportion opens up between the total demand and the desire for immediacy, which directs action away from its orientation in a destiny toward the attempt to achieve its satisfaction in the present.

19. Ibid., 69–70. This portrayal of self-understanding as projected signals a second point of divergence from Kant. While Kant located the anthropological ground of the self, following Descartes, in the "I think," Ricoeur locates it as the "I will." In other words, it is in acting that the individual recognizes him/herself as a meaningful possibility. This fact further grounds Ricoeur's philosophical anthropology as an anthropology of capability, i.e., of agency, and not as a transcendental philosophy.

20. Paul Ricoeur, "Phenomenology and Hermeneutics," in *Hermeneutics and the Human Sciences: Essays on Language Action, and Interpretation*, ed. John B. Thompson (Cambridge: Cambridge University Press, 1981), 116.

21. Paul Ricoeur, *Time and Narrative III*, trans. Kathleen Blamey and David Pellauer (1988), 220–21.

22. Ibid., 222.

23. Ibid., 222–23.

24. Ricoeur, "Phenomenology and Hermeneutics," 117.

25. Ricoeur, *Fallible Man*, 45–46.

26. Paul Ricoeur, "Life in Quest of Narrative," in *On Paul Ricoeur: Narrative and Interpretation*, ed. David Wood (New York: Routledge, 1991), 33.

27. Ibid., 21.

28. Ibid., 21–22.

29. Ricoeur, *Oneself as Another*, 142.

30. Ricoeur, "Life in Quest of Narrative," 22. This threefold function of narrative is revealed in Ricoeur's idea of discursive understanding in general. Ricoeur argued that any discourse is a dialectic of *event* and *meaning*. Discourse is actualized in the event of the utterance of a spoken sentence or in the composition of the written work. It is understood in the meaning that arises out of the relationship between sense—grammatical structure, mood, etc., and reference—that toward which the event of discourse refers. But, the advent of written discourse introduces a wrinkle into this event-meaning structure. First, the meaning of the discourse becomes fixed, through the system of written signs, in such a way that it is disengaged from the event of the discourse. The meaning receives an enduring quality that is not present at the level of spoken discourse. At the same time, the referential function of the discourse is problematized; at the level of the spoken sentence, reference is tied to the event. At the level of written discourse, the event is no longer the context for reference; rather, the referential function of the written discourse becomes fixed in the sense, i.e., in the written structure of the text. The textual structure becomes the source of reference rather than the authorial intention.

31. Ibid., 26.

32. Paul Ricoeur, "Narrative Identity," in *On Paul Ricoeur: Narrative and Interpretation*, ed. David Wood (New York: Routledge, 1991), 188.

33. Paul Ricoeur, *Le Volontaire et l'Involontaire* (Paris: Aubier, 1950).

34. In this sense, *personnage* is an ideal mediating term between the narrative synthesis of literary characters and the self-reflective identities of actual persons. Unfortunately, Kathleen Blamey's translation of *Soi-Même comme un Autre* (Paris: Éditions du Seuil, 1990) makes no mention of this shift of terminology. Thus, the distinction is completely lost in the translation and it is left to the reader to infer Ricoeur's subtle change of emphasis from the context of his argument.

35. Ricoeur, *Time and Narrative I*, 64.

36. Ibid., 65.

37. Dan Stiver has recognized an ambiguity in Ricoeur's thought in the move from an earlier "hermeneutical arc" to this second that Stiver calls a "mimetic arc." The first version, which initially appeared in *The Symbolism of Evil*, the moves from a precritical "first naivete" through a hermeneutical engagement to a second, postcritical reappropriation that Ricoeur called the "second naivete." Stiver favors the first version of the hermeneutical arc, claiming that it offers more possibility for appropriation for orthodox Christianity (Stiver, *Theology After Ricoeur*).

38. Ricoeur, *Time and Narrative I*, 71.

39. Ricoeur, "Narrative Identity," 198.

40. Ricoeur, *Oneself as Another*, 154.

41. Ibid., 158.

42. Ricoeur, "Life in Quest of Narrative," 33. Ricoeur examines four reasons to doubt such a simple reduction of life to narrative structure. First, he argued that one cannot discern the author of a life story so easily as we can a literary narrative. Thus, in considering my life as a story I take on the roles of "Narrator and character, perhaps, of a life of which, unlike the creatures of fiction, I am not the author but at most . . . the coauthor." Secondly, the effect of literary closure, which applies to fictional narratives, simply does not apply to lived experience; my life can never be grasped as a totality the way a literary work can. Thirdly, the text produces its own world which is relatively closed to other textual worlds. This is not the case with life; my story is inextricably intertwined with the stories of others. Finally, narratives are oriented toward the past; what is recounted is past once it is recounted. As I have been arguing, however, life is lived not only in reflection on the past, but in anticipation of the future: "[I]n self-understanding, *mimesis praxeos* appears able to cover only the past phase of life and to have to be joined to anticipations and projects. . . ." It is in this anticipatory dimension of living that action is both supported by *and* breaks away from narrative configuration (Ricoeur, "Life in Quest of Narrative," 159–61).

Ricoeur's refusal to draw a "community of form" between narrative structure and life has led narrative historian David Carr to the charge that Ricoeur's account is a version of the "standard view" on narrative. The "standard view," as Carr understands it, makes one principal claim: life is random and chaotic. Given this basic claim, the notion that narrative and life share a "community of form," avoiding for the moment what Carr ultimately means by this, sounds absurd. Rather than adequately conveying the events it recounts, narrative, whether historical or fictional, imposes a structure on an otherwise structureless course of events. Narrative, therefore, cannot be "true-to-life" because it necessarily de-forms events, paradoxically by giving them some kind of meaningful form, some overall coherence.

How did Ricoeur become involved in this view? Does he not rather devote a major portion of his efforts to showing the manner in which life gains coherence through the application of narrative theory? In Carr's opinion, Ricoeur's portrayal of the relation between narrative and life suffers from a similar, though less extreme, drawback as the more staunch defenders of the "standard view": "He does not go so far as to say with them that the real world is merely sequential, maintaining instead that it has a 'pre-narrative structure' of elements that lend themselves to narrative configuration. But this prefiguration is not itself narrative structure, and it does not save us from what Ricoeur seems to regard as a sort of constitutional disarray attached to the experience of time, which in itself is 'confused, unformed and, at the limit, mute'" (David Carr, "Narrative and the Real World: An Argument for Continuity," *History and Theory* XXV, no. 2 [May 1986]: 119). There are, however, some fundamental problems with Carr's criticism.

For one, Carr is never completely clear about his own position for a "community of form" between narrative and life. At times, he seems to argue that narrative and life have the same "beginning-middle-end" structure; at others, he argues that narrative structure and life have a kinship or commonality. If the latter, Carr is not really odds with Ricoeur's position. If the former, however, it seems that Carr imposes a structure on life that is radically outside of experience; life is not experienced as having a beginning, middle, and end, but rather as having a past, present, and future. This leads to a second problem: it seems that Carr has somewhat misrepresented Ricoeur's project in the accusation of the "standard view." Indeed, Ricoeur's engagement with Augustine was the attempt to construct a phenomenology of time consciousness similar to the one that Carr draws from Husserl. (It should be noted that Ricoeur turns to Husserl in this manner in *Time and Narrative III*.)

43. Ricoeur, *Time and Narrative III*, 248–49.

44. Ricoeur traced the development of this tradition from the ambiguity surrounding the term *ousia* in Aristotle's *Metaphysics* and the ensuing ambiguity which results in the term's Latin translation as *substantia*. Citing Aristotle, Ricoeur stated: "Because potentiality is a genuine mode of being, change and motion are rightfully beings. But if we ask what sort of being motion is, we are referred back to the troubling definition of motion in the *Physics*, namely 'the fulfillment . . . of what exists potentially, insofar as it exists potentially.' . . . [D]espite the lofty titles that the idea of potency draws from its so-to-speak transcendental function with respect to physics, this notion is conceived only on the basis of that of actuality: nothing can be said to be potential without reference to some-

thing said to be real, in the sense of actual, completed; in this sense the actual has priority over the potential 'both in formula and in substantiality' . . . and even in relation to substance, which is not without importance for our discussion. In fact, the intersecting of these two primitive significations of being, that of being appropriate to the categories (*ousia*, which in Latin is translated by *substantia*) and that of being as actuality and potentiality, leads, it seems, to weakening the ever so precious conquest of the idea of potency and actuality" (Ricoeur, *Oneself as Another*, 304–305).

45. Baruch Spinoza, *The Ethics and Selected Letters*, trans. Samuel Shirley (Indianapolis: Hackett, 1982), 109.

46. Ricoeur, *Oneself as Another*, 316–17, emphasis added.

47. Ibid, 303.

48. Paul Ricoeur, "Nabert on Act and Sign," in *The Conflict of Interpretations: Essays in Hermeneutics*, ed. Don Ihde (Evanston: Northwestern University Press, 1974), 222.

49. This, as many have pointed out, represents the fundamental point at which Ricoeur parted company with Sarte's existential phenomenology.

50. Jean Nabert, *Elements for an Ethic*, trans. William J. Petrek (Evanston: Northwestern University Press, 1969), 57–58.

51. Ibid., 111.

52. Ricoeur, *Fallible Man*, 146, emphasis added.

53. Ricoeur, 'Guilt, Ethics, and Religion," 426. For a complete analysis of the symbols of the confession of evil and the cycle of myths that give rise to speculation on evil, see Paul Ricoeur, *The Symbolism of Evil*, trans. Emerson Buchanan (Boston: Beacon Press, 1969).

54. Immanuel Kant, *Religion Within the Limits of Reason Alone*, trans. Theodore M. Greene and Hoyt H. Hudson, cont. John R. Silber (New York: Harper and Row, Harper Torchbooks/Cloister Library, 1960), 32.

55. Paul Ricoeur, "Hope and the Structure of Philosophical Systems," in *Figuring the Sacred: Religion, Narrative, and Imagination*, ed. Mark I. Wallace, trans. David Pellauer (Minneapolis: Fortress Press, 1995), 215.

56. Ibid., 203.

57. Ricoeur, "Guilt, Ethics, and Religion," 437.

58. Paul Ricoeur, "Freedom in Light of Hope," in *The Conflict of Interpretations*, ed. Don Ihde, trans. Robert Sweeney (Evanston: Northwestern University Press, 1974), 406–407.

59. Paul Ricoeur, "Manifestation and Proclamation," in *Figuring the Sacred: Religion, Narrative, and Imagination*, ed. Mark I. Wallace, trans. David Pellauer (Minneapolis: Fortress Press, 1995), 65.

60. As Mark Wallace points out, this preserves Ricoeur from the criticism of liberal foundationalism leveled at him by the New Yale theologians (Wallace, *The Second Naivete*).

61. Stéphan Mosès, *System and Revelation: The Philosophy of Franz Rosenzweig*, trans. Catharine Tihanyi (Detroit: Wayne State University, 1992).

62. This interplay between creation and eschatology finds an interesting correlary in the ideas of ideology and utopia in Ricoeur's writings on political philosophy; cf., Paul Ricoeur, *Lectures on Ideology and Utopia*, ed. George H. Taylor (New York: Columbia University Press, 1986).

63. André LaCocque and Paul Ricoeur, *Thinking Biblically: Exegetical and Hermeneutical Studies*, trans. David Pellauer (Chicago: University of Chicago Press, 1998), 67.

64. Paul Ricoeur, "The Bible and the Imagination," in *Figuring the Sacred: Religion, Narrative, and Imagination*, ed. Mark I. Wallace, trans. David Pellauer (Minneapolis: Fortress Press, 1995), 165.

65. Paul Ricoeur, "Philosophical Hermeneutics and Biblical Hermeneutics," in *From Text to Action: Essays in Hermeneutics II*, trans. and ed. Kathleen Blamey and John B. Thompson (Evanston: Northwestern University Press, 1991), 90. There is a subtle shift of terminology in this article to which Ricoeur did not attempt to draw attention. At places he spoke of "biblical hermeneutics" and at other places he used the term "theological hermeneutics." It is unclear whether he intended these two synonymously. I will argue in concluding, however, that there is reason to uphold a distinction between the two terms.

66. Ibid., 94.

67. Ibid., 96.

68. In raising the question of the distinction between biblical hermeneutics and theological hermeneutics, David Klemm asks, "Does the name God manifest the divine being only within the world of the biblical texts, or is the name the trace of an absolute otherness that breaks out of the world of biblical texts to show itself in the act of interpretation itself?" Klemm offers an answer to this question in terms of what he calls the "cross of interpretation" whereby the God who is named in biblical discourse breaks into experience in a transformative way; he argues, "The divine breaks into the cross of interpretation where interpretive syntheses break down and reveal the dependence of the I on something other than itself. The divine also shows itself in the open horizon

against which we discern meanings. . . . Ricoeur's hermeneutics enables us to see that the cross of interpretation is the final site of human action and passion" (David Klemm, "Theological Hermeneutics and the Divine Name: Ricoeur and the Cross of Interpretation," in *Meanings in Texts and Actions: Questioning Paul Ricoeur*, David E. Klemm and William Schweiker [Charlottesville: University of Virginia, 1993], 259, 269).

69. Paul Ricoeur, "Toward a Hermeneutic of the Idea of Revelation," in *Essays on Biblical Interpretation*, ed. Lewis S. Mudge (Philadelphia: Fortress Press, 1980), 106.

70. Ibid., 108.

71. Paul Ricoeur, "The Hermeneutics of Testimony," in *Essays on Biblical Interpretation*, ed. Lewis S. Mudge (Philadelphia: Fortress Press, 1980), 142.

72. Ibid., 143.

73. VanHoozer, *Biblical Narrative in the Philosophy of Paul Ricoeur*, 257.

Chapter Four. Practrice

1. Ricoeur, *Oneself as Another*, 317.

2. Edmund Husserl, *Cartesian Meditations: An Introduction to Phenomenology*, trans. Dorion Cairns (Dordrecht: Kluwer, 1995), 100.

3. Ibid., 115.

4. Emmanuel Levinas, *Otherwise Than Being, or Beyond Essence*, trans. Alphonse Lingus (Pittsburgh, PA: Duquesne University Press, 1998), 139.

5. Ibid., 110–11.

6. Ricoeur, *Oneself as Another*, 339.

7. Ibid., 294.

8. Ibid.

9. Ibid., 294–95; c.f., Hans Jonas, *The Imperative of Responsibility: In Search of an Ethics for the Technological Age* (Chicago: University of Chicago Press, 1984).

10. Paul Ricoeur, *Memory, History, Forgetting*, trans. David Pellauer (Chicago: University of Chicago Press, 2004), 89.

11. Ricoeur, *Oneself as Another*, 293.

12. Ibid., 189.

13. Ibid., 190.

14. Gabriel Moran, *A Grammar of Responsibility* (New York: Crossroad, 1996), 70.

15. Ibid., 71. Incidentally, Moran suggests that the answer to the question of "to what and to whom am I responsible?" implies a fundamentally religious sensibility. He states: "Does the very existence of the question I am asking . . . imply a religious answer? Undeniably, the idea of responsibility arose in the religious context of a divine day of judgment. . . . Does the project self-destruct without a religious answer for 'to whom am I responsible'? I would say that a religious attitude of some kind is implied, though the imagery and the institutions that grew up around divine judgement are not necessarily implied" (ibid., 72).

16. Ibid., 85.

17. Ricoeur, *Oneself as Another*, 170.

18. Ibid., 172.

19. Aristotle, "Nicomachean Ethics," in *The Basic Works of Aristotle*, ed. Richard McKeon (New York: Random House, 1941), 1028.

20. Ibid., 937.

21. Ricoeur, *Oneself as Another*, 185.

22. Aristotle, "Nicomachean Ethics," 1060.

23. Hannah Arendt, *The Human Condition* (Chicago: University of Chicago Press, 1959), 200.

24. Ibid., 200–201.

25. Ibid., 204.

26. Paul Ricoeur, "Teleological and Deontological Structures of Action: Aristotle and/or Kant," in *Contemporary French Philosophy*, ed. A. Phillips Griffiths (Cambridge: Cambridge University Press, 1987), 106.

27. Immanuel Kant, *Grounding for the Metaphysic of Morals and On a Supposed Right to Lie Because of Philanthropic Concerns*, 3 ed., trans. James W. Ellington (Indianapolis: Hackett, 1993), 42.

28. Ibid., 7.

29. This positive evaluation of desire is due principally to a very different understanding of freedom. While Kant asserted that true freedom is autonomy, self-legislation, Ricoeur's concern was to articulate an understanding of *capability*. As I showed in chapter 2, capability is an only-human freedom residing in the reciprocity of voluntary and involuntary structures. To some degree, humans are always partially caused by forces beyond our control; but they continue to exercise initiative within these preexisting structures. Human capability is this capacity for initiative.

30. Kant, *Grounding for the Metaphysics of Morals*, 36.

31. "The respective merits of the negative formula . . . and the positive formula . . . balance one another; the interdiction leaves open the range of things that are not forbidden and in this way makes room for moral invention in the order of what is permitted; on its part, the positive commandment designates more clearly the motive of benevolence that prompts us to do something on behalf of our neighbor" (*Oneself as Another*, 219/*Soi-même comme un autre*, 255). The degree to which prohibition necessarily entails proaction may be disputed; it is unclear whether or not the prohibition against violence necessarily leads to the motive of benevolence. As I will show in the next chapter, the motive of benevolence outlined in the commandment to love one's neighbor as oneself radically alters the ethical relation to the other.

32. Ricoeur, *Oneself as Another*, 221.

33. Ibid., 222.

34. Ibid., 228.

35. John Rawls, *A Theory of Justice* (Cambridge: Harvard University Press, 1971), 60.

36. Ibid., 62.

37. Ibid., 126.

38. Jean-Paul Sartre, *Being and Nothingness: An Essay on Phenomenological Ontology*, trans. and introd. Hazel E. Barnes (New York: Philosophical Library, 1956).

39. Kant, *Grounding for the Metaphysics of Morals*, 63–67. One might suggest that this example can be dismissed because it is highly unlikely that it would ever really happen. However, the example of those who harbored Jews from the Nazis in World War II stand as important arguments against such a dismissal.

40. Ricoeur, *Oneself as Another*, 263.

41. Ibid.

42. Ibid., 267.

43. Ibid., 268.

44. The importance of the other in the constitution of the self caused Ricoeur to reassess Kant's account of autonomy in its relationship to heteronomy. If the other is reconceived as the one who levels a moral claim, which, in turn, makes selfhood a real possibility, then autonomy can no longer be thought as a self-sufficient reality in opposition to heteronomy. Rather, the question is whether or not we can conceive a dimension of heteronomy that is

compatible with autonomy. Ricoeur states: "From this reinterpretation of the principle of authority [of the other] results the necessity to rework the opposition between autonomy and heteronomy. Two different ideas are henceforth to be distinguished. The first, the one Kant had in mind in speaking of heteronomy, is indistinguishable from the state of 'tutelage' denounced by the pamphlet *What is Enlightenment?* . . . . In its turn, this threefold otherness within the self [receptivity, affectivity, incapacity] joins the properly dialogic otherness that makes autonomy part and parcel of, and dependent on, the rule of justice and the rule of reciprocity. The very idea of others bifurcates into two opposing directions, corresponding to two figures of the master: one the dominator, facing the slave; the other, the master of justice, facing the disciple. It is the 'heteronomy' of the latter that has to be integrated into autonomy, not to weaken it, but to reinforce Kant's exhortation in *What is Enlightenment?*" (Ricoeur, *Oneself as Another*, 275–76).

Chapter Five. Conscience

1. In a similar vein, William Schweiker argues, "Theological ethical reflection does not begin, therefore with what Ricoeur has called the 'night of power' as the crisis of radical evil within the trajectory freedom. It begins with the call of being in the solicitude of the Other sensed and discovered within patterns of interaction. The self from this perspective is not simply the subject that affirms being or questions itself, no matter how radical that questioning appears to be. It is not the self that asks what it can know, what it ought to do, and what it can hope for. The self that is the object of interpretation is one interacting with and responding to other powers and their claim to goodness" (William Schweiker, "Imagination, Violence, and Hope: A Theological Response to Ricoeur's Moral Philosophy," in *Meanings in Texts and Actions*, 220).

2. Paul Ricoeur, "Ethical and Theological Considerations on the Golden Rule," in *Figuring the Sacred: Religion, Narrative, and Imagination*, ed. Mark I. Wallace, trans. David Pellauer (Minneapolis: Fortress Press, 1995), 301.

3. Ricoeur's presentation of the idea of theonomy is remarkably similar to that of Paul Tillich, particularly Tillich's proposal of *theonomous morality* (Paul Tillich, *Systematic Theology, vol. 3* [Chicago: University of Chicago Press, 1963], 266–75). Like Tillich, Ricoeur argues that theonomy is equally resistant to both an independent autonomy and an independent heteronomy. Similarly, theonomy is instrumental in the conquest of meaning over the ambiguities that assail existence, especially moral ambiguities. There is, however, a profound difference in that Ricoeur limits theonomy to a kind of poetic theme within cultural expression.

In many ways, Tillich's understanding of theonomy remains yoked to an idealistic philosophy of Spirit, in the Hegelian sense. Tillich claims: "The Word of God is the *Spirit-determined* human word. As such it is not bound to a particular revelatory event, Christian or non-Christian; it is not bound to religion in the narrower sense of the term; it is not tied up with a special content or a special form. *It appears wherever the Spiritual Presence imposes itself on an individual or a group*. Language, under such impact, is beyond poverty and abundance. A few words become great words! This is the ever repeated experience of mankind with the holy literature of a particular religion or of a theonomous culture. But the experience surpasses the 'holy scriptures' of any particular religion" (ibid., 254, emphasis added). Ricoeur would surely agree that the divine word is not tied to any particular religion or other cultural formation, but he would say that the word only comes to expression in the particular symbols, metaphors, and narratives of a given religion or cultural formation. Cultural expressions of all kinds are the *bearers* of the word, which then reflects back critically on the culture itself. The notion that the Spiritual Presence, one of Tillich's terms for theonomy, "imposes itself on an individual or a group" is simply inconceivable in Ricoeur's position. We are consigned to trace the manifestations of the divine within culture not as an independent movement of Spirit, but as expressions of *human* action and meaning within particular cultures that testify to a reality and a power beyond particularity.

4. Paul Ricoeur, "Negativity and Primary Affirmation," in *History and Truth*, ed. and trans. Charles A. Kelbley (Evanston: Northwestern University Press, 1965), 318 In this article, Ricoeur focused on negation in Sartre's existentialism. While Sartre posits human freedom as the assertion of nothingness which stands in the face of a philosophy of being that equates being with a static essence, and thereby posits value as *lack*, Ricoeur claimed instead that the freedom which negates finitude, i.e., negates the negation, is primordially founded on an affirmation of the value within being reconceived as becoming. Denegation opens onto primary affirmation, *l'affirmation originaire*, through recuperative analysis.

5. Paul Ricoeur, "The Summoned Subject in the School of the Narratives of the Prophetic Vocation," in *Figuring the Sacred: Religion, Narrative, and Imagination*, ed. Mark I. Wallace, trans. David Pellauer (Minneapolis: Fortress Press, 1995), 272.

6. Ricoeur, *Oneself as Another*, 355.

7. Ricoeur, *Oneself as Another*, 343. It is important to point out that Ricoeur believed that Hegel fundamentally misrepresented Kant in posing his argument in these terms; indeed, this interpretation ran counter to Ricoeur's interpretation and incorporation of the Kantian deontological moment. However, in a somewhat

backhanded compliment, Ricoeur claimed, "The artifice of the Hegelian construction is not to be deplored; as an artifice it takes its place among the excesses, transgressions, and hyperboles of all sorts that nourish moral reflection and, perhaps, philosophical reflection in general" (ibid.).

8. Georg Wilhelm Friedrich Hegel, *Phenomenology of Spirit*, trans. A. V. Miller, foreword by J. N. Findlay (Oxford: Oxford University Press, 1977), 396–97.

9. Georg Wilhelm Friedrich Hegel, *Elements of the Philosophy of Right*, trans. H. B. Nisbet (Cambridge: Cambridge University Press, 1991), 173.

10. Nietzsche, *On the Genealogy of Morals*, 84.

11. Ricoeur, *Oneself as Another*, 347.

12. Martin Heidegger, *Being and Time*, trans. John Macquarrie and Edward Robinson (New York: Harper and Row, 1962), 317.

13. Ibid., 320.

14. Ibid., 325.

15. In distinguishing the existential interpretation of guilt from the commonsense, i.e., inauthentic, interpretations, Heidegger argued, "Everyday common sense first takes 'Being-guilty' in the sense of 'owing', of 'having something due on account'. One is to give back to the Other something to which the latter has a claim. . . . 'Being-guilty' also has the signification of '*being responsible for*' ['*schuld sein an*']—that is, being the cause or author of something, or even 'being the occasion' for something. . . . These ordinary significations of 'Being-guilty' as 'having debts to someone' and 'having responsibility for something' can go together and define a kind of behavior which we call '*making oneself responsible*'; that is by having the responsibility for having a debt, one may break a law and make oneself punishable" (ibid., 327).

16. Heidegger, *Being and Time*, 333–34.

17. Ibid., 344–45.

18. "But on what basis does Dasein disclose itself in resoluteness? On what is it to resolve? *Only* the resolution itself can give the answer. . . . *The resolution is precisely the disclosive projection and determination of what is factically possible at the time*" (ibid., 345).

19. Ricoeur, *Oneself as Another*, 351–52. It is important to point out that Ricoeur's preferred translation for Heidegger's *Schuld/schuldig* is debt/indebtedness (*dette/endettement*) as opposed to guilt/guilty (*culpablité/coupable*) (cf., Ricoeur, *Soi-Même comme un Autre*, 404–405). While both are acceptable translations, Ricoeur's choice lends a nuance to the notion of the judgment of conscience which is more amenable to a reclamation of moral conscience.

20. Ricoeur, *Oneself as Another*, 354–55.

21. Ricoeur, "The Summoned Subject in the School of the Narratives of the Prophetic Vocation," 273–74.

22. Paul Ricoeur, "Emmanuel Levinas: Thinker of Testimony," in *Figuring the Sacred: Religion, Narrative, and Imagination*, ed. Mark I. Wallace, trans. David Pellauer (Minneapolis: Fortress Press, 1995), 114–15.

23. The distinction that Jean-Luc Marion draws between the idol and the icon is useful here. Marion argues the idol represents the finite mind's understanding and represention of the divine. In this sense, the idol is actually the unrecognized mirror image of the the finite mind which reduces God to what the mind understands. The icon, on the other hand, is the visual representation of the unrepresentable and is recognized as such. The icon, then, is the point of confrontation between the finite mind which recognizes itself in the countenence of the infinite God. "The idol moves, at least potentially, toward its twilight, since already in its dawn the idol gathers only a foreign brilliance. The icon, which unbalances human sight in order to engulf it in infinite depth, marks such an advance of God that even in times of the worst distress, indifference cannot ruin it. For to give itself to be seen, the icon needs only itself" (Jean-Luc Marion, *God Without Being*, trans. Thomas Carlson [Chicago: University of Chicago Press, 1991], 24).

24. Ricoeur, "The Hermeneutics of Testimony," 143.

25. Ricoeur, "Emmanuel Levinas: Thinker of Testimony," 118.

26. This Kantian strain in Ricoeur's thought has been one of many places where he has recieved criticism for making the Bible subservient to philosophical speculation. Fodor argues that Ricoeur's reliance on Kantian idealism undermines the uniqueness, authority, and special veracity of the biblical texts. Stiver accuses Ricoeur of falling into a tacit positivism that is out of character with postmodern epistemic sensibilities. VanHoozer, most forcefully, accuses Ricoeur of priviledging the Kantian understanding of radical evil and Christ as the image of humanity pleasing to God over the Christian understanding of the transformation of the will through the sacrificial grace of Jesus Christ.

27. Paul Ricoeur, "The Logic of Jesus, the Logic of God," in *Figuring the Sacred: Religion, Narrative, and Imagination*, ed. Mark I. Wallace, trans. David Pellauer (Minneapolis: Fortress Press, 1995), 279. Ricoeur pointed out that a simple arithmetic equality is inadequate due to differences in contribution and ability. Thus, it is Aristotle's notion of proportional equality that he adopts. Following Rawls, Ricoeur argued that a fair distribution is achieved in the balance of two principles of justice: the arithmetic equality of rights and chances, and the proportional equality of benefits, privileges, and responsibilities.

28. Ricoeur, "The Logic of Jesus, the Logic of God," 281.

29. Ibid.

30. Robert Tannehill, *The Sword of His Mouth* (Philadelphia: Fortress Press, 1975), 63, 66.

31. The concept of "the gift" is exceedingly ambiguous, as Marcel Maus and Jacques Derrida, among others, have shown. More problematic still is Ricoeur's formulation "economy of the gift." Whether or not this is one of Ricoeur's characteristically veiled ironic twists is hard to tell. I will explore the ambiguities of this formulation and what Ricoeur may have been trying to do with it in the final chapter.

32. Paul Ricoeur, "Theonomy and/or Autonomy," in *The Future of Theology: Essays in Honor of Jürgen Moltmann*, ed. Miroslav Volf (Grand Rapids: Eerdmans, 1996), 285.

33. Ricoeur, "Ethical and Theological Considerations on the Golden Rule," 297–98.

34. Ibid., 298.

35. Ibid., 299.

36. Ibid.

37. Ricoeur, "Theonomy and/or Autonomy," 284.

38. Kant, *Religion Within the Limits of Reason Alone*, 40–41.

39. Ricoeur, "Theonomy and/or Autonomy," 297–98. The notion that autonomy is "expelled" from moral philosophy is somewhat puzzling here. I take Ricoeur to mean that autonomy itself becomes inscrutable within a pure moral philosophy. In this sense, Kant's moral philosophy demands a complementary philosophy of religion.

40. Ricoeur, "Theonomy and/or Autonomy," 284.

41. Ibid., 285.

42. Abraham J. Heschel, *The Prophets* (New York: Harper Torchbooks, 1962), 16–17.

43. Ricoeur, "Toward a Hermeneutic of the Idea of Revelation," 86.

44. Ibid., 87.

45. Ricoeur, "Theonomy and/or Autonomy," 287.

46. Cf., Mosès, *System and Revelation*.

47. Franz Rosenzweig, *The Star of Redemption*, trans. William W. Halo (Notre Dame: University of Notre Dame University, 1985), 176–77.

48. Paul Ricoeur, "Love and Justice," in *Figuring the Sacred: Religion, Narrative, and Imagination*, ed. Mark I. Wallace, trans. David Pellauer (Minneapolis: Fortress Press, 1995), 320.

49. Rosenzweig, *The Star of Redemption*, 177.

50. Ibid., 214–15.

51. Ibid., 218.

52. Ricoeur, "Theonomy and/or Autonomy," 289.

Chapter Six. The Economy of the Gift and the Poetic Imperative

1. Ricoeur, "Ethical and Theological Considerations on the Golden Rule," 300–301

2. Ricoeur has taken up this topic again, and in a similar vein, more recently in *History, Memory, Forgetting*, see especially pp. 479–86.

3. Adam Smith, *An Inquiry Into the Nature and Causes of the Wealth of Nations* (Indianapolis: Liberty Fund, 1981), 26–27.

4. Marcel Mauss, *The Gift: Forms and Functions of Exchange in Archaic Studies*, trans. W. D. Halls, introd. Mary Douglas (New York: W. W. Norton, 1990).

5. Claude Lévi-Strauss, *Introduction to the Work of Marcel Mauss*, trans. Felicity Baker (London: Routledge, 1987).

6. Pierre Bourdieu, *The Logic of Practice*, trans. Richard Nice (Stanford: Stanford University Press, 1990).

7. Jacques Derrida, *Given Time: I. Counterfeit Money*, trans. Peggy Kamuf (Chicago: University of Chicago Press, 1992), 7.

8. Jean-Luc Marion, *Being Given: Toward a Phenomenology of Givenness*, trans. Jeffrey L. Koskey (Stanford: Stanford University Press, 2002), 115.

9. Marion, *God Without Being*, 150.

10. Calvin O. Schrag, *God as Otherwise Than Being: Toward a Semantics of the Gift* (Evanston: Northwestern University Press, 2002), 40–41.

11. Paul Ricoeur, *The Rule of Metaphor: Multi-Disciplinary Studies of the Creation of Meaning in Language*, trans. Robert Czerny, Kathleen McLaughlin, and John Costello (Toronto: University of Toronto Press, 1977), 98.

12. Ricoeur, *Time and Narrative I*, 80–81.

13. Paul Ricoeur, "Philosophy and Religious Language," in *Figuring the Sacred: Religion, Narrative, and Imagination*, ed. Mark I. Wallace, trans. David Pellauer (Minneapolis: Fortress Press, 1995), 35.

14. Immanuel Kant, *The Critique of Judgement*, trans. Werner S. Pluhar (Indianapolis: Hackett, 1987), 265–300.

15. Ricoeur, "The Bible and the Imagination," 144.

16. Ibid., 145.

17. Ricoeur, "Love and Justice," 329.

18. Ibid., 328.

19. Paul Ricoeur, "Theonomy and/or Autonomy," 292.

20. Ibid., 296.

21. Ricoeur, "The Summoned Subject in the School of the Narratives of the Prophetic Vocation," 262.

22. Somewhat surprisingly, Ricoeur did introduce the love command into the his philosophical discussion of moral conscience. Citing Rosenzweig, Ricoeur argued that "there is a form of commandment that is not yet a law: this commandment, if it can be called such, can be heard in the tone of the *Song of Songs*, in the plea that the lover addressed to the beloved: 'Thou, love me!' It is because violence taints all the relations of interaction . . . that the commandment becomes law, and the law, prohibition: 'Thou shalt not kill'" (*Oneself as Another*, 351). Oddly, this inclusion addresses neither the theological import of the love command, nor the central place that it holds in Rosenzweig's thought. Indeed, it does not really address Rosenzweig at all.

23. Ricoeur, "The Summoned Subject in the School of the Narratives of the Prophetic Vocation," 274. It may be something of a simplistic reading of Rosenzweig not to assign a similar sense of metaphoric mediation to the idea of the love command. Clearly there is something more subtle going on here, particularly in light of the firm and irreducible distinction that Rosenzweig wishes to establish between Judaism and Christianity as two "paths of redemption." If the love command exists in the form of direct, unmediated address, than it is difficult to see how this distinction could stand; to hold Judaism and Christianity as distinctive yet equally legitimate witnesses would be superfluous. Stéphan Mosès's account of the nature of "transcendent truth" in *The Star of Redemption* offers some important nuances in this direction. Mosès states: "Only truth that has its source in a transcendence could be lived by man as an event of his personal life, as something he must *appropriate*. In the immanence of the philosophical system of Totality, knowledge amounts to anonymous par-

ticipation in universal Reason; but here, on the contrary, the person himself decides to bear witness to what he believes in. . . . Rosenzweig uses here the German word *Bewährung*, which means both 'put to the test' and 'verification.' To believe in a truth is to testify to it. . . . From man's standpoint what he lives for is true; he makes his belief true by living it, and thus bears witness to it as his part of truth. In this sense all human truths are partial ones; not because there is no One-Truth but on the contrary One-Truth is *parceled out* among men, to each according to his situation, to each according to his share" (*System and Revelation*, 270). If Mosès is correct in this assessment, then the character of Rosenzweig's thought was very close to Ricoeur's indeed. The revelatory event of the love command is an event of testimony and witness in a way that fits well in Ricoeur's thought.

24. Ricoeur, "The Summoned Subject in the School of the Narratives of the Prophetic Vocation," 274–75.

25. Rosenzweig, *The Star of Redemption*, 177.

Bibliography

Arendt, H. *The Human Condition*. Chicago: University of Chicago Press, 1959.

Aristotle. "Nicomachean Ethics." In *The Basic Works of Aristotle*, ed. Richard McKeon. New York: Random House, 1941.

Augustine. *Confessions*. Trans. R. S. Pine Coffin. London: Penguin, 1961.

Blamey, K. "From the Ego to the Self: A Philosophical Itinerary." In *The Philosophy of Paul Ricoeur*, ed. Lewis E. Hahn, 571–603. Chicago: Open Court, 1995.

Bourdieu, P. *The Logic of Practice*. Trans. Richard Nice. Stanford: Stanford University Press, 1990.

Bourgeois, P. "The Limits of Ricoeur's Hermeneutics of Existence." In *The Philosophy of Paul Ricoeur*, ed. Lewis E. Hahn, 549–69. Chicago: Open Court, 1995.

Carr, D. "Narrative and the Real World: An Argument for Continuity." *History and Theory* XXV, no. 2 (May 1986): 117–31.

Derrida, J. *Given Time: I. Counterfeit Money*. Trans. Peggy Kamuf. Chicago: University of Chicago, Press, 1992.

Fodor, J. *Christian Hermeneutics: Paul Ricoeur and the Refiguring of Theology*. New York: Oxford University Press, 1995.

Frei, H. W. *The Eclipse of Biblical Narrative: A Study in Eighteenth and Nineteenth Century Hermeneutics*. New Haven: Yale University Press, 1974.

Greisch, J. *Paul Ricoeur: L'itinerance du sens*. Grenoble: J. Millon: Diffusion Harmonia mundi, 2001.

Hegel, G. W. F. *Phenomenology of Spirit*. Trans. A. V. Miller, foreword by J. N. Findlay. Oxford: Oxford University Press, 1977.

———. *Elements of the Philosophy of Right*. Trans. H. B. Nisbet. Cambridge: Cambridge University Press, 1991.

Heidegger, M. *Being and Time*. Trans. J. Macquarrie and E. Robinson. New York: Harper and Row, 1962.

Heschel, A. J. *The Prophets*. New York: Harper Torchbooks, 1962.

Husserl, E. *Cartesian Meditations: An Introduction to Phenomenology*. Trans. D. Cairns. Dordrecht: Kluwer, 1995.

Ihde, D. *Hermeneutic Phenomenology: The Philosophy of Paul Ricoeur*. Evanston: Northwestern University Press, 1971.

Jauss, H. R. *Toward an Aesthetic of Reception*. Trans. T. Bahti, introd. P. de Man. Theory and History of Literature, vol. 2. Minneapolis: University of Minnesota Press, 1982.

Jonas, H. *The Imperative of Responsibility: In Search of an Ethics for the Technological Age*. Chicago: University of Chicago Press, 1984.

Kant, I. *Religion Within the Limits of Reason Alone*. Trans. T. M. Greene and H. H. Hudson, cont. J. R. Silber. New York: Harper and Row, Harper Torchbooks/Cloister Library, 1960.

———. *The Critique of Judgement*. Trans. Werner S. Pluhar. Indianapolis: Hackett, 1987.

———. *Grounding for the Metaphysic of Morals and On a Supposed Right to Lie Because of Philanthropic Concerns*. 3 ed. Trans. James W. Ellington. Indianapolis: Hackett, 1993.

Kearney, R.. *On Paul Ricoeur: The Owl of Minerva*. Burlington, VT: Ashgate Publishing, 2004.

Klemm, D. E. *The Hermeneutical Theory of Paul Ricoeur: A Constructive Analysis*. Lewisburg, PA: Bucknell University Press, 1983.

———. "Searching for a Heart of Gold: A Ricoeurian Meditation on Moral Striving and the Power of Religious Discourse." In *Paul Ricoeur and Contemporary Moral Thought*, ed. J. Wall, W. Schweiker, and W. D. Hall, 97–116. New York: Routledge, 2002.

Klemm, D. E., and W. Schweiker. "Meanings in Texts and Actions: Questioning Paul Ricoeur." In *Meanings in Texts and Actions: Questioning Paul Ricoeur*, ed. D. E. Klemm and W. Schweiker, 1–10. Charlottesville: University Press of Virginia, 1993.

Klemm, D. "Theological Hermeneutics and the Divine Name: Ricoeur and the Cross of Interpretation." In *Meanings in Texts and Actions: Questioning Paul Ricoeur*, David E. Klemm and William Schweiker, 255–72. Charlottesville: University of Virginia, 1993.

LaCocque, A., and P. Ricoeur. *Thinking Biblically: Exegetical and Hermeneutical Studies*. Trans. David Pellauer. Chicago: University of Chicago Press, 1998.

Levinas, E. *Otherwise Than Being, or Beyond Essence*. Trans. Alphonse Lingus. Pittsburgh: Duquesne University Press, 1998.

Lévi-Strauss, C. *Introduction to the Work of Marcel Mauss*. Trans. Felicity Baker. London: Routledge, 1987.

Marion, J.-L. *God Without Being*. Trans. Thomas Carlson. Chicago: University of Chicago Press, 1991.

———. *Being Given: Toward a Phenomenology of Givenness*. Trans. Jeffrey L. Koskey. Stanford: Stanford University Press, 2002.

Mauss, M. *The Gift: Forms and Functions of Exchange in Archaic Studies*. Trans. W. Halls, introd. M. Douglas. New York: W. W. Norton, 1990.

Moran, G. *A Grammar of Responsibility*. New York: Crossroad, 1996.

Mosès, S. *System and Revelation: The Philosophy of Franz Rosenzweig*. Trans. Catharine Tihanyi. Detroit: Wayne State University Press, 1992.

Nabert, J. *Elements for an Ethic*. Trans. William J. Petrek. Evanston: Northwestern University Press, 1969.

Nietzsche, F. *On the Genealogy of Morals*. Trans. W. Kaufmann. New York: Vintage, 1989.

Rasmussen, D. M. *Mythic-Symbolic Language and Philosophical Anthropology: A Constructive Interpretation of the Thought of Paul Ricoeur*. The Hague: Martinus Nijhoff, 1971.

Rawls, J. *A Theory of Justice*. Cambridge: Harvard University Press, 1971.

Reagan, C. E. "Words and Deeds: The Semantics of Action." In *The Philosophy of Paul Ricoeur: The Library of Living Philosophers, vol. XXII*, Lewis E. Hahn, 331–45. Chicago: Open Court, 1995.

Ricoeur, P. *Le Volontaire et l'Involontaire*. Paris: Aubier, 1950.

———. "Negativity and Primary Affirmation." In *History and Truth*, ed. and trans. Charles A. Kelbley. Evanston: Northwestern University Press, 1965.

———. *Freedom and Nature: The Voluntary and the Involuntary*. Trans. and introd. by E. V. Kohák. Evanston: Northwestern University Press, 1966.

———. *The Symbolism of Evil*. Trans. E. Buchanan. Boston: Beacon Press, 1969.

———. *Freud and Philosophy: An Essay on Interpretation*. Trans. D. Savage. New Haven: Yale University Press, 1970.

———. "Freedom in Light of Hope." In *The Conflict of Interpretations*, ed. Don Ihde, trans. Robert Sweeney, 402–24. Evanston: Northwestern University Press, 1974.

———. "Guilt, Ethics, and Religion." In *The Conflict of Interpretations: Essays in Hermeneutics*, ed. Don Ihde, 425–39. Evanston: Northwestern University Press, 1974.

———. "Nabert on Act and Sign." In *The Conflict of Interpretations: Essays in Hermeneutics*, ed. Don Ihde, 211–22. Evanston: Northwestern University Press, 1974.

———. *The Rule of Metaphor: Multi-disciplinary Studies of the Creation of Meaning in Language*. Trans. R. Czerny, K. McLaughlin, and J. Costello. Toronto: University of Toronto Press, 1977.

———. "The Language of Faith." In *The Philosophy of Paul Ricoeur: An Anthology of His Work*, ed. Charles Reagan and David Steward, 223–38. Boston: Beacon Press, 1978.

———. "Philosophy of Will and Action." In *The Philosophy of Paul Ricoeur: An Anthology of His Work*, ed. Charles E. Reagan and David Stewart, 61–74. Boston: Beacon Press, 1978.

———. "The Hermeneutics of Testimony." In *Essays on Biblical Interpretation*, ed. Lewis S. Mudge, 119–54. Philadelphia: Fortress Press, 1980.

———. "Toward a Hermeneutic of the Idea of Revelation." In *Essays on Biblical Interpretation*, ed. Lewis S. Mudge, 73–118. Philadelphia: Fortress Press, 1980.

———. "Phenomenology and Hermeneutics." In *Hermeneutics and the Human Sciences: Essays on Language Action, and Interpretation*, ed. John B. Thompson, 101–28. Cambridge: Cambridge University Press, 1981.

———. *Time and Narrative I*. Trans. K. McLaughlin and D. Pellauer. Chicago: University of Chicago Press, 1984.

———. *Fallible Man*. Trans. C. A. Kelby. New York: Fordham University, 1986.

———. *Lectures on Ideology and Utopia*. Ed. G. H. Taylor. New York: Columbia University Press, 1986.

———. "Teleological and Deontological Structures of Action: Aristotle and/or Kant." In *Contemporary French Philosophy*, ed. A. Phillips Griffiths, 99–112. Cambridge: Cambridge University Press, 1987.

———. *Time and Narrative III*. Trans. Kathleen Blamey and David Pellauer. Chicago: University of Chicago Press, 1988.

———. *Soi-Même comme un Autre*. Paris: Éditions du Seuil, 1990.

———. "Initiative." In *From Texts to Actions: Essays in Hermeneutics, II*, ed. Kathleen Blamey and John B. Thompson, 208–22. Evanston: Northwestern University Press, 1991.

———. "Life in Quest of Narrative." In *On Paul Ricoeur: Narrative and Interpretation*, ed. David Wood, 20–33. New York: Routledge, 1991.

———. "Narrative Identity." In *On Paul Ricoeur: Narrative and Interpretation*, ed. David Wood, 188–200. New York: Routledge, 1991.

———. "Philosophical Hermeneutics and Biblical Hermeneutics." In *From Text to Action: Essays in Hermeneutics II*, trans. and ed. Kathleen Blamey and John B. Thompson, 89–101. Evanston: Northwestern University Press, 1991.

———. *Oneself as Another*. Trans. Kathleen Blamey. Chicago: University of Chicago Press, 1992.

———. "The Bible and the Imagination." In *Figuring the Sacred: Religion, Narrative, and Imagination*, ed. Mark I. Wallace, trans. David Pellauer, 144–66. Minneapolis: Fortress Press, 1995.

———. "Emmanuel Levinas: Thinker of Testimony." In *Figuring the Sacred: Religion, Narrative, and Imagination*, ed. Mark I. Wallace, trans. David Pellauer, 108–26. Minneapolis: Fortress Press, 1995.

———. "Ethical and Theological Considerations on the Golden Rule." In *Figuring the Sacred: Religion, Narrative, and Imagination*, ed. Mark I. Wallace, trans. D. Pellauer, 293–302. Minneapolis: Fortress Press, 1995.

———. "Evil, A Challenge to Philosophy and Theology." In *Figuring the Sacred: Religion, Narrative, and Imagination*, ed. Mark I. Wallace, trans. David Pellauer, 249–61. Minneapolis: Fortress, 1995.

———. "Hope and the Structure of Philosophical Systems." In *Figuring the Sacred: Religion, Narrative, and Imagination*, ed. Mark I. Wallace, trans. David Pellauer, 203–16. Minneapolis: Fortress Press, 1995.

———. "The Logic of Jesus, the Logic of God." In *Figuring the Sacred: Religion, Narrative, and Imagination*, ed. Mark I. Wallace, trans. David Pellauer, 279–83. Minneapolis: Fortress Press, 1995.

———. "Love and Justice." In *Figuring the Sacred: Religion, Narrative, and Imagination*, ed. Mark I. Wallace, trans. David Pellauer, 315–29. Minneapolis: Fortress Press, 1995.

———. "Manifestation and Proclamation." In *Figuring the Sacred: Religion, Narrative, and Imagination*, ed. Mark I. Wallace, trans. David Pellauer, 48–67. Minneapolis: Fortress Press, 1995.

———. "Philosophy and Religious Language." In *Figuring the Sacred: Religion, Narrative, and Imagination*, ed. Mark I. Wallace, trans. David Pellauer, 35–47. Minneapolis: Fortress Press, 1995.

———. "The Summoned Subject in the School of the Narratives of the Prophetic Vocation." In *Figuring the Sacred: Religion, Narrative, and Imagination*, ed. Mark I. Wallace, trans. David Pellauer, 262–75. Minneapolis: Fortress Press, 1995.

———. Interview: Chateney-Malabry, July 8, 1991. In Charles Reagan, *Paul Ricoeur: His Life and Work*, 123–35. Chicago: University of Chicago Press, 1996.

———. "Theonomy and/or Autonomy." In *The Future of Theology: Essays in Honor of Jürgen Moltmann*, ed. Miroslav Volf. Grand Rapids: Eerdmans, 1986.

———. "Ethics and Human Capability: A Response." In *Paul Ricoeur and Contemporary Moral Thought*, ed. W. S. John Wall, and W. David Hall, 279–90. New York: Routledge, 2002.

———. *Memory, History, Forgetting*. Trans. David Pellauer. Chicago: University of Chicago Press, 2004.

Rosenzweig, F. *The Star of Redemption*. Trans. W. W. Halo. Notre Dame: University of Notre Dame Press, 1985.

Sartre, J.-P. *Being and Nothingness: An Essay on Phenomenological Ontology*. Trans. and introd. H. E. Barnes. New York: Philosophical Library, 1956.

Schrag, C. O. *God as Otherwise than Being: Toward a Semantics of the Gift*. Evanston: Northwestern University Press, 2002.

Smith, A. *An Inquiry into the Nature and Causes of the Wealth of Nations*. Indianapolis: Liberty Fund, 1981.

Spinoza, B. *The Ethics and Selected Letters*. Trans. Samuel Shirley. Indianapolis: Hackett, 1982.

Stiver, D. R. *Theology after Ricoeur: New Directions in Hermeneutical Theology*. Louisville: Westminster John Knox Press, 2001.

Tannehill, R. *The Sword of His Mouth*. Philadelphia: Fortress Press, 1975.

VanHoozer, K. J. *Biblical Narrative in the Philosophy of Paul Ricoeur: A Study in Hermeneutics and Theology*. Cambridge: Cambridge University Press, 1980.

Venema, H. I. *Identifying Selfhood: Imagination, Narrative, and Hermeneutics in the Thought of Paul Ricoeur*. Albany: State University of New York Press, 2000.

Wall, J. *Moral Creativity: Paul Ricoeur and the Poetics of Possibility*. New York: Oxford University Press, 2005.

Wallace, M. I. *The Second Naivete: Barth, Ricoeur, and the New Yale Theology, 2ed.* Studies in American Biblical Hermeneutics. Macon, PA: Mercer University Press, 1995.

Index

6886365R00122

Printed in Germany
by Amazon Distribution
GmbH, Leipzig